Oxford Modern Britain

Crime in Modern Britain

Eamonn Carrabine
Pamela Cox
Maggy Lee
Nigel South

Series Editor: John Scott

OXFORD
UNIVERSITY PRESS

OXFORD
UNIVERSITY PRESS

Great Clarendon Street, Oxford OX2 6DP

Oxford University Press is a department of the University of Oxford.
It furthers the University's objective of excellence in research, scholarship,
and education by publishing worldwide in

Oxford New York

Auckland Bangkok Buenos Aires Cape Town Chennai
Dar es Salaam Delhi Hong Kong Istanbul Karachi Kolkata
Kuala Lumpur Madrid Melbourne Mexico City Mumbai Nairobi
São Paulo Shanghai Singapore Taipei Tokyo Toronto

with an associated company in Berlin

Published in the United States
by Oxford University Press Inc., New York

First published 2002

British Library Cataloguing in Publication Data
Data available

Library of Congress Cataloging in Publication Data
Data available

ISBN 0–19–924611–4

10 9 8 7 6 5 4 3 2 1

Typeset in Adobe Minion
by RefineCatch Limited, Bungay, Suffolk
Printed in Great Britain by
Biddles Ltd., Guildford and King's Lynn

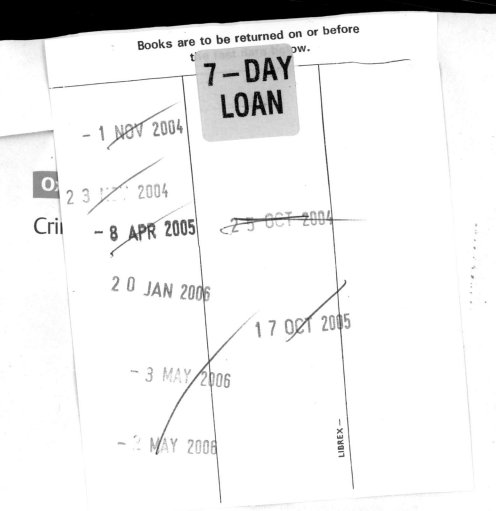

The *Oxford Modern Britain* series comprises the most authoritative introductory books on all aspects of the social structure of modern Britain. Lively and accessible, the books will be the first point of reference for anyone interested in the state of contemporary Britain. The series is invaluable to students across the range of the Social Sciences.

Also published in this series

Kinship and Friendship in Modern Britain
Graham Allen

Religion in Modern Britain
Steve Bruce

Health and Healthcare in Modern Britain
Joan Busfield

Crime in Modern Britain
Eamonn Carrabine, Pamela Cox, Maggy Lee, Nigel South

Women and Work in Modern Britain
Rosemary Crompton

Mass Media and Power in Modern Britain
John Eldridge, Jenny Kitzinger, Kevin Williams

Race and Ethnicity in Modern Britain
David Mason

Age and Generation in Modern Britain
Jane Pilcher

Youth and Employment in Modern Britain
Kenneth Roberts

Foreword

THE Oxford Modern Britain series is designed to fill a major gap in the available sociological sources on the contemporary world. Each book will provide a comprehensive and authoritative overview of major issues for students at all levels. They are written by acknowledged experts in their fields, and should be standard sources for many years to come.

Each book focuses on contemporary Britain, but the relevant historical background is always included, and a comparative context is provided. No society can be studied in isolation from other societies and the globalized context of the contemporary world, but a detailed understanding of a particular society can both broaden and deepen sociological understanding. These books will be exemplars of empirical study and theoretical understanding.

Books in the series are intended to present information and ideas in a lively and accessible way. They will meet a real need for source books in a wide range of specialized courses, in 'Modern Britain' and 'Comparative Sociology' courses, and in integrated introductory courses. They have been written with the newcomer and general reader in mind, and they meet the genuine need in the informed public for accurate and up-to-date discussion and sources.

John Scott
Series Editor

Acknowledgements

WE would like to thank John Scott for suggesting this book project in the first place and thank the anonymous reviewers who provided constructive criticism and encouraging remarks about our original proposal. Patrick Brindle, Angela Griffin, John Grandidge, and Sophie Rogers at OUP have patiently waited for the completion of the manuscript and guided it through to publication. Acknowledgements are also due to the Home Office for permission to reproduce figures from *Digest 4: Information on the Criminal Justice System in England and Wales* (Home Office, 1999).

The Department of Sociology at Essex has provided an intellectually stimulating and convivial environment in which to develop our ideas and extend the boundaries of criminology. Colleagues at Essex and elsewhere as well as friends and families have supported and advised us during the course of writing this book. We are particularly grateful to Patrick Brindle, Bill Hayton, Brian Longhurst, Christine Rogers, Heather Shore, and Deborah Thom for taking the time to offer insightful comments on aspects of the book, and to Chris Ellis, Alison Inman, and Daniel South for their support. Writing this book has been a hugely rewarding, enjoyable, and truly collaborative effort. Plans, drafts, and other matters not remotely connected with this book were discussed at our Fordham 'awaydays' and the part played by Maggy's wonderful lunches in the completion of this book cannot be overemphasized.

Eamonn Carrabine
Pam Cox
Maggy Lee
Nigel South

Department of Sociology
University of Essex
March 2002

Contents

Detailed Contents

List of Figures and Tables

Figures

Tables

Chapter 1

Thinking about Crime

Introduction

CRIME is an integral part of everyday life in modern Britain. It has become a mainstay of political debate and public policy reform. Many people believe that the likelihood of becoming a victim of crime has increased, a belief that tends to persist even in periods where recorded crime rates appear to decline. Criminology has become one of the most popular degree courses, crime programmes one of the most popular television formats, and crime writing one of the most popular literary genres. Crime is clearly something that people think about a lot—whether as policy makers, practitioners, or ordinary citizens, as students and academics reading and writing or as audiences trying to make sense of narratives about crime. Inevitably thinking seriously about crime raises questions. For example, how have patterns and cultural representations of crime changed over time? What kinds of crime have been subject to most political and popular attention, and which overlooked and why? Why has a wealthy welfare democracy produced dramatically rising crime levels? Why do we fear the reality of crime so much while consuming representations of it so avidly? This book sets out to investigate such questions and, in doing so, to provide a critical introduction to the study of crime in modern Britain.

The book approaches these questions and more from four main directions concerned with: histories of crime, everyday life and crime, organizational bases of crime, and popular culture and crime. Each of these directions is pursued in separate chapters, drawing on different literature but with inevitable overlaps. This introduction and the concluding chapter place Britain in contemporary context, exploring the development of professional and practical knowledges and theories about crime and, in the conclusion, looking to the future of research on crime in Britain. The remaining chapters provide distinctive yet complementary ways of surveying the history and forms of crime in modern Britain. First, historical approaches to crime are useful in that they offer both a longer and often a wider view of crime. They allow us to ask what might at first seem to be very obvious questions, such as 'what counts as "modern"?' or 'what constitutes "British" experience of crime?' They also allow us to explore why and how certain kinds of knowledge about crime or approaches to the study and control of crime have come to dominate over others. They provide insights into those wider aspects of social, political, and cultural life that have shaped experiences and understandings of crime in different ways at different times within 'modern' Britain, broadly defined. Second, the investigation of everyday encounters with crime allows us to explore crime as a 'normal' rather than as an exceptional social phenomenon. This may appear extreme, until we consider that one-third of British men are likely to have a conviction by their 40th birthday, that many young people admit to having committed an offence at some time, or that many crimes are committed by respectable people in the course of their everyday jobs. To explore crime as a factor of everyday life is also to raise questions about the conventional ways in which crime and crime risks have been measured, made sense of, and controlled, and to examine the different anxieties generated by these routine experiences for different social groups. The organizational bases of crime are central to the third perspective here. Compared to the crimes of everyday life, crimes committed by the powerful have long received less attention within political, criminological, and popular debates. However, this has begun to change recently. Established discussions of business-related crime and political corruption took on a new significance in the 1980s with a series of city scandals about 'fat cats' and fraudulent traders, and in the 1990s with a series of political scandals around 'sleaze' and 'cash for questions'. Crimes of power and profit organized on a basis that makes them distinct from routine, everyday crimes have long attracted considerable attention in the USA but rather less in Britain. Professional organized crime has featured rather more than business or political crime in academic studies, police and Home Office reports, and the media but bringing all these activities together as based on the use and abuse of organizational resources in pursuit of power or profit is illuminating. The fourth direction pursues crime as 'a product' of popular culture, examining the production, circulation, and consumption of factual and fictional representations of crime and the ways these have developed from the nineteenth century onwards. Chapter 5 considers crime from the perspective of pleasure and entertainment, recognizing that pleasures and fears often go hand in hand and that narratives of crime have come to serve as significant cultural staples.[1]

In short, this book aims to show how the study of crime in modern Britain can be usefully expanded in these four directions and to demonstrate that crime is best understood in firm relation to other aspects of social life. It offers a guide to key aspects of established and emerging studies of crime: Chapters 2 and 5 do this through discussion of historical and cultural work, while Chapters

3 and 4 do it by addressing recent empirical criminological and sociological work. Throughout, the book discusses crime in terms of difference by drawing attention to the gender, class, ethnicity, sexuality, and age of offenders and victims. It encourages readers to take an open view of modernity, Britishness, and criminality through its historical content, through its examination of British experiences of crime in international and comparative contexts, and through its emphasis on broad definitions of crime. 'Modern' Britain is discussed in relation to the 'early modern' period that preceded it (roughly speaking, from 1500 to 1800) and the 'late modern' period that many argue has now replaced it (again, roughly speaking, from the 1970s onwards).

Clearly, questions of crime and questions of the control of crime are not easily separated. Patterns of recorded crime are, after all, to a very large extent determined by efforts made by various kinds of gatekeepers—from the public and the police to the judiciary and the penal system—to report, detect, judge, and punish criminal activities. While this book deliberately focuses on crime rather than its control, it aims throughout to highlight the criminological and cultural importance of different kinds of attempts to contain crime and also aims to refer readers to new studies of the workings of the late modern British criminal justice system.

Defining crime

Crime is generally understood to be behaviour that is prohibited by criminal law. In other words no act can be considered a crime, irrespective of how immoral or damaging it may be, unless it has been made criminal by state legislation. This conceptualization appears straightforward enough but it tells us very little about the criminalizing process whereby certain harmful acts or events routinely come to be identified and recognized as 'crime' in official discourse whilst others are not. For instance, the act of taking a life is not always defined as 'murder'. Thus, 'killing' in wartime is acceptable, even heroic, whereas the killing of the television presenter Jill Dando was regarded as 'evil'; euthanasia is illegal in Britain but legal in the Netherlands. The same is true with 'violence'. Sometimes violence is defined as acceptable and rational, for example within sports such as (male) boxing, whilst at other times it is defined as unacceptable, irrational, and even senseless, for example when associated with hooligans and delinquents. Definitions of crime also change over time. For instance, it was not until 1991 that England and Wales overturned a 255-year-old ruling that had given husbands immunity from prosecution for marital rape (Muncie 2001). Hitherto, the legal definition of 'rape' excluded rape within marriage on the grounds that the marriage contract included a man's 'continual' consent from his wife for sexual activity at any time. Exactly the same behaviour carried out by a stranger in public would result in a lengthy prison sentence but in the privacy of the household and circumscribed by marriage it was not recognized as a crime.

In recent years, some criminologists have also explored the ways in which some forms of culture come to be constructed as crime. For example, Mike Presdee (2000: 24) refers to a process of 'cultural criminalisation' whereby certain popular culture forms have been (re)presented as criminal or criminogenic by politicians, moral entrepreneurs, and 'cultural reactionaries', as the following dichotomies illustrate:

Graffiti is destruction; the oil painting is art.
Cockfighting is cruel; hunting is rural culture.
Glyndebourne celebrates classical music outdoors and is 'cultural'; rave music performed
   outdoors . . . is criminal.
To consent to violence in 'hate' is sport; to consent to violence in 'love' [e.g. s/m] is a
   crime.

Not everyone will agree with the way these contrasts are made and, for example, the second of these will seem to some to be particularly problematic. But Presdee's point is precisely about this kind of problematization, i.e. who decides what is celebrated and deplored, acceptable and unacceptable, what is right and what is wrong?

Criminal acts do not always cause harm to society. 'Victimless crimes' such as some sexual acts between consenting adults and some forms of drug-taking are often cited in this context. Acts of civil disobedience have also been justified on the grounds that the law-breaking is less socially harmful than the law that is opposed (for example, acts against the 'apartheid' laws of South Africa prior to the development of democracy in that country). Conversely, poverty, malnutrition, inadequate health care, unemployment are all equally, if not more, socially harmful than most of the behaviours and incidents that currently make up the 'crime problem' (Muncie 2000). There are therefore no clear, unequivocal criteria for determining whether a particular action is 'criminal' or not. Such judgements are always informed by contestable, epistemological, moral, and political assumptions (De Haan 1990: 154). Questions have been raised in recent decades, both from within criminology (for instance, from the labelling theorists, critical criminologists, cultural criminologists) and from within social movements (such as the feminist movement, human- and animal-rights campaigns, environmentalist groups, anti-racist activists), with regard to what is 'criminal' and how legal conceptions of 'crime' come to be constructed. In the process, the boundaries of traditional social problems have been contested and redefined.

That said, no study of crime can ignore recorded criminal statistics, if only to highlight their partial and problematic nature. Criminal statistics are generally agreed to reveal just as much if not more about crime-recording and prosecution patterns than about patterns of actual criminal activity. Over time, frequent changes in law, court organization, and methods of categorizing and recording offences have frustrated efforts to establish accurate statistical continuities, as the section below on 'hidden crimes' shows (see also Chapter 2). Nevertheless, formal criminal statistics, recorded at a national level in England and Wales from the early nineteenth century onwards, do provide an important starting point for the study of crime in modern Britain. Amongst other things, they show which kinds of offences and offenders have most commonly been prosecuted and how these have changed over time, as well as suggesting when and sometimes why new offences were created and old offences decriminalized. Statistics about crime also highlight the importance attached to social statistics of all kinds within the broader governance of modern Britain from 1800 on. To be able to count the number of criminals (and therefore to be able to estimate future patterns of crime, establish its parameters, and allocate resources to effect its containment) became increasingly essential to the project of modern government. To be able to calculate the number of sick, elderly, poor, vagrant, or criminal subjects was to be able to govern the modern state effectively and efficiently. Thus, while it is certainly the case that no government or police force has ever succeeded in producing totally accurate maps and measures of crime, the modern desire to do so is arguably worthy of study in itself.

Recorded crime and prosecution: 1800–2000

Recorded crime rates followed a distinct pattern in Britain between the late eighteenth and mid-twentieth centuries. The early part of this long period saw a sharp increase in prosecutions (1790s–1810s) that continued to grow, albeit at a steadier rate (up to the 1840s). The middle part (1850s–1910s) saw a distinct slow-down in prosecutions. By contrast, the later part (1910s–1950s) showed a further upward trend, with increases during the First World War and the late 1930s followed by very much steeper rises after the Second World War (see Figure 1.1). The many significant changes in definitions of offences, judicial proceedings, and police and Home Office means of recording crime make it difficult to illustrate this overall pattern with exact figures. The number of

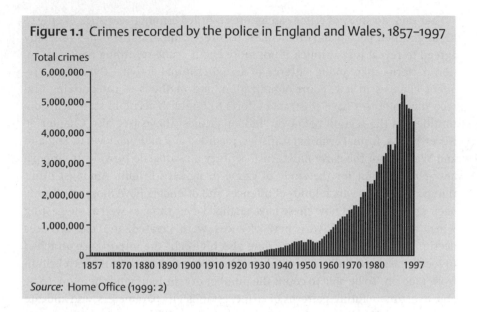

Figure 1.1 Crimes recorded by the police in England and Wales, 1857–1997

Source: Home Office (1999: 2)

crimes recorded by the police (always higher than the number actually reaching court) remained at a steady *c*.100,000 per year from the 1870s to the 1930s, rising to around a third of a million per year up to the early 1950s, and thereafter doubling from half a million in 1955 to a million in 1964 (Maguire 1997: 158–9; see also Radzinowicz and Hood 1986).

From the 1830s onwards, crime was classified into six main types: crime against the person; offences against property (with violence); offences against property (without violence); malicious offences against property; offences against the currency; miscellaneous offences (Emsley 1997: 58). Each type had many more subdivisions, however one kind of crime predominated. According to Clive Emsley, small-scale theft accounted for between 50 per cent and 75 per cent of all crime in the period 1750–1900 (Emsley 1996a: 32). Petty street-based offences were also prominent: taking 1908 as a sample year, proceedings against drunkenness, breaches of by-laws (regulating street selling, street gambling, street entertainments, and so on), vagrancy and assault, accounted for over 60 per cent of all arrests and summons for non-indictable cases (Gatrell 1990: 269). Offences against the person accounted for around 10 to 15 per cent of crimes in the nineteenth century (based on statistics of crimes known to the police and of (non)indictable committals available at different points in the century). Within these figures, reported cases of homicides of—overwhelmingly—wives, husbands, parents, and children, remained relatively low. Between the 1850s and 1890s, the number of homicides reported to the police averaged under 400 per year (Emsley 1996a:

42). This meant that the number of homicides per head of population in the 1870s was similar to that of the 1970s when there were around 500 cases per year but committed within a very much larger population (Home Office 1999)—a fact often overlooked in discussions of 'rising' violence in modern Britain.

Profiles of offenders were similarly stable. From the 1850s to the 1950s offenders tended to be young, male, and poor. Court records show that most were under the age of 30 (the majority in their late teens and early twenties), poorly educated (if educated at all) and employed (if employed at all) in low-skilled, low-paid jobs such as labouring, domestic service and casual work. This pattern then continued into the late twentieth century, regardless of changes in the nature of low-skilled employment.[2]

Most historians, like most criminologists, agree that formal prosecution figures represent only the tip of the iceberg of 'real' crime and that official criminal statistics are more reliable as a guide to the history of policing and judicial mechanisms than to everyday criminal activity. With this huge caveat in mind, historians have explained the pattern described above in different ways. The first sharp rise (1790s–1840s) is variously linked to the combined effects of key changes in British social and economic life, changes identified by some as quintessentially 'modern': population growth; rural dislocation; urbanization and the loosening of traditional social controls, particularly upon young migrant workers; and the economic depression and high levels of unemployment following the end of the Napoleonic wars. All these factors could have meant that more people, especially younger men, were indeed committing more crime. However, historians also stress that changes in the definition and delivery of public order, equally 'modern' in character, were also very significant in producing the apparent crime wave. The changing conception of public order was related to a range of other changes concerned with the administration of criminal justice but also to wider social developments: the creation of more criminal offences, especially around new forms of property ownership, new forms of work, new forms of radical politics, and new concerns to control public space; the establishment of local police forces (themselves employing in the main 'respectable' working-class men); the reorganization of summary courts, which meant that more cases could be tried more quickly in these lower courts as opposed to being heard in the higher courts, or assizes; financial reforms which reduced the cost of bringing a court case and (along with the reform of capital statutes) thus encouraged more ordinary people to prosecute; and finally and crucially, the systematic collection of formal government statistics which allowed crime (and others areas of social life) to be presented for the first time as a distinct 'social issue' that could be judged to be 'improving' or 'deteriorating'. All these factors could have meant that more people, especially younger men again, were subject to increased regulation, control, and statistical surveillance.

The long 'plateau' period where this rise in prosecutions flattened out (1850s–1910s) is more difficult to explain. Although punctuated by periodic moral panics around certain kinds of sensational if rare offences—garotting (or violent robbery) in the 1860s (Davis 1980; Sindall 1987), infanticide in the 1870s (Higginbotham 1989), the killing of women in the wake of the 1880s Ripper murders (Walkowitz 1992), juvenile hooliganism in the 1890s (Pearson 1983)—recorded crime did fall during this time. Social changes of this period seem to have meant that fewer crimes were actually committed, rather than fewer prosecutions brought. Rising living standards, lower food prices, political stability, declining interpersonal violence, and adjustment to new urban industrial lifestyles, combined with the workings of a strong centralized regulatory state seem to have created—temporarily at least—more law-abiding subjects. Historians disagree as to whether this was a sign of contentment or coercion. It was doubtless a mixture of both. Gatrell notably argues that this period represented 'a rare era of success' for the 'policeman-state' (Gatrell 1990: 292). He also argues that, taken together, these kinds of changes constituted a major shift in understandings of civil liberties and social freedoms, which in this context could also be considered as quintessentially modern. Liberty, which had once been defined as freedom *from* the state, was increasingly defined as freedom to be guaranteed *by* the state. Since only a powerful state seemed able to protect the public from criminal disorder, the public at large seemed willing to support the apparent need for such a state (Gatrell 1990).

As Chapters 2 and 3 show, the twentieth-century rise in prosecutions, particularly during and after the Second World War, is commonly viewed in terms of increased opportunities to commit new kinds of crime, trends in the economic cycle, and a breakdown in the fragile public order consensus of the late-Victorian period, especially in the wake of the social upheavals of the two world wars. Recorded crimes rose steeply from about half a million in 1950 to 1.6 million in 1970 and then to 5.5 million in 1991 (Home Office 1999). Property crime, mainly petty theft, continued to dominate criminal statistics. In certain areas of the country, consumer booms (notably of the 1930s and 1950s) generated both more goods for those with disposable income as well as the desire for more goods which very likely resulted in increased property crime. In line with this argument, car-related offences (traffic offences, failure to properly maintain a vehicle, failure to pay licence fees and road taxes, taking and driving a vehicle without consent, and so on), relatively rare in the 1950s when there were few cars on the roads, were among the fastest growing during the post-war years (Maguire 1997; Smerdon and South 1997). More recent recorded crime figures show that property offences continue to dominate. As Figure 1.2

Figure 1.2 Crimes recorded by the police in England and Wales, 1997

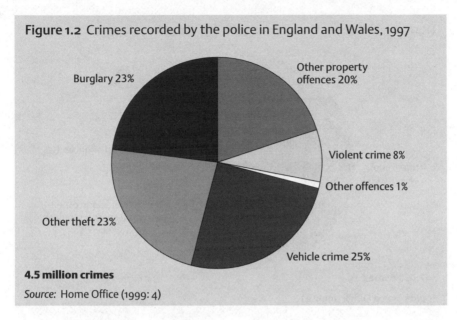

Burglary 23%

Other property offences 20%

Violent crime 8%

Other offences 1%

Other theft 23%

Vehicle crime 25%

4.5 million crimes

Source: Home Office (1999: 4)

illustrates, these accounted for 91 per cent of all notifiable offences recorded by the police in England and Wales in 1997. In particular, over a half of theft offences and a quarter of all recorded crime were vehicle-related theft; 23 per cent of recorded crimes were burglaries. Of recorded crime 1 per cent consisted of drug offences (including trafficking and possession), public order offences, and perverting the course of justice.

Violent crime (including violence against the person, robbery, sexual offences) accounted for around 8 per cent of all recorded crime. Nearly two-thirds of the violent crimes were minor wounding, whilst homicides and more serious offences of violence only accounted for 7 per cent of violent crimes and 0.5 per cent of all recorded crime (Figure 1.3). As Chapter 3 shows, young men dominate official statistics on violence, both as offenders and victims. Crime statistics have consistently found the 'typical offender' to be male (over 80 per cent of offenders known to the authorities) and young (almost half are under the age of 21). For men, pubs, clubs, and the streets provide the main locations for their encounters with violence. For women, the home remains the place of most danger.

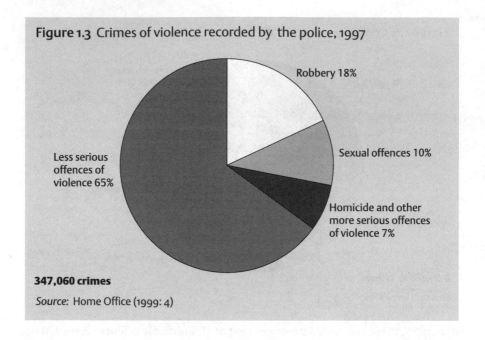

Figure 1.3 Crimes of violence recorded by the police, 1997

Robbery 18%

Sexual offences 10%

Homicide and other more serious offences of violence 7%

Less serious offences of violence 65%

347,060 crimes

Source: Home Office (1999: 4)

Comparative experiences

The majority of industrialized countries have seen parallel increases in recorded crime in the post-war period. With the notable exceptions of Japan and Switzerland, all the available evidence from developed countries points to a pattern of rapid and sustained increase in crime. Such increases in crime have occurred not only in periods of economic downswings and depression but also during times of full employment and exceptional living standards. The 1960s were years of affluence yet against all conventional wisdom, crime continued to rise in the cities of the United States as well as in major centres of European countries, giving rise to vigorous debate about how this might be explained (see Young 1999). In the Dutch case, the largest increase in property crime took place in the 1960s and 1970s, which coincided with a period of growing welfare provision (van Swaaningen 1997).

United States

In the post-war period, high rates of crime became a fact of urban life in the USA, just as they did—albeit on a less dramatic scale—in most European societies. Official crime rates rose sharply from 1960 onwards, reaching a peak in the early 1980s, and then tailing off in the 1990s. Over the period 1989 to 1999, recorded crime in the USA fell by 18 per cent (Barclay et al. 2001). According to the FBI's *Uniform Crime Reports*, the vast majority of recorded crimes are ordinary and mundane, comprising mainly property crimes such as shoplifting, motor vehicle thefts, and burglaries (Felson 1998). What sets the USA apart, however, is that the American urban experience is much more lethal than that of European countries. For the period 1997-9, its homicide rate (6.3 homicides per 100,000 population) was about four times the average rate in the European Union and one of the highest in the industrialized world (the highest homicide rate was found in South Africa—56.5 homicides per 100,000 population) (Barclay et al. 2001). Although violent crimes in the USA constitute a tiny proportion of the major crime total (around two-tenths of 1 per cent), they have come to form the focal point for the public, politicians, and the media alike (Felson 1998). Sensationalist headlines such as 'one murder occurred every 22 minutes, one rape every 5 minutes, and one armed assault every 30 seconds' strongly stir the popular imagination (Body-Gendrot 2000: 33). At the same time, everyday cruelty, hurt, and humiliation have become an integral part of the growing production and consumption of violence as 'popular entertainment' on the internet and on 'reality' television.

The everyday experience of crime (by direct victims or 'consumers') has shaped American people's behaviour and feelings of fear, anger and, in some cases, fascination. Affluent households have fled the cities for the suburbs in great numbers. In the late 1970s and early 1980s, 'white flight' was the term coined to describe abandonment of areas of the city and townships seen as falling prey to black and underclass crime. In the 1990s in some parts of the USA, affluent blacks followed suit. Today, 'around 42 million residents, mostly white, live in ... autonomous communities and about 8 million live in electronically or physically gated communities' (Body-Gendrot 2000: 32). This privatization of safety (South 1994) and the freedom to carry weapons in the public space distinguish the American landscape, as one adult in 50 will carry a handgun on any given day (*Economist*, 26 September 1998) and as Americans spend about $65 billion for their private security each year (Donziger 1996).

The USA is by far the most vocal and visible retentionist advocate of capital punishment, with some 3,500 people on 'death row' in the 38 state (plus federal) jurisdictions that have retained the death penalty (Amnesty International 2001). It also locks up more people than any other Western society. Its prison population tripled from the late 1970s (from 500,000 to 1.8 million in 1998), a population, which, if brought together, would exceed the size of Alaska, North Dakota, and Wyoming, combined (Irwin et al. 2000: 135). What is perhaps more disturbing about the prison population explosion is that the people being locked up are not the sensationalized robbers, rapists, and murderers that the public imagines them to be. Instead, most are defendants who have been found guilty of non-violent or not particularly serious crimes and imprisoned under harsh mandatory sentencing schemes.

Such tough crime policies are not without human and financial costs (Currie 1996; Donziger 1996). The policies currently being pursued in the USA entail unprecedented levels of correctional expenditure, often at the expense of public welfare service budgets: 'States around the country are now spending more to build prisons than they do on colleges, and the combined prison and jail budgets for 1.2 million non-violent prisoners exceeded the entire federal welfare budget for 8.5 million poor people last year' (Irwin et al. 2000: 136). New powers for police, 'three strikes and you're out' sentencing policies, restrictions on the freedom of ex-offenders—each of these carries a price in terms of erosion of civil liberties. Furthermore, a punitive criminal justice system can only have a marginal impact on the rate of crime. For example, between 1987 and 1992 the USA increased its incarceration rate by 33.6 per cent and still witnessed a 2 per cent increase in the nation's crime rate (Irwin et al. 2000: 140).[3] Disturbingly, there is also a clear racial bias within this carceral experiment, as urban African-Americans have borne the brunt of the war on drugs despite the fact that both African-Americans and whites were using drugs at the same rate (Tonry 1995). Thus, one in nine of African-American males aged 20–29 is in prison at any one point, and a staggering one in three is either in prison, on probation, or on parole (Mauer 1997).

Japan

Japan has been characterized as an affluent and highly mobile and urbanized society, which also appears to be safe and secure. It has possibly the lowest level of crime in the industrialized world and is unique in having official crime rates that have dropped in the post-war period in comparison with other industrialized countries—a reduction of 34 per cent between 1950 and 1980 (*Japan Almanac*, Asahi Shimbun 2001: 232). The rate of crime in 1987 was the same as it was in 1966, while during the same period in the United States the rate for serious crime doubled—and more than doubled in Britain (quoted in Crawford 1998: 236).

Many commentators have turned to cultural factors in their attempts to explain Japan's low level of crime—for instance, its cultural emphasis on group loyalties, mutual help and trust, pressures to conform, and the notion of a specific 'culture of shaming' (Bayley 1991; Braithwaite 1989). High levels of interdependency in employment, neighbourhoods, and families are believed to create moral and informal control mechanisms which prevent criminality, while a combination of cultural characteristics and police practices contribute to high rates of criminal confessions, in turn contributing to judicial discretion and low rates of imprisonment.

During the 1990s, however, concerns about prolonged economic recession in Japan have gone hand in hand with fears about growing criminality and violence. Between 1989 and 1999, recorded crime rose by 29 per cent albeit from a low baseline. In particular, there were sharp increases in violent crime and domestic burglary (Barclay et al. 2001). More significantly, some commentators have questioned the idea that Japan is as safe as others suggest. They point to the role of organized criminality—especially *yakuza* (networks of adult male criminal organizations) and gangs of street youths—as a powerful criminal element and culturally visible phenomenon of Japanese society (see Crawford 1998: 241–2; Kersten 1993). According to police estimates, these organized criminal groups have more than 83,000 members and are responsible for 16 per cent of recorded robberies, 6 per cent of murders, 15 per cent of rapes, and most drug and gun smuggling (Bayley 1991; *Japan Almanac*, Asahi Shimbun 2001). There is also an increasing awareness that behind the apparent orderliness of everyday life in Japanese society, organized and corporate criminality are endemic.

European Union

Absolute comparisons of crime levels across the European Union member states are often misleading given the extraneous factors such as differences in reported and recorded crime levels, differences in the definition of crime and in the list of offences that are included in the official crime figures, and changes in official data quality. With this proviso in mind, certain observations can be made regarding crime trends in the EU. Over the period 1995 to 1999, recorded crime fell by 1 per cent in the EU member states. There were reductions in eight countries, the largest being in Ireland (21 per cent), England and Wales (10 per cent), Scotland (8 per cent), and Denmark (8 per cent), but increases in others, including Belgium (18 per cent), Greece (14 per cent), and Portugal (11 per cent). Except for Italy and Portugal, all member states of the EU experienced substantial falls in domestic burglary—England and Wales (31 per cent), Germany (29 per cent), Austria (26 per cent), the Netherlands (22 per cent). There is less of a pattern in other areas of crime. The average rise of 7 per cent in the EU for theft of a motor vehicle tells us little about the sharp increase in Portugal (62 per cent) and Finland (50 per cent) but sharp fall in Germany (46 per cent). Similarly, the average rise of 11 per cent for violent crime in the EU obscures the very high levels of increase in Italy (37 per cent) and the Netherlands (34 per cent) and the modest falls in Luxembourg (17 per cent) and Belgium (7 per cent) (Barclay et al. 2001).

Of all the crime categories, the steep increase in drug-trafficking offences both within and across EU member states is arguably attracting the greatest concern and debate among politicians and in the media. Over the period 1995–9, there was an average rise of 31 per cent in the EU for drug-trafficking offences with the highest rises in Ireland (139 per cent), Greece (128 per cent), and the Netherlands (119 per cent) but there were falls in Denmark (56 per cent), Sweden (32 per cent), Portugal (9 per cent), and England and Wales (6 per cent). Outside the EU, the highest rises were in Eastern Europe – ranging from 170 per cent (in Russia) to a staggering 1,400 per cent (in Estonia) (Barclay et al. 2001). The subjects of drug-related crime and drug trafficking are returned to in Chapter 4.

Britain: crime and internationalism

While it is very useful to be able to compare British prosecution patterns with those of other nations, such comparisons should not be allowed to overshadow the inherent internationalism of modern British life. Modern Britain has been hugely shaped by its engagement with the wider world, not least through colonialism, global trade, war and the formation of international partnerships such as the Commonwealth and the European Union. All of these have arguably shaped British experiences of, and attitudes to, crime.

As a colonial power, Britain did much to reshape the legal and criminal justice systems of its colonies and 'dominions' (Sumner 1982; Carroll-Burke 2000). However, some tactics of colonial rule were brought back home and became integral to 'traditional' law enforcement in Britain itself. For example, fingerprinting, aspects of riot-policing, and the use of 'mediation' agencies to assist in the policing of black immigrant groups all had colonial origins (Cashmore and McLaughlin 1991: 20–9). As a powerful global trading nation from at least the eighteenth century onwards, Britain continually aimed to secure its economic interests through laws governing the production, transport, and exchange of goods. Questions as to who had the rights to produce particular kinds of goods, who had the right to ship them and by what routes, who had the right to import and (re)export them and at what cost were, of course, shaped by the global 'free' market. But these questions and this 'free' market were also shaped by a dense web of commercial laws that Britain aimed to operate to its best competitive and apparent moral advantage. These commercial laws defined many kinds of crime by determining what was lawful and unlawful in trading terms. Modern Britain has also been profoundly shaped by its relations with continental Europe. Britain's membership of European organizations (e.g. Europol) and signing of European agreements has greatly affected its contemporary dealings with crime.[4] However, there are important historical precedents here. For example, trans-European (and North American) conferences and exchange visits on a wide variety of criminal topics including juvenile delinquency, drugs and arms control, prostitution, and prisons took place regularly from the nineteenth century onwards (Leonards 2002; McAllister 2000). Thus, as these and many other examples show, late modern British approaches to crime have long been characterized by an engagement with the wider world.

Hidden crimes

So far this discussion has centred on the official picture of crime. Yet, even as a record of offences known to the authorities, official crime figures are far from complete. In England and Wales, the official crime figures exclude offences recorded by the British Transport Police, Ministry of Defence Police, cases of tax and benefit fraud dealt with administratively by the Inland Revenue, Customs and Excise, and Department of Social Security and, more significantly in terms of numbers, the large numbers of 'summary offences' triable only in magistrates' courts. If different rules of inclusion and exclusion were adopted, the total could be raised or lowered significantly overnight. To give one example: in 1977 the Home Office decided that offences of criminal damage of £20 or less should be defined as notifiable and therefore included in the official crime totals. This decision immediately raised the 'total volume of crime' by about 7 per cent (Maguire 1997). Similarly, new legislation concerning crime and criminal justice has been introduced at an unprecedented rate since the 1980s, creating new offences, modifying the definition of others and, overall, once again changing the 'official' picture of crime in Britain.

Indeed, interpreting official crime figures is fraught with difficulties. As we shall see, in recognition of this point, researchers and policy makers have increasingly turned to alternative measures of crime such as the national British Crime Survey (started in 1982 as a regular, large-scale survey of people living in private households in England and Wales) and other local victim surveys. There is now a widespread acceptance that whatever crime figures tell us, they only represent the tip of an iceberg and politicians and senior police officers routinely warn us against accepting crime statistics as 'hard facts' and refer to the 'hidden figure' of crime *unreported to* and *unrecorded by* the police. The existence of a hidden figure of crime has long been acknowledged although its actual extent was a matter of speculation until the first national victimization surveys in the USA in the 1970s and in Britain in the 1980s. The problem of the hidden figure arises because all quantifiable data depends on how the figures are constructed and interpreted. Not all crimes are reported to the police by the public: because of ignorance that a crime has been committed (e.g. many instances of environmental crime); there seems to be no victim (e.g. certain drug-related offences); the victim is powerless (e.g. in child abuse); the incident seems too 'trivial'; or the victim has no faith that the police will take the offence seriously (e.g. racial harassment or homophobic violence). Nor are all reported crimes recorded by the police. According to British Crime Survey figures derived from regular survey of victim reports, in itself smaller than the 'true' hidden figure, less than half of all offences are reported to the police, of which about half are recorded by the police and appear in the official statistics (Barclay 1995).

Changes in police practices, priorities, and politics will also have a significant effect on the official crime data. Although the police have a statutory responsibility to record crimes, much discretion remains about whether and how to deal with possible offences which do come to their attention. Reports from the public may be disbelieved, or considered to be too trivial, or deemed not to refer to a criminal offence. They may be excluded so as to avoid work or to improve the clear-up rate (Bottomley and Coleman 1981), or as a result of police inefficiency and bureaucracy (Inspectorate of Constabulary 2000). Recorded crime figures can be affected by changes in counting rules. For example, in 1998 the practice of recording only the most serious of a chain of offences in one incident was replaced by recording one crime for each victim. This had the effect of increasing the amount of recorded violent crime from around 350,000 cases in the year ending March 1998 to around 600,000 cases during the next 12 months. However, had the old counting rules still applied, the recorded level would have *fallen* to around 330,000 (Povey and Prime 1999). Equally, the numbers of offences 'discovered' by the police themselves are subject to fluctuations in law-enforcement activities. High-profile planned operations against a particular type of offence (for instance, burglary, drugs, and other street crimes) will inevitably bring about an increase in arrests and the discovery and recording of many new offences in the targeted areas. Conversely, numbers may fall owing to a withdrawal of police interest in a particular type of crime. In the past, high crime figures have been used by police lobbyists to the advantage of the police organization. By examining police inspectorate and committee reports at the time, Taylor (1998) found that the increases in crime between 1914 and 1960 could be largely accounted for by senior police officers 'playing the crime card'. By recording large numbers of minor property offences which were traditionally not recorded, chief constables were able to persuade their police authorities to increase funding. The key message, therefore, is that official crime statistics do *not* provide an objective and incontrovertible measure of criminal behaviour. Instead, they fluctuate according to the organizational constraints and priorities of the criminal justice system.

The dark figure varies considerably with the type of crime committed. Property crime in general has high reporting rates. Burglary with loss and motor vehicle theft have almost 100 per cent reporting rates, presumably in order to meet insurance company requirements (Reiner 2000: 77). In contrast, crimes of violence, sexual assault, and minor theft have traditionally resulted in very low reporting rates (Mirrlees-Black et al. 1996: 24–6). Crimes against certain victims are also more likely to be hidden. In general, the more socially vulnerable the victim and the more private or intimate the setting of the crime's commission, the less visible the crime and the less likely to be publicly recorded. In recent years, there have been a growing number of revelations about the extensive abuse of children who have been in the care of local authorities. By the mid-1990s allegations of sexual abuse by community home staff had surfaced in Leicestershire, Islington, Dumfries, Buckinghamshire, Northumbria, and Cheshire. In 1997 a tribunal of inquiry into abuse in children's homes in North Wales heard evidence from some 300 survivors accusing 148 staff of systematic violence and exploitation (Muncie 1999: 23). Elder abuse is also hidden behind closed doors of private households or care homes. According to one case review of social services in England, some 5 per cent of pensioners regularly suffer victimization. This is almost certainly an underestimate. Non-reporting often results from concerns over domestic privacy, and few cases end up in official statistics let alone in court (Brogden and Nijhar 2000: 48–9). There is some evidence to suggest that more victims come from working-class backgrounds. However, as with other forms of violence in the family, this could be due to the reliance of studies on professional agencies that tend to deal more with working-class clients (Biggs et al. 1995). The capacity of organizations to hide their abuse of power and those in their care is discussed in Chapter 4.

Such findings underline the fact that the problem of crime presented in official figures is both quantitatively inadequate and fundamentally flawed. Indeed, critics have argued that the official statistics provide a skewed vision of the crime problem. Youth crimes dominate the official crime statistics, partly because most take place in highly visible public places—the street, the shopping mall, the football ground. As a result, they trigger the most public anxiety, routinely appear as a part of the political agenda, and command significant criminological attention and research resources. By contrast, many hidden crimes committed—in the corporate boardroom, in the financial marketplace, on the Internet, or in the private sphere of the family—are characterized by 'no knowledge, no statistics, no theory, no research, no control, no politics, and no panic' (Jupp et al. 1999). Even when they *are* reported and recorded, they are often considered to be 'atypical', 'one-off scandals', less serious than 'real crime', and as something distinct from more familiar crises of law and order.

Although crime victimization surveys have sometimes been hailed as offering us 'a more informed picture of crime' (Mayhew and Hough 1988: 157), they too have serious limitations (see Coleman and Moynihan 1996). Most obviously, they only measure criminal incidents where a victim can be identified or where a victim accepts such a status. They depend on victims to be honest and forthcoming in their interviews, which may be difficult especially for sexual offences. Victims of violence at work may also be reluctant to disclose their experiences to interviewers because they feel it reflects badly upon themselves as competent workers (Budd 1999). Respondents may not always remember incidents clearly, a problem which increases with the length of the recall period. The British Crime Surveys, which are household-based, only cover residents in private households and exclude those who reside in communal establishments (e.g. the mentally ill) and other marginalized groups (e.g. the homeless) who may also be subject to exceptionally high risks of crime victimization. Furthermore, most victim surveys suffer from a general inability to tap certain forms of crime where there is no direct or clearly identifiable victim (as in corporate and environmental crime). Their focus on legal (as opposed to social) definitions of crime and discrete incidents can also explain why some respondents fail to perceive themselves as victims. For instance, low-level harassment, not in itself criminal, could nonetheless form part of a continuum of violence and an integral part of victims' everyday experience. In the light of these limitations, the results of crime victimization surveys must be interpreted with caution.

Knowledges of crime

What are the key sources of knowledge about crime in modern Britain and how have these changed? How have academic approaches to the study of crime developed and how do they relate to other kinds of enquiry? In academic terms, crime is studied across many disciplines, from criminology and sociology to law, politics, and psychology to history, cultural studies, and literature. Of these, criminology—one of the fastest-growing degree subjects—is regarded as the primary area of study, although one that can contain elements of all the others listed here.

The development of criminology as an academic discipline has been well documented. Accounts written mainly from the 1980s onwards have typically charted the emergence of post-Enlightenment intellectual approaches to the study of crime and its control, tracing key shifts and splits within them (Rock 1988, 1994; Downes and Rock 1988; Garland 1997). These shifts and splits are often located within a very particular chronology: the classical challenge to pre-Enlightenment notions of arbitrary and violent justice; the positivist challenge to classical notions of rationality and deterrence; the sociological challenge to positivist notions of pathology and degeneracy; the postmodern challenge to sociological notions of socio-structural causes and remedies of crime. Each phase is often told through an overview of the 'foundational' work of key figures: Cesare Beccaria and Jeremy Bentham for classicism, for example; Cesare Lombroso for positivism; Chicago School academics, notably Robert Park, Clifford Shaw, and Edwin Sutherland for sociological approaches; Ian Taylor, Paul Walton, and Jock Young for new deviancy approaches, and so on. This is, of course, an oversimplification of a much more complex literature, although this chronology and these leading characters will be highly, and perhaps wearily, familiar to most criminology students. Such accounts of the emergence of criminology as a discrete field of investigation are useful in offering a map of and introduction to the discipline. But, as with all maps, this one emphasizes certain features over others.

The conventional criminological map has been criticized from various groups inside and outside the discipline. Some feminist criminologists have pointed to its androcentrism (or male-centredness) and its failure to incorporate historical investigations of women's crime other than the more sensational studies carried out by Lombroso and his colleague William Ferrero (Naffine 1996; Gelsthorpe and Morris 1990; Heidensohn 1996; Smart 1976). Transgressive criminologists of various kinds have objected to its failure to link crime and control to wider questions of (dis)order and power (Cain 1990; Sumner 1990). Similarly, cultural criminologists have noted its failure to place criminological landmarks within broader social, economic, and cultural contexts (Beirne 1993, 1994; Leps 1992). Historians of crime, if they were to engage more directly with criminology, might certainly share this latter concern. Some postmodernist commentators have sought to either deconstruct (Smart 1990) or reconstruct (Henry and Milovanovic 1996) criminology, while others have argued in defence of a realist criminology (Matthews and Young 1992) and in appreciation of the diversity of contemporary criminological perspectives (South 1997, 2000).

A further criticism that might be made of the conventional map is that it does not readily encourage discussion of the wider practical impact of academic criminological research upon criminal justice strategies. Students can be left wondering what difference centuries of research have made despite the fact that the effects of much of this work have been considerable. These effects are usefully discussed in terms of policy, position, activism, and critique. Links between academic criminology and government criminal justice policy-making were cemented in 1957 with the establishment of the Cambridge Institute of Criminology, a body directly supported by the Home Office (Garland 1997). More recently, the Home Office's own Research Unit (also opened in 1957) has employed and financed many academic researchers and the Economic and Social Research Council has directed its funding towards research projects (e.g. about crime patterns, victims, the performance of criminal justice institutions) that have clear relevance to policy-making (see Maguire 2000: 127–9). These links have been further strengthened by the appointment of a number of academics to senior policy positions: for example, in recent years criminologists Paul Wiles and Rod Morgan have been appointed director of the Home Office Research Development and Statistics programme and HM Chief Inspector of Probation respectively.

However, the practical influence of criminologists has not been confined to shaping government policy via high-profile institutions. Others have taken a more direct and often much more radical approach by working with campaigners and reformers. Many have been active in penal reform movements of various kinds, in setting up rape crisis centres and hostels for victims of domestic violence and sexual abuse, and in challenging racism within the criminal justice system (see Ryan and Ward 1992; Holdaway and Rock 1998; Cohen 1981). Both policy-making and campaigning could therefore be said to have exercised an influence beyond the immediate search for practical reform in that they have helped to 'set the agenda' through their mainstreaming of wider academic critiques. Nowhere has this been more apparent in recent times, perhaps, than in the close relationship between the philosophies of 'left realist' criminologists of the 1980s and New Labourite politicians of the 1990s symbolized by the statement that governments should be 'tough on crime, tough on the causes of crime' (see Chapter 3).

Another major source of knowledge about crime is the criminal justice establishment itself. The police, courts, probation and prison services, for example, generate a wide range of information, from criminal statistics to annual reviews and research reports to personal memoirs. Their work has of course been studied extensively by criminologists, sociologists, historians, and journalists,[5] interested in pursuing a range of different questions, such as how these organizations have developed, how their agendas have changed, how their operational decisions are made, how they treat different groups of offenders, how they manage their staff, how effectively they serve the public, and so on. However, the fact that all these organizations produce knowledge in their own right should not be overlooked. Most publish their own professional journals, commission research projects, give press briefings, and submit evidence to public inquiries, commissions, and committees. Such texts need, as all texts, to be used critically as Eugene McLaughlin and Karim Murji's (1998) study of the

Police Federation's campaigns to politicize law and order issues shows. Nevertheless, they can provide insights into the everyday work of practitioners and the routine workings of the criminal justice system that are not available to other researchers in quite the same way. Amongst many other things, they show that at any given time, there are many conflicting views as to the nature of crime and the effectiveness or otherwise of favoured models of managing it.

Since criminality concerns the wider community, it is inevitable that other community agencies will also produce information about crime. Welfare agencies of many kinds have been concerned with criminological questions since at least the nineteenth century (and earlier in some cases). Charities and voluntary groups were (and remain) very much involved with crime-related work. Prostitutes, abused children, child abusers, vagrants, drug addicts and alcoholics, battered women, ex-prisoners, and many other groups have all been the subject of specific charitable campaigns, by organizations ranging from the Female Mission to the Fallen to Women's Aid, from the Temperance Movement to Alcoholics Anonymous, from the Howard League for Penal Reform to NACRO (National Association for the Care and Resettlement of Offenders). All such groups produced, and continue to produce, much information about crime. Significantly, they have been hugely overlooked as a source of knowledge about criminality within histories of criminology and theories of crime and deviance. To draw on this vast body of information would be to construct a much broader picture of crime, which would, for example, have a lot more to say on the experiences of women, children, and the elderly as victims and perpetrators of crimes.

Statutory organizations at central and local government level often developed their particular services around the 'idea' of crime. Public health reformers and slum clearers in the mid-nineteenth century consciously sought to improve urban living and to protect and create key commercial spaces for further development. As part of this, they set out to clean up 'dangerous' urban areas and their 'dangerous' inhabitants. In order to do this, they had to identify and map these areas, processes clearly aided by their vivid imaginations as much as by their concrete investigations (see Taylor et al. 1996; Massey 1994). Statutory welfare agencies have also used the threat of criminalization to secure compliance to new social norms. The gradual introduction of new legally enforceable living standards meant that people could be prosecuted for breaching them. Such sanctions began to be applied across many spheres of activity from the late nineteenth century onwards. Residents of an area could face charges for failing to dispose properly of refuse; landlords for keeping unsanitary houses; shopkeepers for selling adulterated foods; parents for neglecting their children and so on. Numbers of these kinds of offences may not have approached those of more 'standard' crimes such as theft, street-based offences, and assault (Gatrell 1990: 269), yet they clearly contributed to the shaping of new cultures of conformity.

Further, welfare agencies have used criminal records to determine a person's eligibility for certain social services. Poor relief was not, for example, automatically given to those who had been convicted of an offence. Similarly, those who had been convicted forfeited their right to an old age pension when these were first introduced although this was later revised (Brown 1978). At one stage, some within the socialist Fabian Society argued that the finger-printing of suspected criminals be extended to all elderly people claiming a pension in order to combat an early form of feared benefit fraud (Webb 1907). Today, certain kinds of public and voluntary provision for homeless people (such as hostels and day centres) can be closed to those known or judged to be violent or heavy users of alcohol and other drugs (Carlen 1996). Certain public sector employers are required to run police checks on potential employees if they are likely to be working with certain kinds of clients. Those with convictions for sex-offending for example are not allowed to work with children.

This attention to individual criminal records as well as the actuarially calculated criminal 'proneness' of certain communities has become an integral part of the work of the modern British financial sector. Insurance companies, banks, credit suppliers, and other lenders seek, store, and exchange information as to the personal character, of those seeking to buy their services. A criminal record can be used as a reason for denying a loan or insurance cover, while the liability of particular residential areas to crime (as calculated by risk-assessors and loss adjusters) can have the effect of making it at best expensive and at worst impossible to secure insurance on domestic and commercial properties. The significance of this commercial knowledge of crime has grown hugely with the increase in home ownership from the 1950s and the massive expansion (through de-regulation) of personal lending and insurance facilities in the 1980s. Risk-related knowledge has thus become central to modern actuarial societies although it should be noted that other legislative developments have countered this in key ways. The Rehabilitation of Offenders Act 1974, for example, removed the duty to declare spent convictions from some categories of minor offender thereby effectively allowing them a 'clean slate'.

Modern knowledges of crime have also been much influenced by broader cultural agencies. Newspapers, novels, and drama from the eighteenth century onwards together with film and television from the twentieth, have done an enormous amount to shape everyday understandings of crime. This is discussed at length in Chapter 5.

Taken together, the work of these various agencies and individuals points to the fact that crime has never been the concern of criminologists and criminal justice professionals alone. It shows that different elements of civil society, broadly defined, played (and continue to play) a major part in the definition, detection, and reform of criminals—some as part of a wider social reform agenda, some as a social duty, some as a form of entertainment. Looking at the history of these diverse contributions also raises further questions about conventional criminological chronologies by suggesting that many conflicting opinions about crime were in circulation in any given period rather than one dominant view or explanation giving sequential way to another. To consider these broad knowledges of crime alongside each other would be to begin to explore the different relationships between them in critical and constructive ways. Different knowledges of crime and criminality have been generated by different organizations for very different purposes. But how have they connected with each other, if at all? How have, for example, 'expert' knowledges related to 'practitioner' knowledges, 'formal' to 'informal', 'policy' to 'popular'?

Knowledges of crime have thus clearly proliferated in modern societies. What have been the wider effects of this proliferation? In one sense, these various knowledges have served to increase the visibility of crime and therefore perhaps to amplify anxieties about it. In another sense, this greater visibility has perhaps made crime a more familiar and less remarkable part of everyday life. It certainly does not follow that the more information gathered about crime, the easier it is to combat. One important reason for this is that their very plurality means that these knowledges inevitably contradict or 'talk past' each other. It might also be tempting to see the spread of this data collection as evidence of the growth of a modern surveillance society where all kinds of social relations are subject to new types of intimate, invasive, and often concealed scrutiny. However, the very many gaps, overlaps, and inaccuracies within this body of information caution against this (Lyon 1994).

Conclusion

As this chapter has suggested, responses to and understandings of crime have changed a great deal in modern Britain. The development of new techniques of counting and countering crime in the early nineteenth century were themselves important modernizing processes. The proliferation of different knowledges of crime, from the gathering of criminal statistics and the emergence of criminology to the spread of client-specific charities and the explosion of detective fiction, has helped to make crime an indisputable part of everyday life. For all this, experiences of crime and reactions to crime have continued to vary greatly. Some crimes, usually the more rare, continue to attract more public and political attention than others. In recent times, the relatively few crimes committed by serial paedophiles, serial killers, and serial joyriders, for example, have attracted far more attention than the more routine thefts and assaults which have dominated criminal statistics since these began to be collated nearly two centuries ago. Those crimes that have been beyond the traditional reach of the police, from sexual abuse and domestic violence within the home to organized corruption within businesses, have come to public prominence only comparatively recently.

New ways of measuring, policing, and understanding crime have had an obvious impact on levels of recorded crime. However, they cannot by themselves explain the dramatic rise in the amount of crime committed and reported since the Second World War in Britain and other Western nations. This rise is a multi-faceted phenomenon, aspects of which are explored in the chapters that follow. The aim throughout this book is to consider crime in a series of wider contexts and to approach it in terms of the historical, the everyday, the organizational, and the cultural.

Chapter 2

Histories of Crime

Introduction

THE study of crime in modern Britain clearly benefits from the combination of historical, criminological, and other social scientific approaches. Historians of crime and social (dis)order can usefully question established criminological chronologies concerning the changing nature of 'modern' crime and its control. They can also, with the obvious benefit of hindsight, consider crime in its broader social contexts by looking beyond changes within the criminal justice system itself to wider changes in, for example, living standards, social reform, cultural life, working practices, gender relations, class relations, and race relations. They can show how moral panics around particular crimes and criminals have arisen and diffused. This is not to claim that it is ever possible accurately to 'reconstruct' any given period in its entirety. Historical knowledge, like all knowledge, is necessarily partial, selective, and subject to change. As this chapter sets out to show, historians' own views as to the causes and remedies of crime have altered considerably since the 1970s, not least with the rise and fall of 'history from below' or social history (see also Emsley and Knafla 1996; King 1999). Historical investigations of the crimes associated with men, women, juveniles, and the 'underclass'—the topics discussed here—have been shaped by different concerns at different times. This chapter identifies key studies in each of these areas in order to show how these different concerns have influenced research directions and how the history of crime has developed as a field of enquiry since the 1970s.

These factors mean that history cannot be put to easy criminological uses. It cannot provide straightforward answers to tempting questions such as 'has crime become worse?' or 'have people become less law-abiding?' or 'how can crime be reduced?' (see also Bosworth 2001). We may not be able to 'learn' self-evident lessons from the past but taking a historical perspective holds numerous advantages for students of crime. One of the most obvious is that a historical approach encourages the use of a much wider range of sources of information about crime, from records of workplace cultures, churches, and charities to social statistics relating to demography, prices, epidemics, and schooling to (un)published writings such as (auto)biographies, memoirs, comics, and diaries.

This is partly because historical researchers, unlike criminological or sociological researchers who can generate 'new' data by conducting surveys, interviews and focus groups, and so on, rely on analysing surviving records and artefacts. In short, historians very often have to cast their research net a lot wider in order to find evidence relating to a particular topic. It is also perhaps because, unlike criminologists and sociologists of deviance, historians of crime have not worked so closely within particular theoretical or methodological schools and have therefore been more free to experiment with different sources and approaches. This can mean that historical investigations of crime can appear to social scientists to be 'under-theorized', yet, as outlined in Chapter 1, a more eclectic approach can demonstrate that knowledges of crime have been generated by many more varied groups than standard criminological accounts would suggest. To draw on this variety is to develop the study of crime in relation to a range of broader cultural contexts.

Overall, a historical approach encourages us to look twice at modern 'facts' about crime, to be wary of contemporary claims that a particular kind of crime, criminal, or criminal justice strategy is 'new', and thereby to ask how, why, and by whom modern claims to truth about crime have been established.

Chronologies

How far has modern Britain produced modern forms of, and ways of thinking about, crime? The answer to this question appears initially obvious. A standard narrative might suggest that modern Britain emerged around the late eighteenth century as the product of distinctly modern processes: industrialization, urbanization, centralization, bureaucratization, rationalization, secularization, and so on. These processes transformed perceptions of crime by offering new ways of diagnosing, punishing, and preventing all manner of social disorders. These new ways of seeing took different and often contradictory forms but despite this drew on a common conceptual vocabulary that was also distinctly modern. Discussions of crime were framed in terms of science (not superstition), class (not rank), cities (not villages), capitalism (not communalism), rationality (not religion), justice (not arbitrariness).

Such an answer rests, however, on a very particular chronology and a very selective view of the pre-modern. It assumes that the emergence of modern

Britain was sudden, complete, and irreversible. It supposes, without investigating these in any depth, that the complex social relations of pre-modern Britain were neatly eclipsed. It stresses change over continuity, difference over sameness, transformation over preservation.

This chronology is, in turn, largely the product of unfortunate if understandable developments within the academic study of crime and social (dis)order. Disciplinary divisions between sociologists of crime and criminologists on the one hand and historians of crime on the other have created a series of parallel universes. Further, even within 'historical' approaches to the study of crime, there is a clear divide between 'modernists' and 'early modernists', a divide based upon assumptions about the fundamentally different nature of capitalist and pre-capitalist societies. This division, long present within the discipline of history, is also deeply rooted in the social sciences through the 'founding' work of Marx, Weber, and Durkheim. As a result, a cross-disciplinary chronological consensus has emerged which presents the modern and the pre-modern as worlds apart.

This is not, of course, to argue that large-scale social changes did not occur or that British perceptions of crime and disorder have altered little since, say, the sixteenth century. That there have been many marked and highly significant changes in the definition, detection, explanation, and treatment of crime is not disputed here. Any student of crime reading the opening pages of Foucault's *Discipline and Punish* (1977) cannot fail to note, and be persuaded by, the dramatic contrast between torture and imprisonment. However, a chronological consensus that so consistently emphasizes change over continuity passes up the chance to investigate crucial questions about crime in more nuanced ways. For all its brilliance, the opening passage of *Discipline and Punish* reads rather differently when considered alongside other historical investigations of pre-modern prisons (Finzsch and Jütte 1997) or late modern torture (Amnesty International 1984).

Historical studies of crime open up larger questions about the causes and timings of change. They also open up a crucial space for the study of (apparent) anomalies, hangovers, and overlaps. Here, historians' work on crime and disorder has been invaluable. For example, Malcolm Gaskill's (2000) argument that the local persecution of 'witches' carried on long after the formal banning of witch trials in 1735 and that the tradition of 'corpse-touching' continued to be used as a formal way of gathering evidence for murder trials until late into the eighteenth century begins to expose the highly complex relationship between science and superstition that characterized the 'modern' period. Vic Gatrell's (1994) argument that public executions continued to draw enthusiastic crowds until they were made private in 1868 complicates the claim that 'modern' punishment focused on the sequestered disciplining of the mind rather than the spectacular assault upon the body (see also Linebaugh 1991). Feeley and Little's (1991) claim that, taking a long view, women's crime rates have *fallen* over time qualifies a contemporary tendency to search for the causes of 'modern' women's *rising* crime rates. Paul Griffiths' (1996) investigation of early modern youth crime insists that the phenomenon of 'juvenile delinquency' cannot be simply reduced to the 'modern' processes of urbanization, migration, and changing authority relationships.

In short, this kind of historical work on British crime—chosen from a wealth of possible examples—shows that many practices and beliefs regarded as 'premodern' survived into the 'modern' period and that, similarly, many of those regarded as 'modern' are also to be found in the 'pre-modern' world. As such, it rightly disrupts established chronologies and thereby demands a new look at old certainties.

Whilst new work on historical knowledges of crime is emerging all the time, most historians of social (dis)order have focused on different types of crime and criminals and changing social responses to these. In Britain, this kind of research tends to fall into three broad categories roughly defined by chronology. Early modern, modern, and contemporary historical studies broadly examine social developments between 1500 and 1800, 1800 and 1945 and 1945 to the present respectively. The first two of these are much more developed as areas of study than the third, although this is beginning to change. These boundaries roughly correspond to what are commonly viewed as epoch-making episodes: early mercantile capitalism and agricultural change; the Enlightenment and industrial revolution; the Second World War and late capitalism.

One unfortunate result of these divisions (institutionalized by schools, universities, and publishers) is that historians of each period do not collaborate as much as they might. The history of crime, like that of other topics, therefore becomes over-segmented. Efforts to counter this have included studies of patterns of violence over several centuries (Cockburn 1991; Sharpe and Dickinson 2001; Archer et al. 2001) and legal historical studies of court organization and procedure (Cockburn and Green 1988). The value of such projects is questioned, however, by those historians and social theorists critical of approaches which privilege any kind of grand narrative (that is to say, approaches which try to explain long-term social patterns in terms of particular dynamics such as class or patriarchy). Foucault's work is an interesting exception in this respect. Although criticized by many British historians of crime for its 'cavalier' use of evidence and 'sweeping' conclusions, it is praised by others for its attempt to re-evaluate conventional periodizations and to re-examine the nature of traditional epistemic breaks, albeit drawing primarily upon French history to do so.

This chapter reviews recent developments within histories of British crime. It focuses on four areas: men, women, juveniles, and the 'underclass'. It does not aim to provide an exhaustive account of the changing illegal activities of these groups, but rather to summarize major debates within key studies on each area produced since the 1970s. Among other things, it shows how, in each area, the rising influence of cultural historians, with their stress on plural identities, shifting subjectivities, discourses, meanings, and the imaginary, has challenged earlier accounts of crime established by social historians, with their stress on social structures, class antagonisms, materiality, and the real.

Masculinities and crime

From the late 1980s onwards, research on gender and social issues across the humanities and social sciences began to focus increasingly on masculinities. Criminology and historical studies of crime were no exception and analyses of masculinities quickly established themselves as exciting new research fields. It could be argued, of course, that men and boys have long occupied the centre ground in histories of crime and disorder in Britain, as well as in the wider West and the developing world. In the British case (as arguably elsewhere) this has been less because of the fact that men and boys have historically dominated prosecution figures of most kinds than because class-bound explanations of crime have dominated such historical research. Such histories began to emerge in earnest from the late 1960s onwards, when radical historians began to turn away from traditional areas of research (high politics, diplomacy, war, state formation, and so on) and to investigate what came to be widely called 'history from below', or 'social history'. 'History from below', with its focus on working-class lives, everyday survival, and political struggles, engaged with crime and disorder in a very particular way. Crime now tended to be cast as a political act, criminals as conscious or unconscious class rebels, policemen as class traitors, and the courts as instruments of brutal class oppression (Hobsbawm 1972, Hay et al. 1975; Thompson 1975; Linebaugh 1976; Fitzgerald et al. 1981). Although this broad view quickly attracted sharp academic criticism (Blok 1972; Langbein 1983; see also Innes and Styles 1993 and Lea 1999), it nevertheless remained dominant into the late 1980s (for overview of these debates, see Philips 1983; Weiss 1999: pp. xiii–xxiv).

Many of these studies focused on the late eighteenth and early nineteenth centuries—a period notable for its new ways of recording, policing, and punishing crime, its (not unrelated) dramatic rise in reported crime, and its sharpening of social tensions in the wake of the intensification of capitalism and urbanism and as a result of the post-French revolutionary wars (trans-European and global wars in which Britain was almost continually involved for over 20 years from 1793 to 1815). In many ways, then, the social processes examined in these studies were central to the making of 'modern Britain'—a 'modern Britain' that produced modern casualties through its redefinition of property, labour, and market. These casualties were generally cast as male in these studies in the form of the many (male) agricultural labourers, (male) industrial workers, and (male) unemployed who were prosecuted in their thousands for poaching, gleaning, arson, animal maiming, smuggling, machine-breaking, rioting for lower prices, protesting to protect customary rights, stealing from employers and landlords, and general low-value theft as well as for setting up illegal political organizations, circulating inflammatory political pamphlets, organizing for higher wages, and agitating for the vote (Thompson 1963; Hobsbawm and Rudé 1969; Jones 1982; Archer 1990). These activities, especially those more directly connected to subsistence, were presented as 'social crimes', or crimes which were believed to be justified by most 'ordinary' people. Thus, in parallel with developments in the radical criminologies of the same period, the working-class male 'criminal' was in many ways depicted by radical social historians of the 1960s, 1970s, and 1980s (and some later texts) as a male class warrior, celebrated as a folk hero rather than condemned as a folk devil.

The dominance of this kind of work within histories of British crime began to give way from the late 1980s onwards with the wholesale questioning of established social historical understandings of class and with increasing attention paid to research (some new, some old) in three key areas. First, studies of early modern societies showed that crime and disorder were more than just by-products of 'modern' social, economic, and political struggles (Beattie 1986; Herrup 1987; Sharpe 1999). Second, cultural historians argued that crime and its control held many and varied social meanings, and that these were as much bound up with issues of nation, race, sensation, and science as they were with economic inequalities (Pick 1989; Walkowitz 1992; Kohn 1992). Third, feminist historians, historians of gender relations, and historians of the family explored many kinds of less than heroic male crimes, including domestic violence and child abuse (Behlmer 1982; Clark 1987; Doggett 1992; Hammerton 1992; D'Cruze 1998; Jackson 2000). This latter kind of work, in particular, opened the way for a series of new historical studies that had, perhaps for the first time, a clear and conscious focus on the shifting construction of criminal masculinities.

These new studies have examined masculinity and crime in distinct ways. Many concentrate on different forms of male violence, examining its social organization and the cultural values attached to it by different societies at different times. A major claim to emerge from different researchers undertaking this kind of work is that British society (in line with other Western societies) became increasingly intolerant of male violence from at least the eighteenth century onwards. This intolerance was displayed through increased penalties for 'everyday' crimes such as assault. Acts of interpersonal violence which may not have been subject to prosecution in the early eighteenth century were punished by large fines, imprisonment, and sometimes the death penalty by the early nineteenth (Wiener 1998). Intolerance of male violence was also expressed through the criminalization of many 'traditionally acceptable' male behaviours, from duelling to bare knuckle boxing to wife-beating. According to Martin Wiener (1998) and others, this shift was closely linked to growing divisions between rough and respectable cultures, divisions variously marked by the physical withdrawal of elites from ordinary communities, by the heightened demarcation of public and private spaces, and by the introduction of the new police as 'domestic missionaries' in working-class communities (Palmer 1988).

This line of argument, which owes much to Norbert Elias's concept of 'the civilizing process' (Elias 1939), thereby discusses crime, class, and masculinity in much more subtle ways than earlier work outlined above. Mark Liddle (1996) characterizes this in terms of ongoing battles between 'bourgeois' men and 'brutish' men. 'Bourgeois' men (middle-class, respectable, civilized men) have, from at least the eighteenth century on, attempted to define themselves by continually distancing themselves from 'brutish' men (lower-class, disreputable, uncivilized men). In this sense, the criminalization of 'brutes' was a clear expression of class power but one that was (and is) ongoing rather than bound to a particular period of history or moment of class formation. It was also an expression of recurrent bourgeois concern to establish new definitions of masculinity, to find new ways of being a powerful man that were commensurate with new respectable lifestyles that continually threaten(ed) to emasculate men through domesticity, consumption, companionate marriages, white-collar work, and gentleman's sports. Further, as Angus McLaren (1997: 13–36) argues, the grouping together of certain men as brutish, degenerate, uncivilized, and sexually perverted was clearly motivated by early twentieth-century anxieties, expressed as concerns to contain homosexuals, child abusers, and migrant workers more generally. These men were, for example, often singled out as still deserving of judicial floggings at a time when the use of corporal punishment was being seriously questioned.

Whilst acknowledging the importance of the increasing expression of intolerance of certain forms of male violence, other historians have stressed the continuing embeddedness of violence in everyday life, particularly among young men. Some of this was more periodic and spectacular, from early modern apprentices' riots (Griffiths 1996), to late nineteenth-century public holiday skirmishes involving hooligans in London, scuttlers in the north-west, and East End boys on day-trips to the seaside (Pearson 1983; Davies 2000) and mid-twentieth-century clashes between teds, mods, rockers, punks, and skinheads

(S. Cohen 1972; Robins and Cohen 1978—see also Chapter 5). Spectacular outbreaks like these seem, however, to have been rooted within more general cultures of 'ordinary' violence among young men. Fights, scuffles, and scraps have a long history in playgrounds, schools, pubs, clubs, and workplaces. The fact that young men have been the chief perpetrators and victims of violent crime across the nineteenth, twentieth, and early twenty-first centuries would seem to bear this out.

Neither these studies, nor this discussion of them, intend to imply that violence and crime is an intrinsic, essential, unchanging, or natural part of modern British masculinities—a line also strongly argued by contemporary criminologists (Messerschmidt 1993; Newburn and Stanko 1994a; Collier 1998). As the above discussion of 'bourgeois' and 'brutish' men shows, definitions of 'acceptable' male violence have been contested between men themselves since at least the eighteenth century. The key point here is that, historically, the negotiation of everyday violence has played a major role in the construction of everyday masculinities and has quite frequently resulted in informal policing directed at, or court appearances by, young men.

This dominant focus on changing patterns of male violence is beginning to be offset by further historical research into female violence (discussed below) and into other aspects of the links between other kinds of crime and masculinities. Petty property crime, by far the most commonly prosecuted offence from the eighteenth century onwards, has also been perpetrated in the main by young men. Some have begun to examine this in gendered terms (Shore 1999b; King 2000), although more studies are needed in this area. It is worth noting here that earlier work on past property crime often based its analysis on fundamental, if often unexamined, assumptions about male nature and male culture. Those writing within the radical social history tradition outlined above often argued that there was a direct connection between economic hardship and theft in the eighteenth and early nineteenth centuries, and that, by extension, men who could not provide for their dependants as ordinary, respectable breadwinners were forced to provide for them by criminal means.

As outlined above, this view has certainly had its critics. However, this kind of logic, albeit often more latent than clearly stated, has shaped many criminological investigations and theories from the 1930s onwards. Theories based on the concept of social strain and anomie posited the young working-class man as the principal victim of market inequalities and of the failure of apparently meritocratic systems to deliver social mobility and social status (Merton 1938; Cloward and Ohlin 1960). It followed that because women and girls were not subject to the same pressure to succeed in terms of work, wages, and prospects, they were not subject to the same pressure to use illegal means to find either status or material resources, or both. These theories were largely framed in

North America but had a profound influence on criminologists and sociologists of deviance in Britain. From the 1970s and 1980s, strain-style theories of crime were given a new racial dimension. Hall et al. argued in their ground-breaking text, *Policing the Crisis*, that class inequalities were greatly compounded by racial inequalities, and that young, poor, inner-city black men in particular had come to bear the brunt of the repercussions of an urban capitalist economy undergoing its own crisis of control (Hall et al. 1978). However, this work has also come to be criticized from within criminology and elsewhere (see Chapter 5).

Historical studies of white-collar crime have also traditionally focused on men (Robb 1992). Recent work has taken a new look at old gendered questions, although again, elements of earlier strain theory logic can still be seen here. Maurice Punch (1996) and James Messerschmidt (1993), for example, argue that white-collar cultures have created particular pressures for the men who work within them: pressures to succeed, to out-perform, to out-do and so on, and that these pressures have led men to break the law in pursuit of status. This point is of relevance to the further discussion of crimes of profit and power in Chapter 4 and is returned to in the concluding chapter.

Sexual offences make up a final strand within British historical work on men and crime. This literature falls into two main types: that dealing with men as sexual abusers of women and children; and that dealing with gay men as victims of abusive and intrusive sexual laws. The first type has its origins in the work of feminist, family, and gender historians outlined above. Histories of women and children's (predominantly girls') experiences of rape, sexual assault, incest, and domestic violence (Clark 1987; D'Cruze 1998; Jackson 2000) have used a variety of sources, including court records, institutional records, newspapers, and diaries, to reconstruct the circumstances in which men's intimate violence could be challenged. This is an important theme within this work: only certain women and girls who presented themselves in certain ways and spoke within certain 'victim' discourses were likely to succeed either in bringing their case to public attention or, rarer still, securing a conviction. A common claim in these studies is that those cases that did make it as far as court were a tiny minority of the possible total. A related suggestion is that male victims of intimate violence, whether this was performed by men or women, found it almost impossible to speak out about the experience even if they thought or sought to do so. This hidden history has yet to be explored in depth, although the silence of conventional sources on this question would appear to make this very difficult.

The second type of literature—on the historical experiences of gay men, variously defined—has its origins in studies of sexuality inspired by the liberation movements of the 1970s (Weeks 1977) and work by (and on) Foucault, which exploded in the 1980s (Foucault 1979). Homosexual practices between men had long been criminalized by British ecclesiastical courts but this criminalization was greatly extended from the 1860s to the point where any 'acts of gross indecency' between men either in private or in public could lead to a criminal conviction. Same-sex practices between women were, infamously, never criminalized although an attempt was made in 1921 (Doan 1998). Decriminalization of male homosexuality did not occur until 1967 and even then certain consensual homosexual acts between adult men remained, and continue to remain, illegal, as does the 'promotion' of homosexuality in schools under the notorious Clause 28 of the 1988 Local Government Act. Modern Britain has certainly had an uneasy relationship with modern sexualities. The messages of historical studies in this field are, overall, rather mixed. Some condemn unjust laws and seek to show above all how men were policed, punished, and pathologized (Weeks 1989; Jeffery-Poulter 1991; Higgins 1996) and how, by extension, they were 'liberated' by later law reform. More recently, others have stressed the different ways in which different groups of men were made subject to these laws (Moran 1996) and also celebrated men's ability to circumvent these laws altogether and to sustain vibrant sexual and social cultures in the decades long before (de)criminalization (Carter 2001, 124–62; Houlbrook 2000, 2002).

Femininities and crime

Academic historical research on women and crime in modern Britain began in earnest in the 1970s (Beattie 1975) and has since developed in many directions.[1] Much of this work has focused on the early modern period, and within this, on witchcraft (Sharpe 1996; Briggs 1996; Gaskill 2000) but also on the more 'ordinary' crimes committed by women such as property crime, slander, assault, and infanticide (Kermode and Walker 1994; King 1996). Perhaps contrary to modern expectations, women have always been a significant presence in the courts, albeit in much lower numbers than men. Some historians, however, argue that the gap between male and female rates of prosecution has not been static, but has actually *widened* over time. For example, Feeley and Little (1991; and Feeley 1994) have argued that women's prosecution rates for serious crimes have in fact fallen from the early modern period onwards and have only risen again relatively recently (in the period after the Second World War).

This apparent fall is attributed to three connected factors. First, many historians argue that women played a much greater public role during the sixteenth and seventeenth centuries than in the nineteenth. Central to this was the fact that all but a relatively small number of elite women were economically active, working in many areas, including agriculture, brewing, baking, and textiles, to support themselves and to contribute to the support of their families. Women did, of course, undertake domestic work and childcare but in conjunction with many other activities. Early modern women thus engaged more fully in public, street, and neighbourhood life (Wiesner 2000; Eales 1998; P. Sharpe 1998). They therefore had more opportunity to commit crime than their nineteenth-century counterparts who were more likely to be confined within private domesticity as modelled on the emergent middle-class home.

Moreover, and secondly, those that did engage in crime were apparently more likely than their later counterparts to be held to account for their actions. Feeley and Little (1991) argue that where modes of law enforcement were more informal and community-based, as they were in early modern societies, they were more likely to be brought to bear on women who had broken the law. As law enforcement became more professionalized and more formally masculinized (with, for example, the appointment of local police officers in the 1830s and 1840s), women became less likely to be prosecuted.

A third reason for the fall in female prosecution rates over the course of the eighteenth and nineteenth centuries is said to be linked to the gradual reframing of punishable offences and the down-grading of the seriousness of certain kinds of crime. Many of the 'serious' offences for which women in the early modern period appeared in court (such as slander, scolding, and defamation) seem very minor to modern eyes. Of course, in a society where so much rested on personal reputation and good name, defamation of character *was* a serious offence. However, in a society like that of the eighteenth or nineteenth centuries where reputation was so much more bound up with property and wealth, and where there was increasing concern to punish crimes against property and physical crimes against the person, such offences carried much less weight and therefore resulted in fewer prosecutions.

However, this overall argument regarding women's falling prosecution rates can be criticized on many fronts. Some argue that the growing gap between male and female prosecutions had more to do with the 'Victorian criminalization of men' (Wiener 1998) and the dramatic increase in charges against men outlined earlier. Others would object strongly to the idea that the more 'open' early modern boundary between public and private spheres gave way to a much more rigid boundary 'somewhere' during the eighteenth century (Vickery 1993). They would doubtless argue that since women's public life remained very active, despite the coming of capitalism and its heightened gendered divisions of labour, space, and time, women's opportunity and readiness to commit crime remained the same.

Others might look to the proliferation of new kinds of offences in the nineteenth and twentieth centuries and their clear connection to women (Zedner 1991). Women appeared frequently in courts on charges of, for example, habitual drunkenness or failure to care for their children in various ways. More 'traditional' female crimes such as prostitution and infanticide assumed new significance amongst the social tensions of the nineteenth-century city (Mahood 1990; Bartley 2000; Higginbotham 1989; Arnot and Usborne 1999). Women's involvement in certain kinds of crime may have therefore declined, but may have increased in others. A fuller historical survey of the activities of lower courts would throw some light on this.

Further, while it may be true that the formalization of law enforcement led to a reduction in the number of women charged with offences, it is also true that the nineteenth century saw a proliferation of 'modern' ways of dealing with deviance, many of which were thought particularly suited to women. The inebriates' reformatory, the religious rescue home, and, up to a point, the asylum and the mental hospital all housed large numbers of women who had committed deviant acts, some of which were criminalized, others of which were not (Zedner 1991). Women and girls could be sent to such places (which survived in different forms well into the twentieth century) by their families, religious charities, and sometimes by the police and the courts for a range of reasons, including vagrancy, destitution, debt, drunkenness, theft, violence, prostitution, sexual promiscuity, illegitimate pregnancy, abortion, and infanticide. Some of those concerned were prosecuted as offenders, others were not: a great deal depended on individual circumstances, the nature of the referring agency, and the availability of funds to pay for such confinement. Clearly, sexual deviance was very significant here, but it was rarely the only reason for a referral. Further, it should be noted that some women and girls approached these institutions themselves, though the 'freedom' of such a choice was often highly constrained (Cox forthcoming). Modern Britain may have thus allowed some women to slip through the criminal justice net but it also created many extra-judicial ways of sanctioning others.

The argument that women both committed more crime and were prosecuted more frequently in the early modern period because they had more social freedom is very similar to a more familiar argument often made about the modern period and the present. The idea that women's social liberation has led them to become both more criminal and more likely to face the same punishment as men has been used by many criminologists to explain 'rises' in women's prosecutions (in Britain as well as in Europe and the United States) from the 1970s onwards. Criminal statistics do indeed suggest that this rise has been 'real' at particular moments (see Chapter 3). Freda Adler's 1975 text, *Sisters in Crime*, interpreted such rises in an unequivocal way: a 'new female criminal' was on the loose and rapidly became a new marker of modern times.

Others totally rejected Adler's claims. Box and Hale (1983, 1984) argued that women might have become more socially liberated in the late twentieth century but that they also remained economically marginal (see also Smart 1979). Structural inequalities meant that as a group they had, historically, always been poorer than men (occupying more menial jobs, combining periods of paid employment with periods of unpaid childcare, earning less during their working lives therefore having fewer savings and reduced pensions, and so on). If women were committing more crime it was because of their social marginality, not their greater equality. More recent studies have repeated this view, variously arguing that the rise in women's prosecutions from the 1980s onwards is explained by a rise in specific areas, all related to continuing and worsening levels of female poverty: benefit fraud, TV licence evasion, prostitution and drug-related offences (Carlen 1988 and 1998; Pantazis 1999; Taylor 1993). Some link the rise in the numbers of women sent to prison not so much to rising female crime rates, but to broader changes in sentencing and penal strategies (Bosworth 1999). Others link the rising numbers of women in general caught within the criminal justice system to the sharp rise in the numbers of black women in particular being detained, charged, and imprisoned (Chigwada-Bailey 1997; see also Home Office 2001), many of them migrants (allegedly) involved in the drugs-trafficking business (Green 1996).

All this shows that there are conflicting explanations of patterns of women's crime in modern Britain. These difficulties are compounded by the fact that some women were and are processed within the criminal justice system, others were, and continue to be, clearly diverted out of it. Their treatment by police, magistrates, and juries compared to that of men has been more lenient in some instances and more harsh in others. In the final analysis, however, any discussion of shifts in patterns of women's crime rests on relatively few cases. Throughout the period discussed here, both during eras of 'rising' and 'falling' female crime, women have accounted for a small minority of cases passing through the various levels of the criminal justice system. Even increases of 100 or 200 per cent in levels of women's prosecution would leave them far behind male levels. The ongoing public fascination with, and fears around, women's crime perhaps say more about fascination and fears connected to wider social questions about order and disorder, stability and change, imagined traditions, and imagined futures.

Further, as some feminist criminologists have long argued, to conduct these discussions in terms of the differences between 'women' and 'men' can be very unhelpful because to do so is to ignore differences between women themselves (as well as between men). It is perhaps equally important for historians and criminologists to ask a set of alternative questions. Why are certain women more subject to policing and not others? Why are certain women arrested and not others? Why are certain women found guilty by magistrates and juries and not others? Why are certain women sent to prison and not others? Why are certain women referred to psychiatric treatment and not others? Important as gender difference is in shaping crime patterns, it is by no means the only difference that counts.

Indeed, many criminologists have pursued exactly these questions. They have found that, on the whole, women who present themselves as more traditionally feminine, and above all as respectful and remorseful tend to get treated more 'leniently' than other women (Carlen and Worrall 1987; Worrall 1990; Heidensohn 1996). Most of this work has focused on women born after the Second World War. In historical terms, work on the early modern period and eighteenth and nineteenth centuries has done much to address these questions and has found similar patterns (Kermode and Walker 1994; Zedner 1991). There remain, however, significant gaps in detailed knowledge of women's crime (and crime more generally) in Britain from the 1900s to the 1970s. This was a period of accelerated social changes which transformed many women's lives through, for example, access to the vote, to equal rights to divorce, and to wider forms of paid work through war, public sector growth, and economic diversification. These changes affected different women in different ways. The questions of how they affected issues of crime and control have yet to be properly addressed. At the very least, the fact that women's prosecution rates remained low across this period would demand an even more critical look at the claim that women's liberation has led (more than once) to their criminalization.

Youth and crime

Prosecuted crime is committed overwhelmingly by young people. This statement is as true for the early twenty-first century as it has been for at least the previous four centuries. It implies two things: that young people (and young men in particular) commit more crime of a kind likely to be reported (by their families and by the public) and that younger offenders are more likely to be pursued formally and informally by the criminal justice system (Lee 1998).

Research into the history of youth crime varies in focus and approach. As outlined below, some have concentrated more on disorderly youth cultures while others have tracked the development and administration of youth justice procedures. Many of these studies have one important element in common, however, in that they all tend to stress the fact that youth crime is not simply a 'modern' problem, but rather has a long and complex history. Notwithstanding the fact that definitions of childhood and youth have changed over time, it is possible to point to the long-standing involvement of boys, and to a lesser but significant extent, girls, in riotous street cultures, subcultures and gangs, property crime of all kinds, and violent crime, from assault and vandalism to manslaughter and murder (Griffiths 1996; King 1998; Shore 1999a; Pearson 1983; Davies 1999, 2000; Humphries 1981; Cox forthcoming). Since the mid-nineteenth century, children and young people have also been brought into the criminal justice system for their own 'protection', both as victims of crimes (such as neglect and physical or sexual abuse) and in attempts to stop them becoming criminals in later life. This kind of 'welfare policing' has been most commonly studied through the experiences of girls (Gelsthorpe 1989; Mahood 1995, Jackson 2000; Cox forthcoming) but was, and is, also extended to large numbers of boys.

The view that delinquency is far from 'new' was perhaps set out most comprehensively by Geoffrey Pearson (1983) in his now classic text, *Hooligan*. The book charted a series of panics around disorderly youth starting with that of the early years of the Thatcher government and its attempt to deliver a 'short, sharp, shock' to young offenders and going back to the late nineteenth-century outrage caused by so-called 'hooligan' rioters in different parts of the country. Pearson's analysis of these events is summed up in his chosen subtitle: these events tell us more about the 'history of respectable fears' than they do about the history of youth crime. The implication was that boisterous youth cultures had not substantially changed across this period yet continually generated new rounds of public and media comment based around a familiar set of concerns: unruly behaviour in public space, lack of respect for traditional values, unwillingness to knuckle down to a stable job, or to settle down to stable family life. In his later writing on this question, Pearson (1994) explained this repeating pattern in terms of repeating inter-generational tensions. The ageing process has meant that adults and older people have always experienced the social worlds of children and the young as unfamiliar, and, to a degree, as posing a threat to 'established' ways of life, whatever these might be. He does not suggest that this is a timeless process but one which has instead been exaggerated in 'modern' times with their accelerated paces of socio-economic change. Again, modernity is linked here to the social changes wrought by early nineteenth-century urbanization, industrialization, and capitalism.

There is support for this general view among many historians of British youth and delinquency. Peter King (1998) and Heather Shore (1999a) have argued that the early nineteenth century represented a watershed in both definitions of, and responses to, what came to be called 'juvenile delinquency' around this time. Recorded prosecutions of children and adolescents, particularly in urban areas, rose dramatically from the 1780s onwards. In part a result of massive population growth and a simple increase in numbers of people under the age of 30, this youth crime wave was more commonly explained by authorities at the time as a result of the collapse of traditional social controls upon young people. As a group, the young had long left parental homes to work as apprentices in agriculture or in small-scale industry or as domestic servants, but now these traditional areas of employment were themselves being restructured. The demand for more flexible, mobile, and adaptable labour in this phase of economic expansion meant that old contracts between young workers and their employers were undermined. Apprentices, for example, were bound to work for the same employer for a set period of time (commonly seven years), often for very low wages. In return, they gained a training, sometimes board and lodging, and, crucially, longer-term job security. Young people may therefore have left home and started work early by today's standards but, in theory at least, they swapped parental discipline for employer discipline. Further, it was expected that they would eventually marry and thus subject themselves to the discipline of their own family life. The breakdown of apprenticeship, together with wider changes in the relationship between employers and workers, therefore disrupted this established pattern, giving young workers a freedom (though also an economic vulnerability) that few of their parents and grandparents had known.

Similarly, youth migration in itself was not new but the urban destinations of many of this early nineteenth-century generation of young workers certainly were. Expanding urban spaces are argued to have contributed to the new phenomenon of juvenile delinquency in two key ways: by providing more opportunities for dissolute leisure activities (Springhall 1986, 1998), but also by providing more possibilities of surveillance and regulation. Towns and cities may have been home to coffee-houses, gaming rooms, pubs, and brothels, but they were also home to moral vigilante groups (such as the Society for the Promotion of Christian Knowledge, or various societies for the 'reformation of manners'), Christian crusaders (such as Anglican evangelists and Methodists), thief-takers, prosecution associations (South 1987), and later public health reformers and the police themselves. The socio-economic changes of this period are most often read in terms of dislocation, breakdown, alienation, and anonymity. Yet this reading overlooks the fact that many steps were taken by many contemporaries to prevent, contain, and ameliorate these processes. The 'invention' of juvenile delinquency in the early nineteenth century was therefore as much a product of attempts to develop new forms of community and new forms of control as it was evidence of a loss of these in their traditional forms.

It should be noted here that the 'modernity' of juvenile delinquency is questioned by many early modern historians who stress the fact that youthful disorder was a major concern for authorities *prior* to urbanization and industrialization. Systems like apprenticeship did not, after all, *guarantee* good behaviour. Griffiths (1996, 2002) details the wide range of measures taken against unruly youths in early modern England by the church, employers, poor law authorities, and the courts. European studies offer a similar picture. Recent work has shown that parents, and elite parents in particular, were prepared to go to great lengths to punish their young sons for immoral behaviour—from drinking and gambling to fighting and promiscuity—which they feared would ruin their family's good name, with dire economic consequences. Some seventeenth-century Dutch parents sent their sons to work in the Dutch East Indies (Roberts 2002), while some eighteenth-century Spanish parents sent their sons to correctional orphanages, sometimes for several years (Tikoff 2002). These were admittedly extreme measures, but nevertheless show the seriousness with which early modern youthful disorder was viewed. They also highlight the often overlooked fact that the sexual and moral behaviour of young men as well as young women was, up to a point, subject to stern regulation.

These two competing claims about the 'modern' and 'pre-modern' nature of juvenile delinquency are not easily reconciled. To some extent, this may be because they are using different approaches to address different stories about societies. For example, early modern accounts often focus on local responses to disorderly behaviour by older youths, some in their twenties. By contrast, histories of nineteenth-century delinquency and beyond tend to examine the development of more national and more statutory responses to illegal behaviour by those under the age of 16. If each were to apply the other's approach to their own period, a less sharply differentiated story might emerge.

However, there seems to be no escaping the fact that ways of dealing with deviance in general changed dramatically in the course of the nineteenth century, as did experiences of childhood and youth. Taken together, the increasingly formal division of law-breakers by age, gender, and seriousness of offence, the increasing readiness and ability of the state to initiate, finance, staff, and monitor criminal justice and penal services and, later, the gradual removal of young children from work to state-sponsored schooling alongside the development of a range of state-sponsored welfare and judicial measures (such as the creation of juvenile reformatories, juvenile courts, and child protection legislation) enacted 'in the name of the child' (Bailey 1987; Harris and Webb 1987; Cooter 1992; Hyland 1993; Hendrick 1994) helped to create a new kind of British society that treated crime and young people in new kinds of ways.

Histories of twentieth-century juvenile delinquency and youth justice are marked by rather different questions. These might be divided into two broad areas of work: studies of youth (sub)cultures (see Chapter 5) and studies of the evolving juvenile justice system. More contemporary juvenile justice studies are less concerned with when and why delinquency was 'invented' (often because they simply assume that it was a modern phenomenon), than they are with when and why formal responses to delinquency became more hard-line or more liberal.

A broad consensus has emerged here which identifies the 1960s and early 1970s (the 1969 Children and Young Persons Act in particular and its subsequent partial implementation by the newly elected Conservative government in 1970) as distinct periods of welfarism in which traditional concepts of criminal justice (crime, individual responsibility, punishment) were to be replaced by welfarist notions about a child's needs and the family life of the 'pre-delinquent'. Care proceedings and community-based treatment or residential care became favoured over criminal proceedings and custodial responses, and the discretionary powers of social workers were enhanced and those of magistrates reduced (Pitts 1988; Morris and Giller 1987; McLaughlin and Muncie 1993; Muncie 1999). This drive to 'liberalize', which according to Victor Bailey (1987) had strong roots in the pre-war period and according to Thomas Bernard (1992) is cyclical, is argued to have been the product of a post-war political consensus across social policy issues in general. The exception was drugs, in relation to which enhanced regulation rather than liberalization was the order of the day (South 1997).

With this caveat in mind, it is clear that there emerged a consensus encompassing political opinion on the Left and the Right broadly agreeing that social problems, from poverty and poor health to social disadvantage and criminality, were best addressed by a raft of more generously state-funded measures, from health, education, and policing to social security, social work, and social housing. In practice, however, rather than replacing the old structures of juvenile justice, the new welfarist principles were simply grafted onto them. The treatment–punishment continuum was merely extended. Welfarist principles were simply added to the range of more punitive interventions and disposals already available to the court. Subsequently the welfarist model of juvenile justice began to break down for two key reasons: when faith in social work's ability to diagnose the causes of delinquency and to treat these with non-punitive methods increasingly came under attack by justice-based models which stressed the importance of rights (the liberal version) or self-responsibility (the conservative version) (see Hudson 1987); and when social policy issues, law and order firmly included, became a new political football in the much more polarized politics of the mid-1970s onwards.

The point is that welfare (meeting needs) or justice (punishing deeds) do not exist in pure forms, nor have either achieved total ascendancy in the history of youth justice. In the 'new' climate, which remains evident in the post-1997 Labour governments, the policies and practices of youth justice continue to be characterized by compromises and contradictions between care and control, and the increasing influence of managerialist concerns of the state.

While there have been a series of backlashes against welfarist juvenile justice measures since the mid-1970s, historical work on earlier periods shows that such clashes have occurred regularly since at least the mid-nineteenth century. Practically every major procedural or service development (from the removal of children from prisons to reformatories and industrial schools in the 1850s, to the development of juvenile courts in the 1900s, to the restriction of birching in the 1930s, to the introduction of the first short sharp shock detention measures in the 1940s) has been held up by some as too lenient and by others as too punitive.

Wider historical debates would, then, tend to support the general Foucauldian view that there is no easy divide between 'punishment' and 'welfare' (Garland 1985; Harris and Webb 1987). Further, accounts which argue for a clear post-1970 move from the 'liberal' to the 'hard-line' tend to base their case on changes in the treatment of delinquent boys. In doing so they overlook the fact that the treatment of delinquent girls, which has often been regarded as being generally more lenient (in the sense of being more informal, more community-based, and so on), could be incredibly 'hard-line' despite its 'welfare' setting (Ackland 1982; Gelsthorpe 1989; Cox forthcoming).

Studies of twentieth-century youth (sub)cultures as outlined earlier in this chapter describe a very different scene to that documented by juvenile justice studies. With their focus on the more spectacular world of the changing public presences of older teenagers and the tensions between differently identified groups (mods, rockers, skinheads, punks, and so on) they could be said to have more in common with early modern studies of disorderly, but not necessarily, law-breaking, youths. Clearly, these investigations have an important place in the teaching of criminology, not least because they mark a defining episode within the sociology of deviance and also because they stretch definitions of deviance beyond the criminal law. To play loud music, wear outrageous clothes, go clubbing, or simply hang out near a corner shop is not illegal, yet all these actions have been and are read by large sections of parents, press, and the public as incredibly threatening to social order—so much so, indeed, that periodic attempts have been made to criminalize aspects of them through a range of minor public order offences, most recently via the 1994 Criminal Justice Act (Muncie 1999). Yet these more spectacular behaviours have accounted, on the whole, for only a small number of juvenile court appearances from the late twentieth century onwards.[2] Together, more mundane cases of shoplifting, burglary, car crime, petty drugs crime, and child protection account for the vast majority. There are overlaps between the spectacular and the mundane, yet these need to be investigated critically rather than assumed.

Dangerous classes, underclasses, and crime

Knowledges of crime from the professional and academic to the philanthropic and popular have been heavily shaped by the idea of the 'underclass'. Ways of describing this group have changed a great deal within modern Britain. Nineteenth-century terms such as the 'dangerous', 'perishing', 'slum-dwelling', or 'vicious' classes have gradually given way to more contemporary references to those who live in 'inner cities' or 'sink estates' or who are considered otherwise 'socially excluded' (Morris 1994). It could be argued that these changing vocabularies denote clear changes in conceptualizations of this group or that they should not be discussed as a singular trans-historical social formation at all since this implies that they are static, ever-present, and unchanging. However, one good reason for analysing historical continuities here is that this allows a critical consideration of the recent claims of key criminological and sociological texts which have argued that British society has moved from being more inclusionary to highly exclusionary (Levitas 1998; Lister 1998; Young 1999). This shift is seen as a predominantly late modern phenomenon, rooted in the 1980s' attacks on the welfare state and workers' rights, and in the 1990s' consolidation of those attacks by a new political centre-ground acting in the name of social democratic reform.

Historians of crime and urban disorder in the nineteenth and early twentieth centuries in particular would question this chronology (Davis 1989a, 1989b; Wiener 1990; White 1986) as might those social scientists that have taken a longer view (Morris 1994; Crowther 2000). Concerns about the dangerous classes were part of everyday life in Victorian Britain. Politicians debated them, newspaper editors serialized reports about them, novelists narrated stories about them, urban planners tried to sweep them away, social improvers tried to reform them away. These concerns and debates had several recurring elements, all of which have echoed throughout the twentieth and early twenty-first centuries. These elements might be summarized as space, race, pathology, and poverty. All were connected to ideas about crime.

In terms of space, the dangerous classes, like the socially excluded today, were seen as closely linked to poor urban areas both in the sense that such people created such areas and that such areas created such people. Together, these two forces generated crime and confounded control. Tenements, rookeries, and cheap rooming districts exercised a huge symbolic power over the public imagination as centres of vice, squalor, drunkenness, traffic in sex and stolen goods, and general depravity. Yet, for the police these were ambivalent spaces. At one extreme they regarded some of them as no-go areas, yet at the other, they saw them as offering unique sources of information about criminal activity and, significantly, as means of supplementing their own salaries through protection rackets and corrupt dealings of various kinds (Davis 1989a; Emsley 1996b).

Discourses of dangerousness and exclusion have also drawn on racial discourses. Such discourses, then and now, have been framed not simply in the narrow terms of appearance and skin tone (in terms of 'black' and 'white'), but have made use of the wide-ranging markers of difference and otherness. In the nineteenth century, the dangerous classes were framed as predominantly poor, urban, and white. They were nevertheless also commonly framed as a 'race apart', as a distinctive breed, type, or strain (Davis 1989a, 1989b; Cox 2002). This became more pronounced in the 1840s with the arrival in mainland Britain of thousands of poor Irish immigrants escaping famine by heading to cities to work, and from the 1860s with the spread of social Darwinist concepts of racial degeneration and the burden apparently placed by the 'unfit' upon the 'fit'. Popular and scientific thinking on white 'races' and 'species' found expression in the criminal justice system through a series of measures (such as the 1869 Habitual Criminal Act and the 1879 Habitual Drunkards Act) designed to detect and detain 'habitual' criminals of various kinds. In this climate, Lombroso's later efforts to define 'criminal types' (through their faces, figures, expressions, tattoos, heredity, and other factors) were clearly part of a much broader cultural turn towards the positivist, the pathological, and the promise of science (Lombroso 1895).

Given this context it is also possible to see how readily other racial discourses of crime were later generated around non-white immigrants of various kinds. Beliefs about the deviant dispositions of 'foreigners' have been attached to many groups over time from Irish and Eastern European Jewish migrants, Malay merchant seamen, and Chinese laundrymen of the nineteenth century to West Indian and Kenyan Asian migrants of the mid-twentieth to today's Roma refugees (Gilroy 1987; Jefferson 1993; Kohn 1992; Crowther 1997; Cox 2002; and see Chapter 4). It is important to note here, however, that concerns about 'foreigners' of all kinds have very often been accompanied by concerns about white underclass behaviour. The cafés, clubs, drugs, and music that have historically grown up around certain migrant cultures have played a crucial part in constructing cosmopolitan, bohemian, mixed urban spaces—spaces viewed by some as vibrant and electric, but by others as degenerate melting pots where 'fixed' cultural values dissolve into dangerous moral relativism.

Of all these groups, however, the experiences of West Indians (mainly young men) within the criminal justice system have attracted most modern criminological attention. These studies of race and crime have been closely connected to studies of class and crime. For Hall et al. (1978), historical moral panics around white underclass criminality took on new politicized forms when they settled on a new target: post-war West Indian, particularly Jamaican, migrants and their children; and the 'new' kinds of criminal behaviours they apparently brought to the deprived inner-city areas where they largely settled: 'mugging' (in fact simply a new name for the old crime of 'aggravated robbery'); 'hustling' (petty criminality involving gambling, prostitution, and unlicensed gatherings); and marijuana-linked crimes (which represented a new phase of a much longer history of British drug use, which included use of opium, cocaine, and morphine).

Other writers extended Hall et al.'s work, critiquing the heavy and often injudicious policing of young West Indians (notably through the use of notorious 'sus' laws—being stopped 'on suspicion' of being involved in criminal activities) in turn fuelling inter-ethnic tensions and migrant frustrations, which ultimately exploded into the fierce urban race riots of the early 1980s in London, Birmingham, Manchester, Liverpool, and Bristol (Scarman 1981; Lea and Young 1982; Holdaway 1996; Keith 1993). For much of the 1980s, perceived links between class and crime were highly racialized, with urban 'black' people (a term which continued to conceal the clear focus on young Jamaican-British men) viewed by liberals and hard-liners alike as among the most seriously socially excluded and, by extension, among the most likely to commit crime. Of course, liberal and left-leaning commentators, including most criminologists writing on this subject, also argued that high rates of crime and imprisonment among young blacks were also the product of the systematic racial discrimination against this group operating at all levels of the criminal justice system (Smith 1997; Gordon 1983), what Macpherson would later call 'institutional racism' in his report into the death of black teenager, Stephen Lawrence in 1993 (Macpherson 1999; South 2001a).

The idea that the criminal justice system itself did a great deal to construct and reinforce (negative) racial identities has become very influential among criminologists and sociologists of crime (Keith 1993; Jefferson 1993; Kalunta-Crumpton 1999). Recent research has focused on the experiences of Asian youths (from British-Pakistani, British Kenyan-Indian, and British-Indian communities) in this respect (Webster 1997). In relation to drugs offences, some of these studies have explored the high levels of alienation from and suspicion of the 'white state' experienced by many young men in Asian communities (Pearson and Patel 1998; Akhtar and South 2000).

For some largely discredited commentators, both popular and political, the link between race and crime was more pathological than social (see Gilroy 1987). However, the idea that criminality within certain groups has primarily pathological causes, that criminal types are 'born' rather than 'made', that offenders are different 'sorts' of people, has certainly been a powerful one since at least the nineteenth century. The power of this view helps to explain why issues of crime have so often been linked to issues of sex, particularly among the 'underclass'. In short, wherever criminality is seen to be in any way 'inherited', the sexual and reproductive cultures of disorderly groups, and especially disorderly young women (from wayward girls of the nineteenth century to teenage single mothers of the twenty-first), are invariably both a cause of social concern and a site for social regulation (Cox forthcoming).

Fears of a 'degenerate' and 'expanding' underclass, characterized by generations of criminals and misfits within individual 'dysfunctional' families, have shaped debates about class and crime from the late-Victorian period on. Early American criminological studies into the 'criminal family phenomenon' seem to have been highly influential in Britain. Richard Dugdale's now infamous 1875 study of the Jukes family, which showed how murderers had married prostitutes, how petty thieves had impregnated mentally defective women, and so on inspired similar studies in Britain (Hahn Rafter 1988). Some of those pushing for greater control of the so-called 'mentally defective' argued that individuals in such families, 'the lowest tenth' of the population, should be institutionalized to prevent them from reproducing (Thomson 1998). Cyril Burt, Britain's first state-appointed educational psychologist and author of the 1925 text, *The Young Delinquent*, included similar family trees among his data, despite the fact that he firmly believed delinquency to be caused by inter-linked social, biological, and psychological factors (Burt 1925).

In the post-war period, a new term, 'problem family', became common amongst social workers dealing with delinquency. At one level, this was a positive development as it signalled a shift of focus away from the individual delinquent boy or girl and onto relations within the wider family of which they were part. However, at another level, it could not help but replicate these earlier characterizations of degenerate families. More recently, and controversially, American Charles Murray's interventions in British debates on the underclass have further continued this pathological line of enquiry (Murray et al. 1990; see also Lister et al. 1996).

Pathological approaches more generally have influenced many twentieth-century theories of crime, from theories of 'moral defect', 'kleptomania', and 'criminal personality' to 'psychopathy' and today's 'attention deficit disorder' (see Mednick et al. 1987; Valier 1998; Hahn Rafter 1988, 1997). It is no exaggeration to say that disagreements between criminologists linked to this psycho-medical scientific tradition (often grouped together and disparaged as 'positivists') and those linked to socio-cultural environmental traditions have divided the subject for over a century.

However, 'positivism' is far too broad a term to do justice to the many varieties of research often negatively associated with it (Brown 1990). Historically, 'positivists' have strongly disagreed with each other and refuted each other's findings. Further, there are more connections between such work and other kinds of criminological work than might first appear to be the case. Psychological, psychiatric, and medical approaches to crime invariably draw on social and environmental factors in some way, while public health approaches do so intrinsically. Similarly, social criminological approaches have very often rested on assumptions (albeit unexamined) about, for example, the 'natural dispositions' of different social groups (men, women, the young, the old, the gay, and so on). Furthermore, the dominance of critiques of 'pathology' and 'positivism' has arguably prevented criminologists from contributing to important discussions of the body emerging within sociology and cultural studies (Turner 1996; South 2000).

Social criminological approaches in modern Britain have been largely shaped by the assumption that crime has a primarily economic root. The majority of those passing through the criminal justice system were indisputably those with access to fewer conventional economic resources. They might fall into crime because of material need or as a way of gaining status denied to them through mainstream means (work, career, higher wages) or because of a combination of the two.[3] Left realist writers of the early 1980s seeking to challenge earlier constructionist views of crime, did much to establish this orthodoxy (see Chapter 3). In their view, crime was a 'real' problem with 'real' economic causes committed and suffered by 'real' people, albeit a problem with (sub)cultural solutions. Moreover, the links between economy and crime could be measured and mapped, as a series of studies on crime and unemployment, prices, disposable income, urban environments, and so on sought to demonstrate.

This view has had some historical support (though notably, again, the period 1900–50 has been somewhat neglected in this respect). Gatrell, for example, has argued that the marked slow-down in prosecution rates between the 1850s and the First World War can be explained in part by the sustained rise in living standards across those decades as well as by the fragile but real consensus between the public and the police that created temporarily shared meanings of (un)lawful behaviour (Gatrell 1990). Such arguments, both historical and contemporary, are an attempt to recapture radical economic ground, to recast the relationship between crime and poverty in positive ways, to argue that if poverty causes crime, then the best antidote to crime is the combat of poverty.

Such economic correlation or determinism have generated different kinds of critiques. As outlined earlier, this kind of analysis has often been based on highly gendered assumptions about men's 'natural' role as providers and protectors that have been challenged by feminist criminologists, although as also outlined earlier, similar economic arguments have been frequently used by those seeking to argue that any 'real' post-war rise in women's crime has been caused by a 'real' post-war increase in women's relative poverty. The gendered assumptions implicit in some left realist approaches have been recently revisited by researchers of masculinities and crime in a reworking of 'the economic' which considers the cultural determinations of 'market' issues (Messerschmidt 1997).

Secondly, research on criminal networks and the experiences of those for whom crime is a means of supplementing or making an everyday living has placed more emphasis on the agency and choices of those 'choosing' to adopt such a lifestyle. This is a complicated and controversial area, not least because to attempt to document the historical existence of 'professional' or 'organized' criminal groups is, for many, to move uncomfortably close to conservative attempts to prove the existence of an inherently or irredeemably 'criminal class'. Nevertheless, old and new historical work in this area (Samuel 1981; McMullan 1984; Shore 1999c and forthcoming) has shown that studies of 'professional' lower-class criminal networks should be included in wider discussions of changing perceptions of the 'underclass', although, clearly, professional and other forms of organized crime extend far beyond working-class communities (as Chapter 4 demonstrates).

The aim of this discussion of the underclass is not to insist on continuities over change. The experience of social exclusion within a welfare society differs, of course, in many ways from that within a pre-welfare society. Access to state education, housing, health care, and income maintenance schemes (such as benefits and pensions) has transformed the nature of *absolute* poverty in modern Britain. *Relative* poverty, however, remains a very live issue. This is partly because late capitalism, like early capitalism, generates inequalities alongside opportunities. But it is also because modern welfare mechanisms have themselves generated new ways of being excluded through new mechanisms of entitlement and, necessarily, exclusion. Experiences of poverty, and the social meanings attached to poverty, certainly change. As this discussion has shown, at certain times structural explanations carry more economic and cultural weight than individualized explanations, social explanations are more powerful than pathological, and racialized explanations more influential than de-racialized. Invariably, though, all these discourses have been in play at any given modern historical moment. The trans-historical presence of the poor in modern Britain, broadly defined through these discourses and others, has dominated trans-historical concerns with crime and deviance, law and order, social control and social justice.

Conclusion

This chapter has mapped some of the key changes in historical writing on crime in Britain over the last 30 years. It has shown how the emergence of radical social history, or 'history from below', in the late 1960s and early 1970s was closely linked to the emergence of the concept of 'social crime' through which crime was seen as essentially caused by the inequalities of capitalist class relations and crime control as essentially a form of class control. This view, although recast many times over since then, has remained very influential in subsequent historical and criminological work. Along with other kinds of early class-based analyses, this work focused almost entirely on men and later boys yet did not examine the variations between different forms of masculinity (for example, bourgeois and brutish, white and black, gay and straight, young and old). By extension, it tended to exclude the criminal and criminal justice experiences of different groups of women and girls. Historical research on both areas, fuelled by the work of feminist and cultural historians, began in the 1980s and has since produced a series of important studies that have helped to broaden the definitions of both 'Britishness' and 'crime'. Such work does not deny the fact that whether the focus of analysis is workplace crime, race and crime, underclasses and crime, juvenile crime, property crime, or violent crime, the history of recorded crime is largely a history of changing patterns of male prosecution: rather, it seeks to explain this phenomenon in a broader range of terms that examines class alongside other variables.

This chapter has also shown how certain chronologies (or accounts of why and when social changes occur) have come to be established within studies of British crime. In particular it shows how divisions have come to be drawn between periods described as early (or pre-) modern, modern and late modern, and how and why those divisions have each been contested by different kinds of writers. Overall, it suggests that although historians cannot provide concrete answers to criminological questions, historical work can clearly enrich criminological work in numerous ways.

Chapter 3

Crime and Everyday Life

Introduction

MURDER, rape, assault, robbery—these are the events people tend to associate with crime. They are also generally represented as shocking aberrations and understood in terms of an individualistic analysis of pathology organized around 'the criminal'. In particular, 'the criminal mind' is the object and subject of analysis, fear, and fascination, and this is reflected both in the history of criminological thought (Downes and Rock 1988) and popular media portrayals of the 'professional criminal' (the Krays) and 'serial killers' (Fred and Rosemary West) from the nineteenth century to the present (see Chapter 5). Whilst the types of crime mentioned above have horrific impact on victims and their families, they are extreme cases which constitute a small fraction of all criminal acts.

As was seen in Chapter 1, violent crime accounted for around 8 per cent of all notifiable offences recorded by the police in England and Wales in 1997 and predominantly involved minor wounding (Home Office 1999). Many cases of homicide and assaults (including sexual assaults) are perpetrated by the victim's own family, (ex)lovers, or acquaintances, and generally in the context of a long standing dispute or relationship between offender and victim. Furthermore, some of the most serious incidents of violence, injury, and harm are perpetrated during the ostensibly normal and legitimate conduct of business by people in positions of power and authority (the 'trusted criminals' of Friedrichs 1996). Focusing on predatory acts by pathological strangers (or indeed their 'criminal personality') skews our understanding of the transgressions, crimes, and risks that are so staple a feature of our society today.[1]

It is undeniable that some people commit more serious crimes than do others, and that some people are more committed to criminal or antisocial behaviour than others. Edwin Sutherland's (1937) classic formulation of professional thieves demonstrated their characteristics as a specialist occupational group defined by a level of commitment to illegal economic activities as a means of making a living. This insight paved the way for much subsequent criminological rethinking and empirical work on the 'all-purpose criminal' who makes crime a career choice and uses it 'as a form of work' (Letkemann 1973); from the 'full-time miscreants' and locally organized forms of serious criminality in a British town in the early 1960s (Mack 1964), to the contemporary highly flexible serious-crime groups that possess the resources, networks, and abilities to straddle both the underworld and upperworld in their entrepreneurial activities and to make a global impact (Hobbs 1995). These forms of crime are discussed further in Chapter 4.

What is often overlooked is that towards the other end of the spectrum lies the vast range of illegal behaviour committed by 'ordinary' and socially acceptable people who neither see themselves, nor tend to be viewed, as criminals. As Thomas Gabor (1994: 7–8), in his book *Everybody Does It!*, argues many of us may have done one or more of the following: taken home linens, silverware, art, and other 'souvenirs' from hotels in which we have stayed; made inflated insurance claims following a fire or theft; illegally copied computer software or videos; used prohibited drugs or abused prescription drugs; exhibited disorderly conduct in public; physically struck another person intentionally. 'Somewhere in-between those deeply committed to an antisocial lifestyle and those only casually or episodically taking a plunge into illicit activities is a mixed bag of people' (Gabor 1994: 12), ranging from amateur thieves and con-artists, to fiddlers and others who are involved in an irregular 'street' economy of hustling, wheeling and dealing, and business 'off the books'. The central premise of this chapter is that crime in general is not the exclusive domain of abnormal or psychologically maladjusted individuals or occasioned by unusual circumstances. The aim is to advance a critical understanding of crime and victimization—the prevalence of different kinds of crime, the social distribution of different forms of crime risks, and the sets of anxieties associated with them—firmly located within the changing social landscape of everyday life in late modern British society.

Everybody does it?

There is evidence to suggest that there is widespread involvement in criminality by the general public. Indeed, crime was rampant during the Second World War even though it was commonly regarded as a golden age of community spirit and national pride. The war created massive opportunities for both conventional and new forms of crime for everyone—from organized gangs, professional criminals, to 'ordinary' and 'respectable' people. Blackouts and bombed buildings made looting especially easy; because of rationing, many people took to fiddling and forging their food, petrol, and clothes coupons; profiteering and the black market boomed (Calder 1991; Fraser 1994).

In the contemporary context, deviant or criminal behaviour (of some form or another) is engaged in (at least on occasion) by the majority of citizens. Consider the following statistics: around one-third of men in England and Wales (and 8 per cent of women) born in 1953 had been convicted of at least one standard list offence[2] before the age of 40 (Home Office 1999); self-report studies consistently show that a majority of young people have committed a crime at some point in their lives (Anderson et al. 1994; Flood-Page et al. 2000; Graham and Bowling 1995; Rutter and Giller 1983). Some Home Office statements have even suggested, in classic Durkheimian fashion, that a certain level of crime is normal and inevitable and that it is unrealistic to expect any set of policies to drastically reduce the crime rate (Young 1992: 104). All that governments can do, according to this 'normalization of crime' perspective, is to work with a range of commercial and not-for-profit organizations (for example, private security or surveillance firms, NACRO), responsible citizens (by taking charge of the security and insurance of homes and businesses), and the community (through 'self-help' groups such as Neighbourhood Watch Schemes) to reduce the opportunistic crime rate.

Crime, rather than being abnormal and uncommon, may be considered a routine part of life. This is especially true if we consider how various forms of pilferage, theft, and minor fraud relate to the way different kinds of work are organized and the occupational socialization that people experience. Gerald Mars (1982: 1) has provided a typology of 'cheats at work'—or what he described as 'normal crimes of normal people in the normal circumstance of their work': for instance, traders dealing in cash to evade VAT (Value Added Tax); taxi drivers who fiddle their takings; warehouse employees who overload and undercharge their friends and relatives; catering and hotel employees stealing food, wine, cutlery, or linen; shop assistants and cashiers in the retail trade 'voiding' a transaction or overcharging customers and pocketing the cash. Indeed, the 1997 Retail Crime Survey conducted by the British Retail Consortium calculated that staff theft during the year cost shops a total of £374 million. The survey also showed that the cost of staff theft was more than double the losses caused by burglaries, eight times greater than the cost of robberies, ten times greater than the cost of criminal damage, and fourteen times greater than the cost of fraud (quoted in Park 2001).

Mars contends that 'fiddles' are part of the elasticity of some occupations which emphasize individual entrepreneurship, flair, adaptability, professional autonomy and where group control of the work force is low. For store managers, travelling sales representatives, journalists, academics, medical consultants, and other relatively 'independent' professionals, for example, the conditions of work may create a criminogenic environment that opens opportunities and rationalizations for rule-bending and rule-breaking. Their fiddling covers a wide spectrum. For example, store managers can 'customize' their own 'shoplifting' by recategorizing goods as old or damaged or altering stock records; journalists can fiddle their travelling expenses and slush money (funds with an ambiguous allocation, such as 'entertainment') and rationalize this as 'perks' that come with the job. Professionals such as lawyers, doctors, and other health professionals (particularly in the private sector) have been involved in billing 'scams'; they can also sell their specialist skills and expertise in the hidden economy. By contrast, in occupations which are highly structured and characterized by controlling rules, minimal autonomy, and tight work-groups (e.g. in cargo-handling areas at airports, distribution centres and docks), fiddles take place in the context of teamwork. As Mars's study of dock workers shows:

The pilferage of thirteen of a consignment of a hundred men's suits provides a good example . . . The hatch-checker knew from his bills of lading what sort of cargo was in transit. The vessel team then engineered an 'accidental' fall of two crates. The damaged crates were moved normally with the rest of the cargo to the shed. The shed team then engineered the undisturbed pilferage of the suits. To do this the fork-lift truck driver had to stack other cargo in such a way as to block off what was happening from the superintendent's line of vision . . . The next day the hatch-checker reported that two crates were missing. By then the suits had disappeared—smuggled out of the dock under the men's clothes. (Mars 1982: 104–5)

Some of the major and more serious 'fiddles' and fraudulent activity committed by legal institutions that have come to light in recent years now constitute a complex field of enquiry in their own right. What is apparent is that many coordinated schemes of fraud are committed by people of 'respectable' professional backgrounds. For instance, a report by a consultancy organization in London in 1991 concluded that one in 20 mortgages in Britain involved coordinated, fraudulent efforts of 'rings' of local solicitors, mortgage brokers, and valuers who entered into schemes (e.g. double remortgaging the same property) with a view to defrauding banks and building societies for personal gain (Taylor 1999: 153).

Similarly, police deviance in Britain and elsewhere has been well documented (Mollen Commission 1994; Newburn 1999; Punch 1985, 2000a). Maurice Punch (2000a: 321) has argued that police misconduct and corruption should not be seen as individual aberrations by 'bad cops' but as 'persistent and recurring hazards that are generated by the nature of work, organizations and society in relation to policing'. Police corruption can take many forms, including corruption of authority, opportunistic theft (e.g. stealing from arrestees or

crime victims), acceptance of bribes for not following through a criminal violation, protection of illegal activities, planting of evidence (particularly but not
exclusively in drug cases), and direct criminal activities (Punch 2000a: 303).
Most officers facing criminal or disciplinary procedures are from the lower
ranks, but they also include some senior officers (HMIC 1999). In 1998, the
Commissioner of the Metropolitan Police acknowledged that there may be up
to 250 corrupt police officers serving in his force, which suggests that the pursuit of an unknown number of criminal investigations may have been seriously
compromised. In response, a special squad of anticorruption investigators,
including accountants and private surveillance experts, was established to target officers believed to be implicated in offences that include planning and
carrying out armed robberies, large-scale drug dealing, threats of violence
against the public, and contract killings (Carrabine et al. 2000). Detectives were
also exposed as 'moonlighting as private eyes, illegally bugging members of the
public and selling highly sensitive police secrets' (Leppard et al. 1997). More
recently, five police officers from the Derbyshire and Nottinghamshire police
forces, including two serving with the elite National Crime Squad, were
arrested for allegedly dealing in cannabis and cocaine (Goodchild and Morrison
2001).

Finally, figures from the Inland Revenue provide clues as to the scale and
prevalence of fraud in tax avoidance and evasion by individuals and businesses.
In 2000–1, the Inland Revenue of the United Kingdom reported that 'the total
additional [tax] liability identified as a result of action against non-compliance'
was £4.5 billion: this presumably referring to taxation owed that might otherwise have not been available to national government (Inland Revenue 2001: 16).
In particular, criminal proceedings and investigations conducted by the Special
Compliance Office into 'the most significant cases of suspected fraud, evasion
and avoidance' identified an additional tax liability of £378 million (Inland Revenue 2001: 19). Of course, this figure does not include the outright avoidance of
taxation by wealthy individuals and corporations moving their bank accounts
'off shore' to one or other of the growing number of tax havens in different
locations made possible by the globalization of markets in recent decades (see
Chapter 4).

Late modern society as a crime-prone society

Recorded crime increased enormously during the twentieth century. As shown in Chapter 1, the main features of long-term trends in official crime statistics since their inception in the nineteenth century are: a relatively unchanged picture until the 1930s, a steady increase up to and through the Second World War, and a pronounced and dramatic rise in the decades after the war. In the years between 1955 and 1964, the number of crimes recorded by the police in England and Wales doubled from roughly half a million a year to a million, doubled again over the next ten years and yet again by 1990 (Maguire 1997: 159). Total recorded crime peaked in 1993, and then went on a general decline (Povey et al. 2001). Changes in reporting patterns have certainly contributed to some of the apparent increases in crime. The 1992 British Crime Survey, for example, explains an increase in the reporting of certain offences (e.g. car theft and burglary with loss) from 1981 to 1991 with reference to increases in telephone ownership and wider ownership of property. In turn, many of these crimes require the reporting of theft or damage before a claim can be made under home-contents and car-insurance policies. Changes in police recording, enforcement practices, and priorities also have a significant effect on the official crime data. However, the sheer scale of a cross-national pattern of sustained increase in crime seems to support David Garland's (2001: 90–1) assertion that there is 'a causal link between the coming of late modernity and society's increased susceptibility to crime'. Others have written of the prevalence of 'economies of crime' in 'post-Fordist market society' (Taylor 1999) or the emergence of 'risk society' where individuals have to negotiate a qualitatively and quantitatively higher level and range of 'risks' and contingencies unknown to previous generations as they go about their daily routines (Beck 1992).

Garland identifies key social, economic, and cultural changes of the second half of the twentieth century which have posed new problems of crime and insecurity. First, the consumer boom and technological revolution of the post-war decades put into circulation a mass of portable, high-value goods (e.g. televisions, radios, stereos, computers) that presented attractive new targets for crime. This increase in the number of circulating commodities generated a corresponding increase in opportunities for criminal victimization. For example, car crime had risen because there were many more valuable cars available on every city street at all times and often unattended than there were before the Second World War. Of course, this argument can be extended beyond the expansion of conventional property crime to the emergence of 'new' everyday crimes: development of the Internet and web-based information and communication technologies have generated new forms of and opportunities for law-breaking—such as software piracy, hacking, sales frauds, hate crime, pornography, and harassment (Mann and Sutton 1998; Thomas and Loader 2000). However, these forms of cybercrime remain massively under-represented in the official crime statistics and under-policed by law-enforcement agencies (Wall 1997, 2001). Technological advance has enabled audio and video tapes and compact discs to be easily copied and fakes are often difficult to detect. The expansion of automated banking and the increased use of 'plastic money' have also posed a new set of risks to the banking industry and customers. The fraudulent use of stolen credit and bank cards was described as one of the fastest-growing, and most favoured, of financial crimes at local and street level in many societies in the late 1980s (Tremblay 1986). The availability of cheap technology, such as swipe machines, and simple techniques, such as 'skimming', which involves reading and copying secret coded details on cards, has pushed up the costs of credit card fraud even further. According to one recent estimate, counterfeit cards accounted for frauds amounting to £138m. in 2000–1 (*The Times*, 5 November 2001).

Second, changes in the structure and lifestyle of families, notably the rise of the 'dual-career' household family, increased privatization of family life and 'acceleration' of everyday life (characterized by increasingly complicated personal and domestic timetables, a reduction in the amount of personal leisure time but corresponding intensification of consumerism), have further weakened established situational controls and diminished the presence of adults for the more general surveillance of youthful activity in local neighbourhoods during the day. Shifts in social ecology and cultural norms have had a similar effect. The depopulation of inner cities; the creation of detached homes of suburbia, stripped of the natural controls of close neighbours or passers-by; an emphasis on individualistic morality and private freedoms in our consumer society—all of these have arguably reduced situational, self, and informal social controls. 'Social space became more stretched out, more anonymous and less well supervised, at the very time that it was becoming more heavily laden with criminal temptations and opportunities' (Garland 2001: 90–1).

Here, one can also refer to Marcus Felson's (1998) discussion of the ways in which criminal opportunities are structured by, and arise out of, the recurring transactions and routines that characterize daily life in the American context. Felson demonstrates how our social arrangements and everyday routines of life associated with work, school, transportation, recreation, consumption, and other patterned activities serve to disperse activities away from family and community settings, reduce levels of control, and increase crime opportunities. Take the example of grocery shopping in out-of-town supermarkets. It involves weekly trips by car as opposed to daily walks to stores one or two blocks away. This in turn helps detach people from their immediate neighbourhood, thus reducing their ability to act as 'capable guardians' of their property. At the same time, the expansion of large 'self-service' stores and the flow of customers through the stores makes shoplifting easier.

The third key trend relates to changes within the demographics of society, in particular the arrival of a large cohort of teenagers after the Second World War. In his study of long-term crime trends in post-war Britain, Simon Field (1999: 8) found that thefts and burglaries are both associated with the number of young males in the crime-prone age groups: 'for every 1 per cent increase in the number of males aged 15 and 20, burglary and theft increase by about 1 per cent' (conversely, the downturn in recorded theft and burglary in the 1990s occurred when the number of young men in the crime-prone age groups had been falling). Self-report studies, which in the main have been directed at young people asking them to list crimes they have committed (detected or otherwise), confirm the prevalence of crime as an everyday part of young people's lives. There is widespread youth involvement in offending regardless of class background (Anderson et al. 1994; Graham and Bowling 1995). Young people are also the age group most prone to highly visible criminal behaviour and over-policing in public space, as crime statistics show the peak age of known offending to be 18 for males and females (Home Office 1999).[3] However, and this is significant, any focus on young people as the perpetrators of crime should not be allowed to obscure or divert our attention away from the worryingly high levels of victimization that young people suffer from their peers and adults (see below).

Taken together, as Garland (2001: 91) suggests, these broad trends have made late modern society a more 'crime-prone society'. Others have stressed the link between property crime and the economy, although the precise nature of such a link is still subject to debate. For those on the margins of the labour market, McDonaldization and casualization (Ritzer 1993) have transformed the kinds of opportunities available. In particular, the scale of economic restructuring that followed the oil crisis in the early 1970s effectively meant that lifetime job security has become a relic of the post-war past and ushered in a polarized labour market wherein low-paid, low-future, part-time 'McJobs' stand in stark contrast to highly mobile, lucratively paid, yet precarious employment that is susceptible to the force of global markets. Some commentators have argued that for those young people who are *without* the protection of employment, family, and welfare, or trapped in the 'magic roundabout' of different training and enterprise schemes, they are most likely to adopt one of the transient lifestyles or alternative 'careers' thrown up by local hidden economies, including 'fencing' stolen goods, unlicensed street trading, acting as 'lookouts', 'touts', and 'hustlers' (Carlen 1996; Craine 1997). For example, Janet Foster's study of a neighbourhood in south London in the 1980s documents the increasing sense of reliance of local young men on their own devices to legitimize their routine involvement in different kinds of 'rackets'. Perhaps significantly, many of their illegal activities were not considered as crime, just ordinary work (Foster 1990: 165; see also Taylor and Jamieson 1997 and Chapter 4).

In an increasingly polarized society in which only 40 per cent of the population have secure employment, while the others are split between those in insecure employment (30 per cent) and a marginalized underclass of the unemployed (30 per cent) (Hutton 1995), the gap between benefit entitlements and realistic standards of living in a consumer-oriented society is widening, with quite obvious implications in terms of the relative deprivation thesis (Lea and Young 1984; Young 1986, 1999). Jock Young (1986) has argued that even an absolute increase of prosperity at a national level tells us little about the relative deprivation of certain sections of society. According to the relative deprivation thesis, people have different expectations depending on what they feel they deserve. They may compare their economic situation to a reference group and feel relatively deprived when these expectations are not met. The argument is that, faced with signs of evident wealth and possessions in neighbouring communities, unemployed youth could be motivated to commit street and property crimes because of emotional frustration, latent animosities, and lack of opportunities (Lea and Young 1984).

In his recent reappraisal of patterns of recorded crime over half a century in post-war Britain, Field (1999: 7–9) found interesting correlations between trends in the economic cycle and patterns of recorded crime. He argued that there is a demonstrable link between general economic growth—represented in terms of the growth in criminal opportunities associated with the stock of consumer goods—and growth in some acquisitive offences. 'For every 1 per cent increase in this stock, burglary and theft have increased by about 2 per cent.' This long-term link determines what is described as the 'equilibrium' level of crime—recognizing that this equilibrium level itself changes over time. Short-term fluctuations adjust as follows: when the crime level falls below the 'equilibrium', property crime growth increases, drawing the crime level back towards the 'equilibrium'. The reverse adjustment occurs when actual crime rises above the 'equilibrium'. The model is seen to provide an explanation for the downturn in recorded property crime (16 per cent fall in recorded theft and 14 per cent fall in recorded burglary between 1992 and 1996): a combination of a correction to the dramatic crime growth in the early 1990s arising from economic recession and the stabilizing of the stock of consumer goods (Field 1999: 11–12).

Insofar as the link between unemployment and property crime is concerned, Chris Hale (1998) found unemployment to be a factor in explaining short-run fluctuations. Field (1999: 15) found no evidence of any relevance for unemployment once the other economic factors were taken into account, either because unemployment has 'a relatively small impact on property crime, and the link between crime and the business cycle is mediated instead through factors like wage rates, the availability of overtime and short-time working and the buoyancy of the black economy', or because 'these aggregate data obscure a strong link'. Certainly, in more specific analyses of links between unemployment and criminality e.g. in relation to drugs, high unemployment and associated social deprivation have been noted to be correlated (Peck and Plant 1986; Pearson 1987; ACMD 1998).

Finally, no discussion of everyday crime should be confined to the 'ordinary' street crimes that dominate the official statistics. If we therefore shift the focus of attention from crimes on the street to 'crimes in the suites', we will find that trends of increasing globalization of markets, deregulation, and privatization have also generated multiple opportunities for criminal enterprise. Additionally, technological innovations such as 'computers . . . international direct dialling, telephones, telexes, computer aided despatch systems and facsimile senders' (Levi 1987: 3) have enabled fraudsters to attack information and/or money where it is most vulnerable and from a distance. Indeed, the acceleration of free market policies, the internationalization of major speculative financial activity, the deregulation of stock exchanges in 1980s, the growing bureaucratic complexity of the corporate enterprise, and the concentration and centralization of capital into larger and larger units administered by 'professional managers', have expanded the range, the scale, and the opportunities for corporate business wrongdoing, insider trading, and money laundering (Hughes and Langan 2001: 269–70; Taylor 1997a: 288–90).

Social distribution of crime risks

Although crime is increasingly regarded as a common, enduring feature of the social order, the actual impact and experience of crime remains highly differentiated and stratified. Individuals are differentially placed in respect of crime — differentially vulnerable to crime, differentially fearful about crime, and acquiring differential 'readings' of media information and other types of knowledge about crime. Indeed, there is evidence to suggest that the risk of crime victimization is unevenly distributed within and between different localities and various sections of the population. Existing British Crime Surveys and various research studies have highlighted social class, ethnicity, age, geography, and gender as key and intertwining variables in the patterns and rates of crime victimization.

Social class

Crime victimization surveys have shown that the risk from crime is unequally distributed among the population, with the poor generally bearing the greater burden. Successive British Crime Surveys have consistently shown that people living in inner-city areas, in council accommodation, and with low income and few home security measures, are exposed to particularly high risks from property crime (Mirrlees-Black et al. 1998; Kershaw et al. 2000). Burglaries and vandalism that take place in deprived areas may have particularly severe impacts on the poorest, many of whom are also subject to repeat and multiple victimization (Trickett et al. 1992; Pease 1998).

The significance of class in crime victimization has been a key issue from one particularly influential perspective in British criminology since the mid-1980s. As Young (1986: 21) puts it, the central tenets of 'left realism' are to recognize that crime is 'a very real source of suffering for the poor and the vulnerable' and to 'take crime seriously'. John Lea and Jock Young in their pivotal work, *What Is To Be Done about Law and Order?* (1984), drew attention to the fact that most crime is intra-class and intra-racial, committed by relatively disadvantaged perpetrators on similarly relatively disadvantaged victims. Thus working-class crime (street crime, burglary, personal violence) is seen as a problem of the first order. The task of the Left, so they argue, is to accept this reality, try to understand it and do something about it, rather than deny or over-dramatize it. To contextualize this position, this is a response to the views of 'critical' criminology, which from various standpoints are committed to a political-economic analysis of class, class relations, and the functions of crime. Of central importance to critical criminology is the connection between class, crime, and the state with crime control providing the coercive means through which threats to the established social and economic order are identified and controlled. From this perspective there is a direct relationship between economic crises and political responses of the state and judiciary, leading to marginalization and criminalization of some groups and not others (Scraton 1987; Scraton and Chadwick 1991; Hall et al. 1978).

Left realists carried out several high-profile local victimization surveys and influenced the design of a number of other local crime surveys aimed at discovering the 'lived reality' of people at risk, notably in Islington (1986; 1990), but also in Merseyside and Edinburgh. By focusing on particular localities these surveys attempted to pinpoint the higher levels of crime prevailing in socially deprived inner-city areas and to highlight the disproportionate victimization of women, of minority ethnic groups, and of those on the lower end of the social scale; and to set crime in its broader social context by including questions about racial and sexual harassment, drug abuse, and other forms of antisocial behaviour (Crawford et al. 1990; Kinsey 1984; Mooney 1993).

However, critics have argued that, by focusing on crime as perceived by individual victims, left realism is inevitably trapped within the narrow confines of the discussion on highly visible intra-class (and youthful) crimes of the street. It tends to overlook other (non-youth) crimes and harmful activities such as fraud, environmental pollution, and corporate crime (though see Pearce 1976) and, therefore, fails to challenge the class-based nature of law and political and media-driven definitions of what constitutes 'serious crime'.

Ethnicity

The various British Crime Surveys have found that minority ethnic groups are generally at greater risk of crime victimization than whites (Fitzgerald and Hale 1996; Percy 1998; Clancy et al. 2001), but there are important variations. According to the 2000 British Crime Survey, minority ethnic groups (especially Pakistanis and Bangladeshis) are more at risk than whites of household crimes. Indians remain more at risk of burglary than other groups, after taking into account factors such as living in high-risk areas. There are less marked or less consistent differences in risks of personal crimes (Clancy et al. 2001). It is of course extremely difficult, if not impossible, to isolate ethnicity as a discrete variable in explaining patterns of victimization. Socio-economic factors and wider processes of racialization may be at work here, if we take into account the fact that minority ethnic households are more likely than whites to experience poverty (that is, with incomes below half the national average) and to live in socially disadvantaged areas (Berthoud 1997). Smaller-scale, local area studies have revealed even more complex patterns of risk of victimization and variations within and between different groups (for instance, some studies found black women and elderly Asian men to be more vulnerable), localities, and offences (Brown 1984; Jones et al. 1986; Crawford et al. 1990; Jefferson and Walker 1993).

Minority ethnic groups are also routinely subject to acts of racial violence and harassment that range from murder, damage to property (including racist graffiti), to verbal and other forms of abuse of an isolated or persistent nature. There are also well-documented cases of harassment directed at Jewish communities and desecration of tombstones and synagogues (Holdaway 1996: 47–9). Clearly, members of all groups can be victims. The British Crime Survey estimates that in 1999 around two-thirds of the 280,000 racially motivated incidents were directed against white people, reflecting the much larger population in white groups. Minority ethnic groups were the victims in around one-third of the racially motivated incidents, even though they only make up 5.9 per cent of the population of England and Wales (Clancy et al. 2001). In other words, the risk of being a victim of a racially motivated offence was much higher for ethnic minorities (especially for Pakistanis and Bangladeshis) than for whites. There is some evidence to suggest that the majority of perpetrators of racially motivated incidents or threats against Afro-Caribbeans and Asians are young white men. However, as Rae Sibbitt (1997: 8) has argued, victim reports are likely to be biased insofar as they predominantly relate to face-to-face violence or threats and miss out incidents of non-direct or low-level racial harassment. 'Thus, for example, the descriptions may miss those who have stolen washing from the line, vandalised cars, smashed windows, made malicious and threatening telephone calls, posted threatening notes or noxious substances through the letter box' (ibid.). Indeed, Sibbitt's study in two London boroughs found the perpetrators of racial harassment and violence to be of all ages—very young children, adults (men and women), older people (including pensioners)—often acting in groups of friends or families. Even seemingly minor acts of criminal damage which are not regarded by the police as being serious enough to merit careful investigation can have a profound cumulative effect upon the victims, and in some instances escalate into serious episodes of violence and intimidation.

Perhaps more damagingly, minority ethnic groups have pointed to persistent police failure in taking racially aggravated incidents seriously and in protecting them from victimization. Such criticisms have gathered momentum following the police mishandling of one particular landmark case. On 22 April 1993, Stephen Lawrence, a young black teenager, was stabbed to death in a racist attack carried out by a group of white youths whilst waiting for a bus in south London. The Metropolitan Police investigation was flawed in many respects, and serious allegations of racism, corruption, and collusion between the police and criminal families in south London were made during the inquiry that was eventually launched into the police failure to bring the murderers to justice. Following relentless campaigning, a private prosecution by the Lawrence family, a flawed internal review by the police, an inquest, and a Police Complaints Authority investigation, in 1998 the Labour government launched a judicial inquiry (a proposal resisted by the previous Conservative government) led by a former High Court judge, Sir William Macpherson. Not only did the Macpherson Report (1999) expose professional incompetence, failed leadership, and a catalogue of errors made during the murder investigation, it also found 'institutional racism' to be pervasive within the Metropolitan Police (and by extension elsewhere, South 2001c).

Seen in this light, the experience of policing presents a very different reality of urban street life for blacks from that experienced by whites. In Britain, as in the USA, a 'zero-tolerance' approach to policing, combined with the racialization of law and order (Butler 1993; Keith 1993) has routinely produced high rates of 'stop-and search' and generalized surveillance of black people. Between 1997 and 1998, black people were five times more likely to be stopped and searched by the police than whites. In 1998 through 1999, they were six times more likely to be searched, at a time when the proportion of stops leading to arrests for crime had actually *declined* (Lea 2000). This over-policing of particular sections of society has serious implications, especially against a background of continuing revelations about police misconduct and corruption, miscarriages of justice, police violence, and successful claims against the police for civil damages (Carrabine et al. 2000; Newburn 1999; Punch 2000a).

Age

Age is another key determinant of risk of crime victimization with the young being most at risk. Contrary to popular imagination, children under the age of one are more at risk of being murdered than any other age group; many of the victims are killed by their parents or carers (Home Office 1997). There is also evidence to suggest that the elderly experience less violent crime than do younger people: British Crime Survey data shows that the risk of violence is lowest for men and women aged 65 or above (Kershaw et al. 2000; but see discussion on 'elder abuse' in Chapters 1 and 4).

Specific questions about victimization of younger people under 16 were not included in the British Crime Survey until 1992. Since then, British Crime Surveys have repeatedly shown that young people experience relatively more serious problems as victims of crime irrespective of class, gender, or place. Amongst the 12 to 15-year-olds, a third claimed they had been assaulted at least once, a fifth had had property stolen, a fifth had been harassed by people their own age, and a fifth harassed by an adult. Furthermore, the risks of theft and assault were substantially higher than for the adult population (Maung 1995). Young men aged 16 to 24 had the highest risk of violent victimization (Kershaw et al. 2000). Also, the second Youth Lifestyles Survey found involvement in fights to be the most common offence type committed by boys aged between 16 and 21, and the second most common offence type (after buying stolen goods) committed by boys 14 to 15 years of age (Flood-Page et al. 2000). Studies in Edinburgh (Anderson et al. 1994), Glasgow (Hartless et al. 1995), and Teesside (Brown 1994) produced startlingly similar results indicating routine experience by children and teenagers of different forms of abuse in the home and on the street, harassment by adults and other young people, as well as other forms of serious crime (including physical assault and theft from the person). Few of these experiences are reported to the police, however, and youth victimization (as opposed to youth offending) remains low on the priority lists of the police and politicians.

In response, young people often have to forge a number of routine strategies to enhance their personal safety and to develop a mental mapping of the local landscape and its dangers—for instance, the routine pooling of resources for a taxi home in the evening hours, identifying 'no-go' areas, avoiding certain situations of perceived risk, and/or avoiding groups of youths believed to be 'trouble' (Loader 1996; Hollands 1995). In one study of the 'strategies of avoidance' adopted by different publics in the cities of Manchester and Sheffield, researchers found that young Afro-Caribbean men made use of a distinct indicative map to inform their strategic use of the broader 'white city'. Similarly, gay men spoke of having extended 'routes' which they would use in the hope of avoiding harassment (Taylor et al. 1996). In this way, young people become 'experts' in their own safety; they acquire and monitor a practical knowledge which helps them 'go on' in routine activities and retain a sense of what Anthony Giddens (1991) called 'ontological security'. The problem, however, is that the safety-enhancing strategies of some young people—most notably that of 'hanging around' in groups—can have a detrimental impact upon the safety and well-being of others (especially girls) and provide a source of conflict between young people, local residents, and the police (Loader 1996: 63–5).

Geography

Crime victimization surveys have consistently shown a higher risk of crime victimization for urban areas than for rural areas. The British Crime Survey data show the risk of being a victim of violent crime and burglary to be significantly higher in non-rural areas than in rural areas (Kershaw et al. 2000; Aust and Simmons 2002). A Home Office study also highlights the significant risk of burglary victimization suffered by students in the private rented sector: they tend to live in poorer and cheaper parts of cities and towns where there may be higher prevailing crime rates, and in properties filled with a good supply of desirable items for theft (e.g. portable stereos and other expensive electronic goods) but left empty for many hours during the average weekday (Tilley et al. 1999).

Certain routine practices of an urban lifestyle have been associated with an increased likelihood of crime victimization. For example, risk of vehicle-related crimes is found to be closely related to living in cities, especially inner cities, parking in the street at night, and driving a good deal. Young men living in inner cities and going out at night are found to be particularly at risk of crimes of violence: most at risk are those who are single, under 30 years old, drink heavily several evenings a week, visit places of entertainment such as pubs and clubs, and who assault others (Mayhew et al. 1989). However, such analysis does not take into account the likelihood that assaults in the family setting (mostly against women) are massively under-reported even in crime surveys. Furthermore, by concentrating on the urban lifestyle and behaviour of some victims, crime surveys run the risk of reinforcing the notion that there are two types of victim—innocent and blameworthy. Put simply, the innocent victim is typified by an elderly woman or child who is considered 'helpless' and an 'ideal' subject for concern whereas young men, homeless people, the drunken victim of an assault, the woman whose demeanour or dress suggests that she was 'asking for it' are considered less deserving of sympathy because of their risk-taking behaviour (see Christie 1986).

Writing from a different perspective, Ian Taylor (1997b, 1999) highlights the shifting 'urban fortunes' behind the massive increase in crime in specific localities and regions from the late 1980s to early 1990s. As Taylor (1999: 134) claimed, 'the highest rates of increase in reported crime have occurred in those industrial areas, like South Yorkshire, with the most recent loss of what was locally assumed to have been a secure labour market, where the smallest increases in crime have occurred in areas like Greater Manchester, the "youth capital" of the North of England with one of the largest post-Fordist labour markets in the North, not least in its night-time economy.' For Taylor, the vast and disproportionate increase in crime in some localities reflects the differential capacity of cities to respond to global economic competition, de-industrialization and the challenge of workplace restructuring, and the level of development of 'hidden economies of crime' in particular localities.

It is not just the inner cities that have become synonymous with the 'crime problem'. Geographical research on crime and the use of computer-generated analyses of patterns of reported crime in different local police force areas (e.g. Crime Pattern Analysis) have pointed to particular concentrations of so-called 'hotspots' of crime. Research evidence in Minneapolis in the USA and Merseyside and Newcastle in Britain suggests that even high-crime areas have their relatively safe micro-locations, as well as their specific 'trouble-spot' areas where the night-time leisure population and people going about their daily business were especially vulnerable (Sherman 1995; Hope 1985; Hirschfield et al. 1995). In addition, households in council estate areas experience much higher rates of burglary compared to those in non-council estate areas in Britain (Mirrlees-Black et al. 1998; Kershaw et al. 2000). Many of the most depressed housing estates are found in areas evacuated by business and industry. Geoffrey Pearson (1987) illustrated the sequence of how drug-related crime problems in a locality can lead to closure of local shops and other amenities, increased 'bad reputation' for the area with consequences for credit and insurance availability for residents. Indeed, there is evidence to suggest that the development of 'place-myths' (Shields 1991) and reputations is 'materially crucial to the declining or ascending paths of neighbourhoods and towns ... processes of polarization which show every sign of having intensified in the United States and Britain in recent years' (Girling et al. 2000: 11; see also Bottoms et al. 1992; Davis 1990).

Gender

Gender is another key variable in understanding crime and the risk of crime victimization. Crime statistics show that, in 2000, 19 per cent of known offenders in England and Wales were women (Home Office 2001). When women are convicted it is more likely to be for offences involving theft and handling stolen goods, fraud, and forgery. The dramatic increase in the number of women in British prisons in the past decade (the number has tripled to 4,045 since 1990) has been linked to their increased involvement in violent crime and, more significantly, in drug-related crime (including as drug 'mules') (Rumbelow 2001; see also Home Office 2001). But as Pat Carlen (1998: 56) argues, 'there is a consensus amongst analysts and commentators that the steep increases in the numbers of women received into British prisons in the 1990s can best be explained by the increased numbers of women in the social categories of economic need and social deprivation who have traditionally been more vulnerable to imprisonment . . . and by the increased punitiveness of the courts towards female offenders in general.'

The issue of the 'maleness' of perpetrators of crime has long been a subject of debate within feminism and between feminism and criminology (Cain 1990; Gelsthorpe and Morris 1990; see Chapter 2). In recent years, James Messerschmidt (1993) has developed and applied Bob Connell's (1987, 1995) notion of 'multiple masculinities' to argue that crime provides a means of 'doing masculinity' for certain men in certain situations when other resources are unavailable. Crime and the different forms it takes, Messerschmidt argues, vary according to how different class and ethnic groups come to define their masculinities in a racist and heterosexist society. For example, lower working-class racial minorities assert their masculinity in the street gang whilst for white middle-class youth, crime takes the form of vandalism, minor theft, and drinking outside the confines of school (for a critique, see Jefferson 1997).

In respect of violent crime, victim surveys and official statistics have consistently shown that men are more likely to be the victims of violent attacks, particularly by strangers and by other men in public spaces. Women on the other hand are more likely to be victimized at home (Mirrlees-Black et al. 1998; Mirrlees-Black 1999; Kershaw et al. 2000). In cases of murder in 2000/1, 42 per cent of women homicide victims, compared with only 4 per cent of men, were killed by a current or former partner (Home Office 2001). Women are the major victims of reported (and unreported) sexual violence; they are also more likely to have experienced persistent and unwanted attention (i.e. 'stalking') than men (Kershaw et al. 2000; Budd and Mattinson 2000). The highest esti-mates of domestic violence have come from local victimization surveys, which probably reflects the problems of using narrow legal definitions in understand-ing sexual victimization and interviewers' insensitivity to women's personal and often painful experiences in earlier national crime surveys. For example, the first two British Crime Surveys revealed only one (unreported) case of attempted rape and 17 and 18 cases of sexual assault respectively in the 1983 and 1985 reports. By contrast, the first Islington Crime Survey (Jones et al. 1986) showed that one-third of the households in that area contained people who had been sexually assaulted during the previous year, and that young white women were 29 times more likely to be assault victims than women aged over 45. A survey of over 1,000 married women also suggests that 14 per cent had been raped by their husbands at some time. Rape by husbands was found to be twice as likely as rape by acquaintances or boyfriends, and seven times more likely than rape by strangers (Painter 1991). In another North London survey, Jayne Mooney (1993) found that one in three women reported having experienced domestic violence (ranging from mental cruelty to assault, or rape or both) at some time in their life, and one in ten claimed to have been victimized during the previous year. Using a broad definition of sexual violence, Jalna Hanmer and Shiela Saunders (1984) also found that almost half of the women they inter-viewed in Leeds had experienced incidents of 'threats, violence or sexual har-assment' during the previous year, and 21 per cent of these incidents had occurred in their own homes. All these studies suggest levels of sexual crime against women higher than those revealed by national victim surveys and certainly far higher than those indicated by police records.

By contrast, male-on-male violence is more likely to take place in public spaces, although there is evidence to suggest that adult men are also victims of domestic violence, in both hetero- and homosexual households (Watson 1996; Newburn and Stanko 1994a). There is relatively little information available on non-consensual male buggery (now legally defined as rape). Although it appears to be far less common than male–female attacks, male rape probably occurs more often in closed institutions such as prisons (Jones 2000: 92). Many work-based injuries also take place where assault and intimidation commonly occur between men—either from managers or colleagues, as a result of unsafe work-ing practices (Stanko et al. 1998), or in the course of providing services to the public (especially in occupations such as the police, security guards, nursing staff, publicans and bar staff) (Budd 1999). But as Michael Levi (1997: 858) has argued, there is a gap between the perceived 'dangerousness' of certain jobs and the actual occupational death rates. For example, most of us see the work of police and prison officers as more dangerous and probably involving more 'violence' than that of miners or oil workers, even though police and prison officers have a far lower risk of death on duty (an average of one per 100,000 employees annually) compared to 87.3 deaths per 100,000 employees in oil and gas extraction annually. 'The construction industry had the largest *number* of fatalities. Coal mining, followed by the railways industry, had the highest injury rates' (ibid., italic in the original).

Fear of crime

Not only are social groups and individuals differentially vulnerable to crime victimization, they are also differentially fearful about crime. Fear of crime has come to be regarded as a 'problem in its own right' (Hale 1992), quite distinct from actual crime and victimization, and distinctive policies have been developed that aim to reduce levels of fear. British Crime Surveys now regularly investigate the levels and character of this fear, categorizing and measuring the emotional reactions prompted by crime. Generally, the term has been used to refer to perceived threats to personal safety in crime victimization surveys. Respondents are asked questions which focus on how safe they feel walking alone at night in their area, how safe they feel when they are alone in their home, how much they worry about different kinds of crime happening to them, and so on. The 2000 British Crime Survey data shows that those who were most concerned about crime were notably women, the poor, those in unskilled occupations, and those living in the inner cities, council estate areas, or areas with high levels of disorder. Concern about crime was in general higher in London, the North, and the Midlands. The young were most concerned about car-related theft; young women were particularly worried about being raped or physically attacked. Women (especially older women) were far more likely to feel unsafe at home or out alone after dark than men. Black and Asian respondents were far more worried about all types of crime than white respondents. People in partly skilled or unskilled occupations were found to be more fearful than those in skilled occupations. Those who considered themselves to be in poor health or who had a limiting illness or disability also had heightened levels of concern about crime (Kershaw et al. 2000: 47–9 and table A7.9).

But what exactly does such data tell us? Questions about how to define and measure 'fear of crime' have been perennial points of debate in criminological and policy discussions. First, crime victimization surveys have produced data that appears to show a mismatch between people's expressed levels of worry about crime and their antecedent levels of risk of victimization. People who are most likely to be victimized, i.e. young men, are the least likely to feel unsafe, whereas ostensibly low-risk groups such as women and the elderly express heightened levels of fear (Maxfield 1984). Such data has given rise to extended debate about the rationality or otherwise of people's expressed fears. Left realists, in their criticisms of early victim surveys and the conclusions they drew, argued that national surveys failed to relate fears of crime to respondents' everyday experience of crime (see Young 1986, 1987). If people live in high-crime areas their fears are more likely to be related to their perceived risk of victimization. In addition, women's anxieties about rape appear far more rational when the extent of unreported rape is taken into account. The argument is that for those sections of the population who have a low level of social resources, fear has its 'rational kernel' and to suggest otherwise is a complacent talking-down of the scope of their predicaments (for a critique, see Sparks 1992b). Fear cannot be accounted for simply with reference to the likelihood of victimization. Instead, it may be generated by any combination of personal, cultural, or environmental factors. For example, the higher levels of fear among the elderly and the poor may reflect the more severe impact of crime on these groups in physical, emotional, or financial terms (Kinsey and Anderson 1992).

A second strand of the debate concerns whether or not respondents' admissions to fear should be taken as a straightforward measure of their worries about 'crime'. It is extremely difficult, if not impossible, to separate fear of 'crime' from a variety of complex, generalized concerns or anxieties—such as an individual's 'judgement' of government competence to deliver public security (Taylor et al. 1996). People's fears may be linked to anxieties about other aspects of their lives: job security, ageing, and poor health. There is evidence to suggest, for example, that when 'fear of crime' is placed in the context of respondents' worries about financial problems or health, concerns about crime recede in their relative importance (Hough 1995). Research also suggests respondents more often express anger about crime, rather than fear, if given the choice (Ditton et al. 1999). People's anxieties may reflect uneasiness about shifts in racial and ethnic demographics in a given neighbourhood. Or they may be triggered by loud gatherings of young people outside local pubs, activated burglar alarms, or speeding ambulances and police sirens, as one study on the suburbs in South Manchester indicates (Taylor 1995). British Crime Survey data suggests perceptions and experiences of 'disorder' or 'anti-social behaviour' are associated with general problems of living in the city—such as teenagers hanging around, garbage in the streets, broken streetlighting, visible drug use, run-down houses, noisy neighbours, and abandoned cars (Budd and Sims 2001).

In this context, respondents' admissions to fear may in fact be 'defensive, individuated responses to a host of structurally generated public insecurities' (Loader 1997: 156), which require careful deconstruction. Thus for Garland (2001: 10), fear of crime is but one element of our 'fear of strangers' that is inextricably linked to the social, economic, and cultural uncertainties that have come to characterize late modern society. For Taylor (1999: 18–19), fear of the 'Other' is related to a wider set of anxieties about one's own survival and position in a very insecure and competitive post-Fordist market society. Evi Girling et al. (2000: 169–70) argue that 'everyday talk about crime', and the passions, anecdotes, and moral judgements such talk discloses, is a 'device' for registering and making sense of 'a variety of more difficult-to-grasp troubles and insecurities': inability to defend a 'secure local life'; perceptions of national change and decline; stressed social relations of various kinds (e.g. intergenerational conflicts). People's discussions of crime and other matters of concern to them are 'both informed by, and in turn inform, their *sense of place*; their sense, that is, of both *the place* they inhabit (its histories, divisions, trajectories and so forth), and of *their place* within a wider world of hierarchies, troubles, opportunities and insecurities' (Girling et al. 2000: 17, italics in the original). In this sense, people's worries and talk about crime are rarely merely a reflection of 'objective' risk, but are also inextricably linked with how particular places are experienced and imagined and 'bound up in a context of meaning and significance, involving the use of metaphors and narratives about social change' (Sparks 1992b: 131).

Third, many feminists have pointed out that conceptualizing and measuring the 'fear of crime' in separate public/private domains is highly problematic. Their central argument is that women's heightened sense of fear is inextricably linked to the endemic nature of male violence in their lives. Liz Kelly (1988) suggests that women's everyday lives exist along a continuum of sexual violence. Whilst crimes of the psychopathic stranger, the deranged rapist, or the serial killer invariably capture the media attention, the most frequent and routinized forms of male sexual violence are shielded from public view. National or local crime victimization surveys which are based on measuring discrete events cannot fully comprehend the pervasive, underlying threat to security that characterizes the experiences of many women. Women routinely learn to manage their lives structured and informed by their relationships with men they know. In these relationships many women during their lifetime learn to deal with habitual violence, bullying, or prolonged abuse, in what can be described as 'climates of unsafety' (Stanko 1990).

Fourth, some critics have challenged the gendered stereotypes of 'fearless male/fearful female'. Jo Goodey (1997) has argued that we need to understand the shifting meanings of fear and what it is to become a 'fearless' male during the period of late childhood/early adolescence. In her study of children's gendered fear of public place crime Goodey (1997: 407–13) found that, whilst overall more girls (72 per cent) than boys (46 per cent) were worried when outside in public places, at age 11 *more* boys were worried when outside than girls and expressed higher levels of fear of 'older boys'. Their personal experiences of crime and fear are placed 'in their individual biographies of having found things ("syringes"), seen things ("older boys") or imagined things ("in your mind") which have scared them'. It is the point at which boys no longer feel able to express their vulnerability and fear (the 'fearless' stereotype of the late adolescent male) that should be of most interest to criminologists. As Goodey suggests, 'growing up male' and taking on a 'fearless' persona can perhaps be best described as adopting a form of defensive or coping strategy to counter the feelings of marginality and, in the case of young black men, the overt and covert racism which others display towards them.

The question of how fear is constituted, mediated, and experienced thus remains an issue of extensive debate. Indeed, people's fear may escalate not only because of direct or indirect experiences of victimization but also as a result of a range of diffuse anxieties and uncertainties: the campaigning work of pressure groups representing victims; the activities of private security firms; the media's role in instigating or channelling fear (see Chapter 5), and, last but not least, politicians playing the law and order card.

The politicization of crime

In criminal justice on both sides of the Atlantic, the need to reassure and protect the fearful public has been expressed through increasingly punitive policies and practices encapsulated in crowd-pleasing, sound-bite statements: 'Prison works', 'Three strikes and you're out', 'Truth in sentencing', 'No frills prisons', 'Zero tolerance policing', 'Tough on crime, tough on the causes of crime' (Dennis 1997; Garland 2001; Shichor and Sechrest 1996). In Britain, what is significant is the way in which the crime problem has come to take on a new meaning in everyday political discourse. Until the 1970s, no post-war party manifesto suggested that the level or form of crime was itself attributable to the politics of the party in government. That was to change when, against a background of increasing crime and industrial disputes, law and order became a prominent issue in electoral competition. As David Downes and Rod Morgan (1997: 90–3) have argued, crime policy ceased to be a bipartisan issue that can be devolved to professional experts.

The Conservatives under Margaret Thatcher refashioned their traditional claim to be the natural party of government representing the order of established authority. They also espoused a classical theory of criminality (Downes and Rock 1988), stressing the 'needs' of the victim before those of the offender, the need for effective deterrence, and the free will and personal accountability of the individual. Their argument was that the welfarist ideas and policies of the Left, the supposed permissiveness of the 1960s, the lowering of family standards, and the 'professional progressives among broadcasters, social workers and politicians' had eroded individual self-restraint and self-reliance, produced a generation of selfish and violent delinquents, and created 'a fog of excuses in which the muggers and burglars operate' (Riddell 1989: 171; see also Muncie 1999). Utilizing a neo-classical model of human motivation and liberally using terms such as 'wickedness' and 'evil', delinquency was not just repoliticized, it was remoralized (McLaughlin and Muncie 1993: 175–6). In the run-up to the 1979 election the Conservative Party courted the police service (then dissatisfied with Labour reluctance to fully fund a proposed pay award) and simultaneously talked up the law and order issue with attacks on the 'soft' treatment of 'dangerous young thugs' (Reiner and Cross 1991; South 2001a). The Police Federation on its part campaigned actively to expose and exploit the differences between the main political parties and effectively blurred the questions of police pay, resources, and law and order. This set 'the scene for the emergence of a "law and order" climate in which all politicians could not afford to be positioned as being "soft" on crime or offering anything less than un-stinting support for the police' (McLaughlin and Murji 1998: 386).

It is not surprising, given this background, that the criminal justice system received a substantial injection of resources and ideological support in the 1980s: 'between 1982 and 1990 total expenditure on police, prisons, probation and the courts increased by over 70 per cent, an increase without parallel elsewhere in the public sector' (McLaughlin and Muncie 1994: 115). As Stuart Hall (1980: 5) noted in 1980, a year after the Conservatives' first election victory, 'make no mistake about it: under this regime, the market is to be Free; the people are to be disciplined'. The linkage of issues of law-breaking, order-defiance, and morality was critical to this strategy of 'authoritarian populism'. 'The presence, behaviour, and lifestyle of single parents (particularly women), young people, the homeless, scroungers, drug takers, illegal immigrants, and the conventional criminal have been elided into one apocalyptic vision of chaos and breakdown, an unmanageable detritus out of control' (Ryan and Sim 1995: 124; Scraton 1987). This form of political discourse appeared in various guises in the nineteenth century (see Chapter 2) and holds wide international appeal on the political Right in the contemporary context (see Garland 2001: 135–6). The racialization of crime is also significant here—the demonization of black people and family as the criminal 'other', culturally inadequate, and as standing outside the boundaries of 'Britishness' has been a recurring feature of post-war Britain, whether it be 'the "pimp" of the 1950s, the "black activist" of the 1960s, the "mugger" of the 1970s, the "rioter" of the 1980s or the "yardie drug dealer" of the 1990s' (Keith 1993: 42; Cashmore and McLaughlin 1991; Hall et al. 1978).

As Garland (2001: 13–14) observes, whilst 'politicization' sometimes suggests a polarization of positions, the populist form that everyday penal politics has taken has had exactly the opposite effect. Far from there being a differentiation of policy positions, there is narrowing of debate, a general shift away from the old correctionalist orthodoxy in everyday crime talk amongst politicians, and a convergence of the policy proposals of the major political parties. 'The centre of political gravity has moved, and a rigid new consensus has formed around penal measures that are perceived as tough, smart and popular with the public' (ibid.). This is precisely what has been happening in Britain. In 1997 at his first Party Conference as Home Secretary of the New Labour government, Jack Straw told delegates: 'We said we would make Labour the party of law and order. And we did.' Since this title had previously been the proud claim of the Conservative governments of the 1980s and early 1990s, some on the Left complained that they could see little difference between the criminal justice policies of the New Labour government and those of their predecessors. Notwithstanding New Labour's acknowledgement of links between social conditions and crime and its creation of the Social Exclusion Unit during its first term in office as a policy task force to address issues of social deprivation and community disadvantage, the continuation of demonstrably punitive responses to offending and a tendency to locate the causes of crime at the level of pathological individuals and dysfunctional families has been evident in the everyday language of politics (Brownlee 1998).

However, the actual 'rigidity' of this new consensus has also been characterized by tensions and contradictory forms of punishment (as diverse as incapacitative warehousing, disciplinary retribution, curfew, prisoner enterprise, reintegrative shaming, negotiated restitution) which, according to Pat O'Malley (1999: 185) can be accounted for by the ascent of neo-liberalism. In this revisionist account, it is necessary to recognize that neo-liberalism is not a single, unified political rationality. Rather, it encompasses social authoritarianism (with an emphasis on order, discipline, and traditional forms of obligation) as well as free market individualism (which expounds autonomy, enterprise, and the significance of innovation). In other words, neo-liberalism is an alliance between competing discourses on the nature of governance that finds its most obvious expression in a dislike of welfarism. This terrain is not solely the province of the Right, as fractions of the Left can be equally vocal in their scepticism about new interventions aiming to make a difference, which explains why New

Labour represents a continuation of the tensions in criminal justice policy rather than a transformed horizon of possibilities (Carrabine et al. 2000: 197–8).

The seductions of crime

It is arguable that in order to transform the possibilities of 'what should be done about crime', we need to grasp the lived experience of criminal events, to make marginalized groups 'visible' and be able to 'read' them. To some extent this understanding of crime as 'meaningful action' builds on the classic ethnographic tradition of American sociology, from the Chicago School and the sociology of subcultures to the analytic models of British cultural studies (especially the pioneering work of the Birmingham Centre for Contemporary Cultural Studies in the 1970s on subcultural symbolism and resistance; see P. Cohen 1972; Hall and Jefferson 1976; Hebdige 1979), interactionist sociology (as embodied in concepts such as moral entrepreneurship and moral enterprise in the creation of crime and deviance; see Becker 1964), and the invention of 'folk devils' as contributory to generating 'moral panics' (S. Cohen 1972).

Recent developments in cultural criminology (Presdee 2000) have taken this sense of 'crime as interaction' a step further and emphasized the stylized dynamics of threatening or illicit subcultures (as opposed to the 'substance' of crime). Indeed, British subcultural analysis has been applied to a succession of predominantly working-class, male-oriented, white youth cultures (teddy boys, mods, skinheads, punks) and black youth cultures (rude boys and Rastafarians) in terms which emphasized their dramatic, oppositional styles and modes of resistance (Hebdige 1979; Hall and Jefferson 1976; McRobbie 1988; for a summary, see Muncie 1999). More recently, the convergence of youth cultural consumption and hybrid youth styles points to the fact that 'acceptable' youth subcultures—those organized around music and fashion, for example—and 'deviant' youth subcultures exist not as distinct alternatives, but along a continuum of stylized social marginality. Through the use of language (e.g. ritualized street talk), dress, imagination, drama, and the construction of an 'aesthetics of deviance', young people achieve a symbolic creativity in which their identities are forged, remade, made sense of, and experimented with on a routine basis (Hebdige 1979; Ferrell and Websdale 1999).

Significantly, Jack Katz (1988) and Mike Presdee (2000) argue that only through awareness and analysis of the situational dynamics of criminal events can we understand the 'moral and sensual attractions' in 'doing wrong'. Take, for instance, youthful adventures in crime—vandalism, theft, shoplifting, and other 'sneaky thrills'. In a study of drug takers and property offenders, Mike

Collison (1996) argues that predatory street crime and a heady mix of crime and excessive drug use exemplify life 'on the edge' and provide a more exciting alternative to school and work. Certainly property crime such as shoplifting has to be understood not simply in terms of survival and subsistence—although for some these may well be the primary motives—but also in the context of the creation of needs, the structuring of consumption, and the commodification of desire under late capitalism. Yet according to cultural criminologists, these societal processes alone cannot explain the meaning or situational dynamic of shoplifting. The event of shoplifting can be understood as a version of a thrilling and sensually gratifying game, a dramatic and illicit adventure. Its buzz or 'magical', 'seductive' quality can be as important as any overt or immediate need on the part of the shoplifter for the shoplifted items (Katz 1988: 54). Bank fraud and theft, or manipulating the stock market, all contain the 'thrills and spills of edge-work' (Presdee 2000: 62). The same argument can be extended to computer hacking. For the hacker, there is the excitement of trespassing, the demonstration of superior power in entering systems which are apparently impregnable, and the risk of discovery.

The seductions of crime are also highly gendered. For many economically and socially marginalized young men who are trapped in circumstances of poverty, crime can provide an alternative way of expressing masculinity unavailable through legitimate channels. In the Australian context, Connell (1995: 110) argues that the daily life of these angry young men involved a predictable routine of school resistance, contests of daring, minor crime, heavy drug use/alcohol use, occasional manual labour, talk about sport and cars, and short heterosexual liaisons. These activities, more or less enthusiastically defended by these young men in coarse and aggressive fashion, provide excitement (frequently, in the excitement of violence, so 'making a mark' in the local community by instilling fear and respect) and entertainment in a bleak environment. However, these activities also constantly lead to various forms of trouble with the police, other young men, and women. It is precisely this reworking of themes of masculinity but in a context of poverty and in extreme forms which is so vividly portrayed by Beatrix Campbell in her account of crime and riots of the early 1990s on blighted British council estates (in Newcastle upon Tyne and Oxford). Young men in economically deprived neighbourhoods who were cut loose from the disciplines and controls of the adult labour market became engaged in a militaristic culture of crime: celebrating war and force as ways of sorting things out (Campbell 1993: 323). In the context of car crime and so-called joyriding (or 'fantasies of escape', Davis 1990), Campbell argues that the origins of the compulsions of perpetrators lie in the macho car culture of a consumer society. Joyriders share mainstream fantasies with the typical motorway speeder. They favour the top end of the market, high-performance vehicles which are associated with power and status. The police, suggests, are equally captivated by car culture and exhibit a similar masculinity; in this sense, the car chase has become a symbolic re scenes and themes of risk-focused movies in which *both* joyriders *ana* the po... play out their fantasies.

Indeed, crime, rather than being abnormal, can provide an outlet for the expression of many socially revered values. This point has been consistently made in works from Emile Durkheim (1964) through Robert Merton (1957), to the more recent literature on organizational deviance and corporate mis-conduct (Punch 2000b). As Stan Cohen (1973: 622) reminds us, 'some of our most cherished social values—individualism, masculinity, competitiveness—are the same ones that generate crime.' In the context of the 'enterprise' culture and the highly competitive and volatile environment of business and financial markets, some commentators wrote of a 'culture' of aggressive masculinity (even the language in everyday use in the post-Fordist financial markets and corporate boardrooms is full of sexual and military metaphors), risk-taking, and the daily struggle for gaining a competitive edge over rivals above most other considerations that is actively embraced in everyday work-life and leisure by managers and young city professionals (Stanley 1992; Punch 2000b).

Such observations are particularly pertinent when we take into account the increasingly intimate relationship between legitimate and illegitimate activity in the new global market (Taylor 1999: 162; see Chapter 4). For instance, as Dick Hobbs (1995: 10, italics in the original) reflects on the instrumental aspects of professional crime, 'contemporary professional crim-inals *are* businessmen . . . they merely buy and sell commodities in accord with market'. Of course, this does not mean that an interest in pursuit of hedonism and search for excitement is absent in the serious-crime com-munity. Many of the seasoned criminals in Hobbs's book stressed that 'they get a "buzz" based upon an explicit recognition of the oppositional infer-ences of their deviance' (1995: 118). And if we turn to the world of business, corporations sometimes rely on their managers to perform 'dirty deeds' in covert business activities—for example, to act as spies, phone- tappers, com-puter hackers, moles, safe-breakers, forgers, vote-riggers, saboteurs, debt-collectors, garbage rummagers, hatchet-men, and 'escorts' (Punch 2000b: 265). Furthermore, as Punch (2000b: 262) argues, it is the sense of excitement or 'a sense of machismo in beating the competition' that induces some man-agers to engage in such deviant practices. 'They seem to value some of the same characteristics found in professional criminals—"trouble, toughness, smartness, excitement, autonomy".'

It is important to emphasize that while Presdee, Katz, and many other proponents of the 'cultural criminology' project are keen to develop an empathetic, appreciative understanding of the meanings and emotions associated with crime, they are not necessarily sympathetic to these actors. Recognizing the transgressive qualities of certain forms of behaviour does not necessarily mean accepting such behaviours as a 'magical resolution' of personal and social dilemmas (for example, if we consider the potentially lethal consequences for self or others in the case of joyriding) (Taylor 1999: 89). And in reading of the works of violence of some criminals, Katz expects readers will experience disgust rather than celebration of their worlds and activities. Nonetheless, the point remains that the seductions of crime and deviance are universal not just among those already offending. In different ways, this connects with theoretical re-explorations of the significance of the 'carnival'—as in 'time-out', spaces of resistance—and the 'carnivalesque' in society and history, and fascination with spectacle and transgression. Everyday life may be described as harbouring a great deal of resistance and elements of opposition to the rationalization and regulation of our ordered routines. There is a tendency to promote sociality and the desire to be immersed in collective and frivolous activities—having fun, sex, partying, dancing, drinking and taking drugs, street protests, and so on (Maffesoli 1989). But as E. Van Ree (1997: 93) argues from a neo-functionalist standpoint in the context of drugs as a 'chemical carnival', ultimately such pleasure-seeking activities only provide 'a temporary and reversible slackening of the bonds of reason . . . [whilst they] indirectly serve to strengthen the societal framework'.

Conclusion

Although crime has been a constant focus of public and political attention, this chapter suggests that there is no singular 'crime problem' as such. Instead, there is a wide spectrum of illicit behaviour, misconduct, troubling and alarming events which are widespread and constantly occurring and a variety of ways of conceiving of and thinking about everyday crime. This chapter has therefore tried to provide an overview of these different conceptions and priorities about types of harm, danger, and transgression; different fears and anxieties which are only partly about crime in the legal sense; different experiences, concerns, and responses of social groups within a heterogeneous late modern society.

In the next chapter, several of the themes presented here are revisited but in the context of a focus on crimes related to the pursuit of profits and power. If the focus of this chapter has been placed on individual crimes and victimization, the focus of the next is on organizational dimensions of crime.

Organizational Forms of Crime

Introduction

THE focus of this chapter is organizational forms of crime in modern Britain. These will be defined further below but include: professional or organized crime; business crime (including corporate and white-collar crime); and political crime and corruption. All of these areas of crime and deviance have, in various ways and at various times, been matters of interest to governments and to the criminal justice system, whether as targets for investigation and prosecution or embarrassments to be 'covered up'. Public attention, concern, and fascination have also focused on such crimes and for most readers, the subject matter of this chapter will be familiar. The cases of Ronnie and Reggie Kray and other key characters in the history of British gangsterism are well known and the subject of numerous books, documentaries, and films. Major scandals of contemporary business crime have been detailed and frequently revisited in accounts provided by financial journalists and crime reporters, for example Robert Maxwell's misappropriation of the pension funds of his employees at the Mirror newspaper group, the corruption at the heart of the Bank of Credit and Commerce International (BCCI), the activities of 'rogue trader' Nick Leeson and the fall of Barings Bank, and even the complexities of the Guinness–Distillers affair.[1] The shelves of popular booksellers in Britain feature with increasing prominence titles purporting to be about 'True Crime' and, leaving aside the large market for accounts of the careers of serial killers, much of this shelf-space is given over to biographies of professional criminals and 'inside story' investigations of corporate chicanery. Indeed, the popularity of such books indicates considerable interest in this area of crime and the themes pursued are not dissimilar to those found here: changes in post-war society, in popular culture and consumption, and in the politics and practice of enterprise and making money.

To date, much of the influential literature on organizational forms of crime describes developments in the USA. By contrast, the literature on Britain appears to be surprisingly slim and tends to make repeated reference to the same or similar lists of crimes and cases. One explanation for this may be that Britain simply does not have the same kind of socio-economic and cultural history as those societies, such as the USA or Italy or now Russia, which have provided the most famous accounts of extensive organized and corporate crime, political conspiracy, and corruption. Alternatively, it may be that there are many examples of serious organizational forms of crime so far unrevealed in Britain. While this seems unlikely it is not unknown for institutionally embedded, socially corrosive, and deviant practices to 'suddenly' come to public attention. The perpetuation in the courts of Britain of a long series of miscarriages of justice, since at least the 1980s, is one example (Walker and Starmer 1993). These cases are in large part explainable in terms of the failings of police organizational culture, inadequate control over police deviance, and the criminal suppression of evidence. Another example is the identification of racism as institutionalized within parts of the police service (MacPherson 1999). In the absence of a substantial literature on British cases reference is often made to American sources for purposes of comparison and to illustrate the possible range and diversity of organizational crime. Here, with a focus directly upon Britain (and its location as part of enlarged Europe) over-reliance on American sources is avoided.

However, a comparative perspective remains useful in order to illustrate distinctiveness and specificity, to draw attention to features of crime that may be internationally commonplace, or to indicate emerging global trends. For example, some forms of corruption such as simple bribery may be universal. Other forms of political corruption may be intimately tied to specific features of the political and bureaucratic styles and systems of particular states, differing where religious, royal, or dynastic authority and patronage are dominant or where authority and appointments are based on elite eligibility, on elections, or on merit.

However, the value of comparison in this respect is not the sole reason for introducing an international perspective. Much (although by no means all) of the crime discussed here is increasingly international in scope and/or its implications (Findlay 2000) and this requires attention. Globalization is the relevant context that many commentators now refer to although many would also acknowledge difficulties with defining the term. Les Johnston (2000: 18) neatly suggests this concept reflects 'the growing transnational interdependence of societies and the reduction of temporal and geographical constraints on social processes'. The late modern world of 'globalization' has been one in which, not only are we seeing enormous changes relevant to the traditional frontiers of geography, culture, and politics but also to the traditional frontiers of crime

(Jamieson et al. 1998; Findlay 2000). Awareness of this has been raised by examples of new crimes in cyberspace, offences against the environment and animal life, international financial crime, the increase in drug trafficking and the smuggling of asylum-seekers across borders (all of which are pertinent to Britain, see below), as well as by the terrorist attacks on the World Trade Centre in New York on 11 September 2001. Transnational or cross-border crimes are key features of a globalized world of crime without frontiers. These may be committed in one or more legal jurisdictions (Michalowski and Kramer 1987; Sheptycki 2000b); they may have participants in only one or in several countries; and they may involve receipt or export of commodities across borders (Jamieson et al. 1998; see also Van Duyne and Ruggiero 2000; Farer 1999). Such commodities may themselves be illegal or legal but destined for prohibited use (e.g. arms, Phythian 1999; Ruggiero 1996: 130–7; or pharmaceuticals). Such complex transnational crime issues require understanding of their domestic implications as well as the international context.

This chapter first provides an *overview* of organizational forms of crime and what this idea means, and then illustrates this discussion by providing *further examples* in sections divided as follows: professional organized crime; business crime (including corporate and white-collar crime); political crime and corruption; and state crime.

Defining organizational crimes

Organizational crimes are committed by those holding positions in legal or illegal structures or associations that have an organizational basis or are part of a wider organizational framework, the purpose, exploitation or abuse of which can facilitate the pursuit of profit or power or both. For example, with regard to professional organized crime, Levi (1998: 335) refers to 'the popularly accepted (in Europe) definition employed by the German Federal Police [that] Organized crime is the planned violation of the law for profit or to acquire power'. Correspondingly, Hughes and Langan (2001: 246) adopt a broad definition of corporate crime as follows:

Illegal or harmful activities—both acts of commission and omission—engaged in by business organizations or members of such organizations in pursuit of their goal of maximising power and profit in relatively unpredictable social, political and economic environments.[2]

For present purposes the pursuit of profit and power are central and may derive from or be associated with:

- the enterprises of professional criminals, criminal associations, and gangs (professional organized crime);
- engagement in any of numerous forms of organized business activity and/ or the status of being a professional post-holder within such an organized unit (business, corporate, or white-collar crime);
- employment in, or opposition to, the political decision-making machinery and forms of governance of the state (political corruption, crime, and terrorism) and relatedly, the actions and activity of the nation-state itself (state crimes).

All of these may usually be discrete and distinct domains but one key theme of this chapter is that there are also overlaps. From a Marxist perspective, Frank Pearce's (1976) essays on the mutual interests and cross-over activities shared between the legitimate and the illegitimate spheres of American society demonstrated hypocrisy, corruption, and structural failings in the modern capitalist state, all of which fostered what Pearce influentially called 'crimes of the powerful'. An alternative view of the blurred line between legitimacy and illegitimacy has been influentially noted by the social anthropologist Gerald Mars (1982: 49) who observed that 'there is only a blurred line between entrepreneuriality and flair on the one hand and sharp practices on the other'. As Mars and others have documented, this point would seem to apply to a wide range of occupational scams and fiddles, ranging from the top-floor board room to the basement boiler room. In the USA, such blurred lines and examples of symbiosis between corporate and criminal activity have been found in the entertainment and gambling industries, the arms trade, the waste disposal business, and many other areas (Simon and Eitzen 1993; Woodiwiss 1988; Block 1999).

Various writers have now described such tendencies in neo-liberal as well as post-communist societies (Ruggiero 1996; Ruggiero and South 1995; Hughes and Langan 2001; Rawlinson 1998; Gilinsky 1998). Such authors have reported how operational dimensions of illegal and legal enterprises blur, and how the participants in legitimate business may overlap with or actually be the same personnel as those operating in illicit activities and markets (Punch 1996; Dorn and South 1990). Indeed, Hughes and Langan (2001: 242; Ruggiero 1996) argue that it is problematic to analyse corporate crime and organized crime separately and in a compartmentalized manner, since both are in fact forms of 'organized' criminal activities. Take the following example: in 2001, a case of transnational crime under investigation by Italian police identified a director of a prestigious British banking consultancy as a key partner in an arms trafficking operation using forged documents to smuggle arms into Bosnia in contravention of a legal embargo. The range of other associates implicated included directors of legal companies, politicians, members of the Russian and Ukrainian mafias, and former KGB agents. Offshore bank accounts held in Jersey were used to facilitate transactions (Thompson 2001a).

On the international stage, the banking system and financial markets have offered excellent examples of such symbiosis. The growth of money laundering of the proceeds of various criminal enterprises but particularly from drug-related crime, has now become a major route for the incursion of criminal involvement and influence into the legitimate economic sector (South 1992; Taylor 1992; Rawlinson 1998; Van Duyne 1998). In the response from law-enforcement agencies, the targeting of the financial resourcing of drug traffickers and terrorist groups and networks and, crucially, their support via 'legitimate' use or manipulated corruption of the banking system, has now become a particularly high priority for national and global policing of financial crime.

Other forms of crime within the scope of this discussion also have organizational dimensions—whether crime is committed by and for legal organizational bodies (by business corporations or by states) or within and against them (white-collar crime or political crime, corruption, and terrorism). The sense in which this applies to crimes committed by corporations or states is obvious. Perhaps less obvious and frequently underemphasized as organizational crimes are the offences of individual white-collar offenders. Yet such persons generally employ or exploit the organizational resources of their own employers to commit their crime, almost invariably against their own or another organization (Punch 1996, 2000b).[3] Embezzlement is the obvious traditional example while the newer field of computer crime has produced new variations on old fiddles and scams as well as forms of crime and deviance only made possible by the development of networked computer systems (Wall 1997, 2001; Thomas and Loader 2000). Where the victim or victims are outside the organization (e.g. as individual account holders or consumers in general) organizational resources may be used to commit the crime and then to disguise it, masking it from the notice of the organization and the victim.

Similarly, the politician involved in what seems simply to be individual corruption, in fact derives his or her ability to profit from criminal or deviant activity (such as taking bribes or other improper behaviour) from being part of a powerful and organized elite in society, in other words, from being a holder of office within the organization of local or national government (Doig 1984, 1996). The same applies to corrupt officials in the bureaucracies of government. Most indicatively, given that it has been the subject of considerable controversy, the value of politicians as lobbyists for other powerful individuals and groups follows from this position of respectability and privilege. The position and the advantages enjoyed are only available by virtue of being a part of the organization of government. Thus while the temptation of lobbying in return for substantial fees has been one of the recurrent revelations since the late 1980s about the misbehaviour and undeclared 'outside interests' of individual Parliamentarians, the effect has been to generate perceptions of the British political system as a whole as blighted by a culture of 'sleaze' (Budge et al. 2001: 324–5, 435). Alternatively, the motivations of the politician-offender may be to politically profit or further the cause and power of a political organization. The Westminster 'homes for votes' scandal of the 1980s and early 1990s was a good illustration of this and will be discussed later.

It is this *organizational* element (in the form of criminal associates working together, or the structures of legal businesses, or the machinery of the state) that makes these crimes ones that involve the abusive exercise of power, whether this power be legitimate or illegitimate, usually accompanied by pursuit of profit. This may follow from the exploitation of the enhanced resources and capacity for criminal enterprise derived from 'criminal combination', or via unique access to and corruption of office and privilege in the worlds of commerce and politics.

Professional and organized crime

Whether on a short, medium, or long-term basis, involvement in criminal enterprise as a way of life is what distinguishes the 'professional criminal'—for whom crime is their profession. The British version of professional crime remains, so far, somewhat different from that of the USA. American definitions of 'organized crime' emphasize features such as violence and continuity and it is questionable how far these definitions can be applied to the UK situation. For example, large-scale but short-term frauds perpetrated by professional criminals may involve no violence (Levi 1981; Campbell 1994) while 'Project crimes' (McIntosh 1975) such as the Great Train Robbery in 1963 (Read 1984), the Brinks-Mat gold bullion robbery in 1983 (Campbell 1994: 241–5; South 1992 n. 5; Levi 1991) and a number of other 'Big Hits' as Duncan Campbell (1994: 240–51) describes them, were certainly organized but not on a basis designed to be 'continuing'. What is described as 'organized crime' in American legislation and studies, that is, the large-scale and ongoing 'continuing criminal enterprise', is not yet apparent in Britain. In 1994, the then-Director of the National Criminal Intelligence Service told the House of Commons Home Affairs Select Committee that the UK does not 'suffer directly from traditional organized crime' and the police preferred to refer to 'enterprise' or 'entrepreneurial' crime as a term to describe the activities of home-based criminal groups (Statewatch 1994: 15). Clearly then, this is not to say Britain has no experience of crime gangs, rackets, and organized thieves. For example in 2000, police averted the so-called 'crime of the millennium' when a gang used a JCB digger vehicle to smash into the Millennium Dome in an attempt to steal diamonds worth £350 million (BBC online news, Tuesday, 7 November 2000). In 2001 the House of Commons Treasury Sub-committee heard evidence that 'criminal gangs have infiltrated customs and excise on such a scale that they are stealing duty free spirits and wine worth £1m a week from a single warehouse' (Hencke 2001). But the point is that the extensive nature of such crime is not evident in Britain.

Learning about 'doing the business'

So what are the formative features of the professional crime career in the British context? The process of 'apprenticeship' was once a frequently studied subject in a once flourishing branch of sociology, the sociology of industry (Williams 1957; Eldridge 1973). The decline of manufacturing industry and of this sociological field has left the idea of apprenticeship sounding rather old-fashioned. Yet, apprenticeship was also—and remains—pertinent to the study of entry into professional crime and criminal associations (Ruggiero and South 1995). In the early decades of the twentieth century, apprenticeship could mean learning about a legal trade or alternatively about the rules and routines of delinquent gang membership and assimilation into the criminal life of the local area (Samuel 1981). In the United States this process has been captured in numerous studies of youth gangs and professional criminals (whether the 'explanations' emphasize social structure and social disorganization or social learning and differential association: see for example South 1999b; Hobbs 1995). In Britain, Samuel's (1981) study of Arthur Harding and the illegal street economy of parts of East London provides recollections of such a 'criminal community' in the early years of the twentieth century. Some 80 years later, Foster's (1990: 165) study of 'villains' in a south London locality drew the conclusion that juvenile crime

was an 'informal' apprenticeship and preparation for adult crime. The juvenile years involved learning the basic rules of the community and how to 'play the game' in the highly visible public sphere. This resulted in attention from law-enforcement agencies which influenced the formation of attitudes, allowed the juvenile to learn the rudimentary rules of interaction with the police and how to minimize likely detection, arrest and conviction. These experiences, in addition to the new opportunities which adult status afforded in terms of employment and the utilization of the family network, brought about a transition from the public (i.e. delinquency on the street) to the private sphere of crimes (i.e. professional crime and secretive planning and carrying out of criminal projects).

Like many others in the late-1980s, Foster's case-study community was changing in complexion, even as she was concluding her fieldwork. Tradition and
change coexist as comfortably or uncomfortably in the locales of professional
crime as they do elsewhere. This is the theme pursued next.

Should they ever seek such a dubious distinction, many British towns and
cities can claim a long history of semi-organized criminal communities and
gangs (Pearson 1983) although this is also a history of rivalries and conflict,
defections and disloyalty. In the early 1920s, Birmingham had the Brummagem
Boys led by Billy Kimber; George Mooney and Sam Garvin held together a
Sheffield gang of some notoriety; 'Leeds, Bristol, Liverpool and Newcastle also
had their share of hard men' (Freeman 1996/7: 3), and Glasgow earned a reputation as a 'mean city' with a violent gang culture. The social changes following
the First World War had offered many new opportunities for crime but, as
Campbell (1994: 22) notes, it was on the racetracks of the 1920s and 1930s that
'the idea of organized crime and gang warfare was to have its modern birth.
Street gambling was illegal and the large sums that bookies at racecourses
could make drew a criminal element who offered what amounted to
protection.'

In the post-First World War period American influences (in particular the
new movies) on British popular culture were beginning to overlay the language
and style of some criminal gangs (Freeman 1996/7; and see Chapter 5). Evidently
the breadth of illegal entrepreneurialism and scale of violence engaged in by
American gangsters during the 1920s Prohibition era were not matched by
criminal ambitions in Britain. Furthermore, the social context was considerably
different. Nonetheless the confidence and style of the American gangsters was
noted, envied, and copied.

Such cultural borrowings continue of course and have also been important to
a whole series of deviant or 'resistant' youth and other (sub)cultures (Hebdige
1979; Hall and Jefferson 1976) seeking to establish an identity and a 'reputation'.
From the 1920s to today—young offenders, illegal betting operators, protection
racketeers threatening violence or arson against premises, or vying for lucrative 'door security' contracts at pubs and clubs, drug dealers claiming territory,
as well as professional criminals—have all constructed 'bad' and 'dangerous'
identities partly built up from images that American films have provided of
'public enemies' (Campbell 1994: 145).

In the late 1950s and into the 1960s, London 'gangland' (Morton 1995) became
the focus of much attention with the Kray brothers as central figures, epitom-
izing a 'home-grown' mix of such illegal entrepreneurialism and flamboyant
style. In 1963, the Great Train Robbery proved to be a sensational 'event', a
crime that for its time seemed one of exciting audacity and a key moment in
the social history of British crime. Between them these two sets of images of

criminal style and criminal operation have become the icons of British 'gang-sterism' and organized 'project crime'. This status needs some further atten-tion. The Krays, the Train Robbers, and the decade of the 1960s in general have left an enduring image of what British professional 'organized' crime 'looks like' — despite the fact that this is not what professional organized crime looks like today. As Morton (2000: 4) observes, 'The Krays became the public face of organized crime in Britain but top gangsters do not end their days in prison having spent half their lives there. The successful criminal is the one who is never arrested and of whom the public has never heard.' Indeed the con-temporary high-profile notoriety and tabloid press presence of most popularly familiar underworld characters reflects their efforts to publicize and sell their 'stories' (the True Crime books on the high street shelves), stories that in fact draw attention to their failed projects, marriages, and prison escape attempts, etc.

The Sixties: crime, populism, and style

Foster (1990: 15) suggests that the Train Robbers 'captured the hearts and imaginations of thousands of working class people'. The journalist Peta Ford-ham reported their subsequent trial in terms reflecting the ambiguity of popu-lar opinion concerning the crime, writing that 'the events were so vividly in the minds of the actors that they remember, like Henry V's men at Agincourt, with advantages what feats they did that day' (in Campbell 1994: 134), and Piers Paul Reid 'was to say in his version of events that "politically one might describe the train robbers as Saxons still fighting the Normans"' (ibid.). Numerous factual and fictional accounts of what was called 'the crime of the century' have sup-ported an image of the robbery as a 'shock to the system' and 'the establish-ment' and even senior police officers were grudgingly admiring of the scale of the crime, albeit more likely to emphasize that violence was used against one of the railway staff. Such admiration and affection were later recycled in the 1980s film Buster starring Phil Collins and Julie Walters.

Foster acknowledges Read's (1984) biography of the train robbers as provid-ing a context if not explanation for such top-league 'villainy'. For Read (ibid.: 321–2; Foster 1990: 15) it was important that the robbers be understood in terms of coming from a 'sub-society of working class South London' that had experi-enced 'endemic poverty juxtaposed to conspicuous consumption north of the River'. Professional criminals from such a background were prepared to dem-onstrate 'total repugnance for the rules and formalities of the modern state' (Read 1984: 322).

However, if such 'rules and formalities' need not apply, then what might? A decade or so later, Hebdige's (1977: 30) study of 'criminal performers' in Fulham, West London, drew the following principle from one respondent: 'Straight people say that the people who are beneath the law live in the jungle. But there's a law of the jungle. It's like a religious code. If you are involved in the twilight zone there are certain rules laid down and you abide by them.' The wider literature often disputes such notions of 'honour among thieves' and 'criminal codes of conduct' and Read (1984: 322) asserts that 'the only authority recognised [is] the natural authority of a "name"—another criminal who had earned ... respect through demonstrable qualities of courage, cunning and ruthlessness' (Read 1984: 322; see also Campbell 1994: 64–109). Undoubtedly, certain top-league 'villains' of the day asserted their authority and, in turn, attracted respect. However, in retrospect, it is clear that neither the mail train robbers nor the Krays and their contemporaries were very sophisticated as 'professional' criminals. In terms of the construction and cultivation of image though, the Krays benefited from the new emerging interest in working-class culture and identity and utilized it to help create their own myth (Freeman 1996/7: 10). Their large-scale ambitions and high-profile image created a press and underworld standing that belied the fact that essentially they were medium-scale criminal operators employing small-time crooks. Their notoriety was inevitable. Britain was simply unused to gangs operating in the ways of the Krays or the more financially astute South London Richardson gang (Richardson 1991; Parker 1981; Foster 1990: 18). Press reports conveyed condemnation but also lurid fascination with the 'new criminals' of the 1960s, while the police harboured a culture of hypocrisy that boasted there would be 'no hiding place'[4] for criminals yet was (at least in parts) perhaps more corrupt and permeated by bribes to 'look the other way' than ever before or since (Campbell 1994: 92, 198–211).

The labour market and professional crime in Britain

In Britain, research from authors such as John Mack (1964) to Mary McIntosh (1975) to Dick Hobbs (1999) shows that 'British organized criminals tend to be relatively short-term groups drawn together for specific projects such as fraud and armed robbery, from a pool of long-term professional criminals ...' (Levi 1998: 338). At least since the late 1970s and early 1980s, this pool has been changing in character. For both Ian Taylor (1999) and Hobbs (1997) the rise of market society since the 1980s has meant that traditional and legitimate employment markets of the past have declined or simply disappeared. Ship-building, mining and steel industries, and related factory production have all been run down and face precarious futures, and their communities now suffer problems of social deprivation, crime, and drugs.

Historically, of course, there have always been labour markets comprised of casual and unskilled workers and these remain. However, other kinds of opportunities available in the labour market have been changing, often quite rapidly. New elites have been created in the 'virtual production' sectors of information technologies and finance, new groups of the dispossessed and excluded have been left behind (Young 1999), and new skills of commercial and technical competence are required of the young who are new to the world of work. The 'old' apprenticeships into 'real' work are no longer on offer and instead various work-training and placement schemes have been promoted by governments since the 1980s, serving as 'magic roundabouts' (Craine 1997) to keep trainees in artificial work and out of the official unemployment statistics. Whether this amounts to a well-meaning scheme for social inclusion or a cyn-ical policy of social exclusion of many of an employable age, the result is to yield little real employment and stake in society. For some at least, greater opportunity and reward may seem to be offered by a criminal career.

Organized crime as alien threat

From Dickens's Fagin and Arthur Morrison's *Tales of Mean Streets* (1894), the anti-Semitism and xenophobia of Victorian England (Freeman 1996/7: 3) to recent fears of Yardies, illegal immigrants, and of middle-eastern visitors or residents as possible terrorists, British culture has always found it preferable 'to think of organized crime as an unwelcome foreign import . . . or as an unpleasant work-ing class activity which 'decent people' can well do without' (ibid.). The signifi-cance of media, community, and criminal justice labelling and reaction to the 'threat of organized crime' as associated with minorities, deserves discussion here. The threat of the subversive 'other' has been a frequent and significant feature of official and media discourse about most serious crime in late modern Britain, for example, drug-related crime, organized groups involved in the smuggling of illegal immigrants, and in the running of sweatshop trades with non-resident, exploited labour, and terrorism. Police intelligence agencies and media reporting have also attached notoriety to other overseas crime organiza-tions such as the Russian 'Mafia' (Rawlinson 1998) and Columbian Cartels (Eddy et al. 1989) although so far there has been little evidence of any major encroachment of these operations into criminal associations or organized criminal enterprise in Britain.

Since the early 1990s, media and enforcement focus on Yardie 'gangstas', particularly in the South London drug trade, has been partly a response to fears about the growth of the crack-cocaine trade and to investigation of a number of murders related to the crack and sex trades occurring since the late 1990s. However the true extent of 'Yardie organized crime' is questioned by some writers (Murji 1999; Stelfox 1998) in ways warning against the populist appeal of mythologizing and demonizing issues that wrap together various 'fear of crime' factors—drugs, guns, and young black males.

This issue of ethnicity as symbolic of outsider groups needs to be put in context. In the drugs trade, for example, it is native-white professional criminals who dominate the hierarchy in Britain not 'alien others'. Furthermore, it is the existing state of the market (legal and illegal) and condition of society that enables such enterprise to flourish. Quite contrary to alien conspiracy theories the 'outsiders' do not change the society. Rather the society and its existing structures provide the opportunities for crime and deviance, as well as the accompanying motivations and rationalizations (Ruggiero 2000; Young 1999; Cloward and Ohlin 1960; Hobbs 1997). Nonetheless the attractions and social functionalism of the identification of 'threatening minorities' and 'others' cannot be lightly dismissed and remains a key feature of the way late modern societies understand or imagine crime. This has been the case historically (Chapter 2), finds constant reproduction in various media narratives about crime (Chapter 5), and in the late twentieth and early twenty-first centuries the paradigm cases of alien external threat have been drugs and terrorism.

Recent trends

In 2001 the National Criminal Intelligence Service published the *UK Threat Assessment of Serious and Organized Crime* (London: New Scotland Yard). This report offered an analysis of available police information on the number and activities of organized criminal groups in the UK. Just focusing on London and south-east England it was estimated that 400 'organized criminal gangs' operate in this region with a total profit of around £25 billion per year. Drug trafficking and dealing represented the main source of such profits but diversification has also been a key theme and now involves activity ranging from the smuggling of cigarettes to avoid tax to the smuggling of human beings (often as cheap, illegal 'slave labour') to avoid immigration officials (Ruggiero 1997; Jamieson et al. 1998).

Counterfeiting is a major activity for professional criminals both in Britain and with links globally, involving production of goods or currency and then distribution. Fake designer label clothing and multiple illegal reproduction of popular audio and video tapes are well-known examples. Currency counterfeiting faces the problem that daily use of money makes fake versions harder to pass but this does not mean such counterfeit circulation is uncommon and it can be profitable whether a crude operation passing gold-painted moulded lead as £1 coins or involving sophisticated printing or photocopying equipment to manufacture high-value notes. The introduction of the Euro across much of Europe in early 2002 was predicted to be a boost to professional counterfeiters as this is a currency with which there is no history of familiarity and which is literally conceived and designed to be used in transactions across borders. Smuggling of pornography into Britain has been a long-standing target for Customs and Excise, and since the 1980s child pornography has become a particularly high-profile issue. The international sex trade has found new outlets via websites and mail-order organizations of legal and illegal provenance but organized prostitution remains a mainstay of the trade and numerous reports link the international trade in smuggling asylum-seekers and economic refugees to schemes of exploitation that sell women either into sex work or unpaid domestic service.

For some professional criminals, opportunities for criminal exploitation follow from unsuccessful attempts by society to regulate risks. For example, despite the introduction of food regulations from the mid-nineteenth century, food crimes have become a target for criminal enterprise (Croall 1998: 280). There is a long history of bad business practice on the part of legitimate retailers selling adulterated or out-of-date goods, and this is now paralleled by a trade in contaminated meat products that has attracted criminal gangs estimated to be 'making millions of pounds . . . from the illicit trade of "laundering" meat destined for the pet food industry or destruction' (Harris 2001: 10). The foot and mouth emergency in 2001 led to the mass slaughter of cattle yet much meat classed as unfit for human consumption nonetheless found its way back into the human food chain. Unfit meat can be treated or simply cut away from what appears to be safe meat but can still contain bacteria or other food poisons. Harris (2001) reports that 'meat scheduled for pet food can be bought for as little as 30p per pound but if doctored and sold back into the human food chain it can fetch as much as £2 per pound'.

Enterprises involving both professional criminals and law-breaking legitimate companies are involved in various 'green crimes' (South 1998), for example, the high-profit trades in rare, live animals, birds, or flora, and in products derived from protected plants or from animals killed to supply demand for body organs or skins. Certain forms of traditional 'alternative medicine' use such products, while animal skins have unlawfully been used in the production of shoes, handbags, and other items finding their way into the European luxury goods market. In 1998 government ministers 'from the world's richest nations' launched 'a crackdown on a "phenomenal" increase in green crime. Smuggling banned chemicals, waste and wildlife—often by the Mafia—[was estimated to be] worth up to $40 bn (£24 bn) a year, making it the biggest illegal trade after drugs' according to the *Independent on Sunday* (5 April 1998).

Drugs, drug markets, and crime

Contrary to popular and media images of drug trafficking, the distribution side of the drugs market in Britain can, like British 'organized' crime in general, be characterized as largely 'dis-organized' (Dorn et al. 1992; Hobbs 1997; Lewis 1994). This kind of analysis of the drugs trade and various other illegal businesses and 'rackets' owes much to Reuter's (1984) influential reappraisal of the American idea of 'organized crime' and his argument that this monolithic image actually represents 'fancy' rather than 'fact' (Reuter and Rubinstein 1978). Of course, this is not to say that drugs distribution enterprises and criminal participants lack organizational structures, skills, and abilities, for clearly this is not so. But in the sense argued by Reuter (1984), drugs and many other illicit markets (South 2001b; Ruggiero and South 1997) demonstrate tendencies towards fragmentation and dis-organization rather than towards the forms of monopolistic control of crime markets so feared and dramatized by mid-twentieth-century American mafia-watchers (Hobbs 1997, 1998: 408).

In reality, the British 'drugs market' is a set of markets for different drugs but also for combinations thereof, with many independent, small-group wholesalers and individual retailers involved. Ecstasy, amphetamine, cocaine, and other drugs now associated with the dance and club scene may be sold in particular 'markets' though these markets may also, for example, supply cannabis and skunk. There is no 'rule' about how drug markets operate. Combinations of drugs have always been available from the same dealers (Lewis 1994, 1989) although, as Coomber (1997a, 1997b) notes, this does not mean that some drug dealers do not find it useful to abide by certain rules. In most cases, such rules are based on personal assessment of risk and market logic, often refuting popular scare stories about drugs and 'drug peddlers', for example, avoidance of selling near school premises, or avoiding selling short-weight or adulterated drugs. The market logic applied is that the consequences of such behaviour would lead to a bad reputation and unwanted attention from the police, complaints or reprisal from dissatisfied customers, or simply the loss of custom altogether.

Among users, the arrival of a poly-drug 'pick'n'mix' drug culture was evident from at least the early 1990s (Parker and Measham 1994). Since the mid-1990s, the growing popularity and availability of cocaine, in powder form and as crack-cocaine rocks (Boys et al. 2001; Bean 1993; Corkery 2000) has contributed to the further blurring of markets. As in the legal marketplace where consumer choice and traditional brand loyalties may change, so do they in the drugs market. As availability of popular drugs has grown and their price has fallen, users increasingly choose from a 'smorgasbord' of legal and illegal substances (from alcohol and tobacco to ecstasy and cocaine) to 'fit' their lifestyle, desires and aspirations, and source and amount of income (Sharp et al. 2001; Collison 1996; Parker et al. 1998; Shapiro 1999). Overall, the diversification of illicit markets and their growing capacity to cater to the hidden consumer demand for drugs and other goods and services reflects the 'bazaar' of the late modern city (Ruggiero and South 1997) and a parallel, irregular economy of considerable size and significance.

The maintenance of market share and profit is as central to drug distributors as it is to high-street stores. To minimize law-enforcement disruption, vulnerability to penetration by undercover officers, or betrayal by informers, the use of violence has been evident in cases involving criminal groups since the 1970s (Lewis 1989; Ruggiero and South 1995). Some of these groups involved 'old hands' previously involved in bank robbery and other project crimes but who could see that drugs offered a more profitable and lower-risk alternative venture. For these entrants, some of whom had roots in the 1960s gangland era of the Krays and Richardsons, the 'profession of violence' (Pearson 1972) was simply being carried over into a new arena. From the late 1980s and particularly since the 1990s, newer entrants to the drugs business have proven themselves as capable of such assertive action as any of their predecessors and indeed may now routinize it as part of everyday business (Thompson 2001b; Hobbs 1995). Avoidance of law-enforcement attention is a key risk-reduction goal in such business. But this in turn leads to a 'ratchet' effect of interaction between criminal groups and the police that has important implications. Simply put, as law-enforcement and asset-investigation strategies become more sophisticated it is to be expected that at least some drug distribution businesses will increase their own levels of sophistication. It could also be argued that the move to more arming and use of firearms by the police is less likely to be a deterrent than a provocation to their use by serious criminals. While evidence for or against this view seems inconclusive, it is certainly the case that criminals involved in dealing in illicit markets will find firearms fairly readily available (Taylor 1999: 182, 179–83).

This discussion has moved from the early decades of the twentieth century to the beginning of the new. Clearly much has changed: the nature of some forms of professional crime and criminal communities; media images and reporting; the wider labour market; the increased significance of the global context; and the emergence of the huge drugs-crime arena involving old and new forms of criminal enterprise. Yet certain features are consistent and common: opportunism, organizational frameworks, and the pursuit of power and profit. Unsurprisingly these are also features of criminal enterprise and deviant behaviour in the legal marketplace.

Business crime

Criminal opportunities and enterprise in the legal market are usually characterized by terms such as corporate, white-collar, or business crime. However, many authors have deliberated on the difficulty of compartmentalizing offending into such categories. Indeed, for some critics the different definitions offered are simply muddy and untenable (Ruggiero 2000) while others observe that, despite the substantial literature generated, disputes about terms and definitions remain unresolved (Nelken 1997; Croall 1992). For present purposes, the term 'business crime' is adopted, although not solely in the astute and more precise sense proposed by Clarke (1990) but more broadly as a straightforward, familiar, and comprehensive type or category of crime.

As noted earlier, there is increasing recognition that the lines between professional organized crime and business organizational crime are blurred and overlap. At the same time, while lines of demarcation may be blurring there are also examples of the two areas simply mirroring each other. The hustles, scams, and confidence tricks so well documented in the trade of traditional crooks are also reworked in various ways in the world of legal traders and 'contrepreneurs' (Frances 1988). In this respect, BCCI was a con-trick or 'big sting' operation based on recognition that the assumptions of regulators and account depositors would be that such a 'big bank' must be a sound and above-board institution. Such confidence tricks can also be carried out by individuals or 'con-merchants' claiming to have the organizational resources, expertise, and track record to 'deliver the goods', all of which may be as fraudulent as BCCI's operation.

Such a case was one of the great business crime scandals of the 1990s, revealed in the prosecution of the 'financial adviser' Roger Levitt. Levitt was brought to trial in November 1993 following the collapse of his financial services company in 1990 with debts of £34 million. In large part though, the remarkable nature of this case lay not in Levitt's confidence trick but in the response of the criminal justice system. Indeed, to many commentators, the lenient nature of the subsequent legal judgment against Levitt was even more scandalous than his own offences. As Steven Box (1983) and others have indicated, there is considerable inconsistency in the way in which the criminal justice system treats the crimes of the powerless versus the crimes of powerful business offenders. Furthermore, there are significant practical impediments to the prosecution and punishment of certain forms of crime. Again these advantage business offenders. The journalist Peter Hillmore (1993) was struck by the different sentences delivered in what he called 'bizarre' court judgments made around the time of the Levitt trial:

Roger Levitt was ... a high profile crook, funding a wing at an Oxford college but a common crook for all that. ... He cheated people, who lost their money ... He cooked the books, he lied and his £34 million empire collapsed. ... His behaviour, said Mr Justice Laws was 'thoroughly and markedly dishonest'. Which is why Mr Levitt got ... 180 hours of community service as a punishment. ... Mr Levitt who had been on legal aid, went back to the £750,000 Maida Vale house owned by a family trust. Only his victims have really suffered ... [By contrast] in Ebbw Vale magistrates court ... Sharon Jones was also judged to be a criminal. The 30 year old mother of six is due to give birth to a seventh child in two weeks time. Her offence was failing to pay a £55 fine imposed for not paying her television licence fee. The magistrate ... sentenced her to five days in jail.

Hillmore's juxtaposition of these and other cases neatly reflects the argument of Reiman's (2001) well-known critique of the inequality of the American criminal justice system, 'The rich get richer and the poor get prison'. In Britain, such inequality of treatment for offences of major versus minor financial proportions has been discussed in studies comparing state agency responses to avoiders and evaders of tax payments with the fate of low-income claimants of state welfare benefits prosecuted for fraud (Cook 1989).

The Levitt case nicely stands to illustrate several themes common to criminal justice and other official responses to major business offences in the late 1980s and 1990s. These offences arose in a climate of de-regulation and the law was shown to be inadequate in response. As various commentators have noted, there is an ambivalence in society about the 'seriousness' of such affairs compared to, say, burglary or robbery (Box 1983; Clarke 1990). This ambivalence may partly be related to the fact that in some cases no 'crime' as such may have been committed, though regulations may have been breached, official guidance has been ignored, trust violated, and so on. As a number of court cases have shown, the complexity of the evidence and arguments put forward by prosecution and defence lawyers can baffle even experts let alone ordinary jurors, so a further layer of mystification is added about whether a crime has been committed or not. Indeed, cases may be regarded as too difficult to explain to a jury in a criminal court and are therefore only proceeded with as regulatory (i.e. non-criminal) offences (Dyer 2001). Given that when (or if) such crimes ever do reach court, trials can each cost from £10 to £20 million to stage (Gillard

1996)—for example, the 1980s series of 'City show trials' of the Maxwell Brothers, Barlow–Clowes, Blue Arrow, TC Coombs, Guinness, and Brent Walker and others (see Table 4.1)—then it is unsurprising that calls are frequently made to speed up the process and reform the jury element of such trials (Dyer 2001). The period of the 1980s and early 1990s became notable for the number of such cases coming to light and attracting not merely the private justice of the city

---

Table 4.1 Major business frauds and deceptions, 1986–1995

1986 Guinness–Distillers Affair	A fraudulent share-support operation to strengthen the Guinness attempt to take over the Distillers company	Four senior executives eventually convicted in 1992 for insider dealing and other offences; appeal against conviction rejected in December 2001
1988 Barlow–Clowes collapse	Left 17,000, mainly elderly, small investors with £190 million loss	Managing Director Peter Clowes jailed for fraud
1989 Blue Arrow affair	Deliberate deception of investors	Eleven executives charged
1991 Bank of Credit and Commerce International closed down	Varying estimates of losses: from £760 million including £100 million lost by UK Local Authorities (Taylor 1999: 144) to US $10 billion owed to 800,000 depositors in 1.2 million bank accounts in over seventy countries (Passas 1996)	Closure of bank, prosecution of senior figures
1991 Polly Peck International collapses	£450 million is unaccounted for	Principal executive, Asil Nadir, charged with misappropriation of funds but given bail. In May 1993 he fled to Northern Cyprus
1991 Robert Maxwell reported dead after a mysterious sailing accident	Between £450 and £500 million defrauded from Mirror Group pension funds affecting 32,000 employees	Maxwell's sons Kevin and Ian charged with fraud but acquitted
1995 Barings Bank collapses	£800 million lost on the world commodities trading market by dealer Nick Leeson	Leeson charged and imprisoned (the film *Rogue Trader* was made about the affair)

Sources: Taylor 1999: 144; Hughes and Langan 2001: 241–2; Croall 1998: 282

and financial regulators but the far more public attention of criminal trials. Why was this?

The Financial Services Act of 1986 was designed to free British financial operators working in the market of the City of London from the constraints of custom and tradition and thereby (supposedly) increase competitive effectiveness. Out-of-date arrangements for doing day-to-day business were to be swept away. New systems of oversight were to be introduced but without centrally imposing unnecessary restrictions on the newly released vitality of the market. This idea of releasing the untapped energy of the market in one 'Big Bang' was part of the Conservative government's strategy to 'roll back' the state and 'roll out' opportunities for private enterprise and for public as well as institutional share-holding and trading. This strategy involved the process of privatization of various formerly nationalized services and the encouragement of the general public to buy shares in them, and was also accompanied by a flurry of takeovers, mergers, and buyouts (Taylor 1999: 140–5). As Taylor (ibid.: 143) remarks, 'the scale of the "financial revolution" which liberalization of financial markets had unleashed—and the size and scale of the financial risks and temptations which had effectively been handed over for "market competition"—only really became apparent during the 1990s in a series of well-publicized instances of fraud.' These included the cases listed in Table 4.1 (the list is by no means exhaustive).

Such fraudulent activity represents a particular kind of business crime but these cases also demonstrate the difficulty of either applying precise labels or deriving precise definitions from such offences. Which of the cases described above would clearly be 'corporate crime' and which 'white-collar crime'? Using the general term 'business crime' seems to remain the simplest and clearest way to provide a definitional umbrella.

Of course, business crimes have impacts and implications beyond the financial hot zones of market deals and trading. British businesses have been accused of profiting at the expense of human rights (a topic discussed further below) and the contribution of businesses in various sectors to the rise in green crimes (South 1998) should also be noted. For example, the 'production and pollution' offences committed by the agricultural and chemical industries (Pearce and Tombs 1998), and the relocation by Western transnational corporations (TNCs) of high-pollution industries in less developed countries (Michalowski and Kramer 1987: 37).

The unscrupulous practices of business criminals can lead to loss of pension funds and/or unemployment for thousands of employees. Collusion between supposedly independent scrutineers of business practice and their employing clients can cover up malpractice and misuse of funds. The revelations in 2002 about the energy futures dealer Enron and their compliant auditors Arthur

Andersen was a stark example. Andersen 'overlooked' irregularities in Enron's internal accounting and in its reports to shareholders and the market. The collapse of this global enterprise, with its many European subsidiaries, had ramifications for commercial partners and employees in Britain. It also implicated Lord Wakeham, a member of Enron's management board and a former Conservative minister in allegations of mismanagement, and tainted the Labour Party because of their close relationship with the Andersen group prior to the 1997 election. Andersen provided services to the party free of charge with the alleged implication that the quid pro quo was that should they be elected to government, Labour would favour Andersen in competitions for contracts.

As noted earlier, some forms of business crime are connected to the world of professional organized crime. Interests of profit and power are common to licit and illicit criminal endeavours although, in most senses, these fields of enterprise are still 'worlds apart'. Nonetheless, examples of 'cross-over crime' can be identified and involve different sectors of modern social organization in collaborative crime arrangements.

Cross-over crime: business, professional, political, and state crime

BCCI was a 'legitimate' international corporate entity, supposedly regulated by British and other international banking authorities. Despite this reputable and regulated status, BCCI managed to engage in money laundering and fraudulent transactions on an enormous scale. The bank serviced criminal organizations and, according to various reports, supported the interventions of the Security Services of several states in the affairs of other states.[5] At the same time, some senior staff within the bank were involved in frauds and embezzlement. According to the Governor of the Bank of England, BCCI was dominated by a 'criminal culture' supporting activities and associations such as: 'nepotism, money laundering, misappropriation of depositors' money, blackmail, massive fraud and the provision of finance for illegal arms deals' (Croall 1998: 282; Punch 1996). When the bank lost funds through its stock market trading it simply used the money available to it from depositors, created fictitious loans, and avoided regulatory attention by moving money between countries and different accounts. According to the findings of other investigators, BCCI is only an extreme and particularly well-known example of how intense global commercialization can promote tendencies and opportunities to pursue power and profit via intensely criminal means (Rawlinson 1998).

The 'Arms to Iraq' scandal of the late 1980s and early 1990s is another case where business, political, and regulatory systems were brought into disrepute, and accusations of impropriety and ministerial cover-ups abounded. The Matrix Churchill company, a manufacturer of specialist machine tool equipment, was ostensibly at the centre of this affair and executives of the company were brought to trial but the case was really one reflecting the abuse of trust by those in public office. As Ian Budge et al. (2001: 436) put it, this case was an 'example of the lengths governments can take to conceal facts from Parliament'. The background involves a series of assurances from government ministers to Parliament during the 1980s that Britain was not exporting arms either to Iraq or to Iran. At the time, both countries were engaged in a long war and Western governments had agreed to help prevent escalation of the conflict by not selling arms to either side. In fact the British cabinet, without reference to Parliament, had secretly changed policy. From 1987 onwards the government was actually encouraging arms manufacturers to meet export demands from Iraq. This duplicitous behaviour was scandalous enough when revealed but furthermore the government contributed to what would have been a gross miscarriage of justice by withholding evidence when executives of Matrix Churchill were charged with arranging illegal exports to Iraq in the early 1990s. The subsequent 'disclosure of the facts by an eccentric ex-minister, Alan Clark, led to the collapse of the trial and prevented the wrongful imprisonment of the executives. The disclosure provoked a judicial inquiry, the Scott Commission, whose report strongly condemned the government and various ministers' (Budge et al. 2001: 436).

The activities of the British arms and security technology industries have also been of concern to civil liberties and human rights commentators. This is because their products for the 'free market' can so readily be used—or indeed are intended for use—to suppress other forms of freedom. In other words, the world of business production of the means of force supports the use of force in various examples of state crime and contributes to the blurring of distinctions between crime and politics (Cohen 1996, 2001). For example, there has been criticism of British manufacturers of security technology producing water cannons and rubber bullets that have been used in anti-riot and anti-strike policing on mainland Britain and in Northern Ireland. Critical criminologists, campaign groups, and others would characterize the violent suppression of protest as a crime of the state. But these industries are primarily major exporters overseas and it is arguable that their most damaging contributions to the manufacture of violence occur not in Britain but in various client states. For all the talk of adoption of an ethical foreign policy by the Labour government of 1997 the arms and security industries have continued with business as usual, selling the technologies of crowd control, surveillance, and torture to regimes that have little regard for the principles of democracy or human rights (Cohen 2001). The consequences are undoubtedly 'crimes of the state' (Cohen 1993) and just because these do not take place in Britain does not mean that Britain should not share responsibility for these crimes.

State crimes

In a settled and consensus-based democracy, with a relatively stable internal political system, overt crimes of state inhumanity are likely to be rarer than in dictatorship states, characterized by militarized agencies of control, political conflict and insurgency, and de-legitimated state structures. Britain represents one version of the former, ideal-type. But even so, it has certainly not been immune from criticism for its human rights record (Carrabine et al. 2000). Complaints concerning paramilitary policing, police brutality, the effects of use of CS gas, violent use of restraint equipment, and of course, deaths in police custody or in prison, have been frequent. Some complaints have been upheld by the courts and official inquiries, others rejected.[6] The operations of the British army and security services in Northern Ireland have produced events and legal cases of a kind that many critics would characterize as 'state crimes'. That many such 'crimes', deviations and injurious actions of the British (or any other) state may not actually be defined as crimes is unsurprising. After all, the state itself is the principal source of such definitions. Furthermore, it can be assumed that many activities potentially eligible for such labelling are not known about. Those that do come to wider notice usually do so by accident or by virtue of the conscience of some of those involved who give voice to their concerns or through the persistence of investigators (e.g. journalists and, in some cases, judicial inquiries and the police).

Even in a relatively open democracy, the state has a vested interest in the management of information and the civil service and successive governments collude to conceal secret crimes. This may occur in at least three possible ways. First, secret crimes may be the result of activities of the state security services — by definition a domain of secrecy. Second, they may be the result of intentional failure to act on information and evidence known to the state. Or, third, they may be acts of omission where, in the classic phrase from the 'Spycatcher' trial, the state is 'economical with the truth', that is, it does not reveal all relevant information or it simply tells lies. The history of the health and safety record (and other matters) relating to the nuclear energy industry has been a prime example of the employment of such strategies, usually justified in the name of state security or commercial sensitivity. In the 1950s, at the height of the Cold

War, British, Australian, and American servicemen were exposed to radiation in atom-bomb tests. In Britain, from 1945 onwards the Ministry of Defence station at Porton Down recruited soldiers as guinea pigs for the testing of chemical and biological agents and protective clothing against gas-warfare attacks (BBC News Online, 30 July 2001). Much information about how and why such dangerous exposures were allowed would seem to have been lost or has been disputed by governments but veterans have continued to press for compensation for damages to health. In 2001 police investigations into these cases were opened (ibid.; theage.com, 'breaking news' 29 December 2001). In the Gulf war, and then in the Bosnia and Serbia conflicts, the exposure of British and other soldiers, as well as indigenous civilians, to new forms of military arms that use depleted uranium, has also been controversial (Gunther 1999). The debilitating illness called Gulf War Syndrome has affected a number of veterans and, it is claimed, led to several deaths. This syndrome has been attributed by veterans and some medical evidence to the use of these DU weapons and possibly to the cocktail of anti-chemical warfare medicines given to soldiers. But again the question of evidence, and who holds it, is central (Fine 2001).

More than ever, the Foucauldian formula that 'knowledge is power', and vice versa, applies to the state in late modernity. The exposure of wrongdoing can be circumvented by suppression and manipulation of knowledge and evidence of such action. In the high politics of the state this has probably always been a part of statecraft. However, in a society in which knowledge has become so much more diverse and important, the state can increasingly avoid 'doing' or 'being guilty' of state crime by simply 'not doing': in other words by employing the power to not act on knowledge, and/or preventing others from acting by suppressing or 'overlooking' knowledge or evidence.

The following are simply illustrative examples. The BSE crisis generated numerous scandals of waste, incompetence, and inadequate responses from government but also many cover-ups of other damaging revelations. In 1996 the *Observer* newspaper reported how 'For ten years the Tories hid the emerging truth about BSE. The more damning the evidence the more Ministers gambled with the health of the nation. And in protecting their friends the farmers they sacrificed the population at large' (*Observer*, 24 March 1996: 16). Five years later the *Independent on Sunday* (28 January 2001) newspaper drew upon previously unpublished Ministry of Agriculture documents to show that 'Britain could have spread BSE to 69 countries by selling them meat-and-bone cattle meal knowing that it might have been contaminated with the disease'. The post-1997 Labour government has promoted the 'public understanding of science' yet failed to act on scientific evidence that would not be popular with the Treasury: for example, evidence that car exhaust pollution causes childhood asthma (Lean 2001) with the implication that major investment is needed in public transport as an alternative to the car. Or evidence that suggests that worrying developments in the field of genetic research—an area regarded as a major money-spinner for the British economy—could lead to the imminent availability of biological weapons capable of targeting particular ethnic groups (*British Medical Journal* 1999: 283).

A fuller treatment of this neglected area would enrich British democracy as well as the capacity of British criminology to understand and explore the deviance, criminality, and negligence of the British state. Too readily do British studies of 'state crime' simply cite examples from the USA or developing nations.

Political deviance and corruption

Until relatively recently, political corruption in Britain has been neglected by criminology (Levi and Nelken 1996) although for obvious reasons the subject has received more attention in political science and to some extent sociology. Taking advantage of political office for purposes of enhancing personal position and reward (power and profit) is an abuse of the organizational resources and status available to the office-holder and of the trust placed in her or him (see below). Some instances of political corruption may lead to criminal charges and prosecution and a few recent high-profile cases are noted below. However, most do not reach this stage and, if revealed at all, the only punishment likely to follow is undesirable publicity, minor scandal generated by media reporting, and the occasional official rebuke.

Scandals concerning sleaze and corruption have a long history within British politics and have periodically come to the attention of the public. For example, false claims regarding titles, votes, character, accomplishments, and expenses have been frequent, and misuse of power via formal and informal means, for example, through friendship and professional networks, has also been common. In December 1997, as the new Labour government settled into power on the back of a huge majority and a new image, the Postmaster General in the new government, Geoffrey Robinson, was the subject of controversy surrounding his financial affairs and his management of these. The Prime Minister Tony Blair was criticized for his defence of the minister and before the end of the affair, Robinson and another senior figure in government, Peter Mandelson, had both been forced to resign because of impropriety and scandal related to non-disclosure of a financial arrangement between the two. Again, following the 1997 election, Blair was implicated in a scandal arising from the Labour Party's acceptance of a £1 million donation to its pre-election 'treasure chest' from the Formula One Racing lobby at a time when it was seeking the exemption of the sport from the EU ban on tobacco advertising (Bartlett 1999: 227). Whilst Labour subsequently returned the Formula One money the Robinson embarrassments continued into 2001 when the former minister was found to have further misled Parliament about a payment arising from a previous business connection with the disgraced Mirror newspaper owner, the late Robert Maxwell. In 2001 Peter Mandelson, at the time Northern Ireland secretary, was forced to resign, and in 2002 the former Labour Minister for Europe, Keith Vaz, was disgraced after misleading the parliamentary standards commissioner. Both faced accusations of lobbying for special treatment for the Hindujah brothers in their application for a passport.

That the Labour Party had achieved a dramatic electoral success in 1997 undoubtedly owed something to the taint of sleaze and corruption that had become associated with the previous Conservative governments (Nolan 1995; Ridley and Doig 1995; Bartlett 1999). The Nolan report (1995) on 'Standards in Public Life' referred to the problem of a 'culture of sleaze' (para 1.7) and while the focus was on individual MPs such as Neil Hamilton and their contact with lobbyist consultancy firms such as Ian Greer Associates, this problem was recognized to be a systemic one. Sanctions could be avoided because Parliament and the libel laws protected the private interests of MPs, even when they lied about these (Bartlett 1999: 205-6). The resulting violation of public trust threatened the legitimacy and authority of Parliament (ibid.).

The legitimacy of local government was also occasionally called into question in the late 1980s and 1990s, though again by no means without precedent. Corruption regarding the award of contracts and various scandals involving nepotism dates back at least to the nineteenth century. In the late 1980s and early 1990s the 'homes for votes' 'gerrymandering' scandal of Westminster council drew attention to local corruption of political democracy, but in a particular way. As the District Auditor put it in December 2001 when the House of Lords rejected an appeal by Dame Shirley Porter, former leader of the council, this case epitomized the cynical 'use of council resources to achieve party political advantage'. Briefly, Porter and her former deputy had sold off council homes to potential Conservative voters to boost the election prospects of the party and with no consideration of the loss of public money for the council. This was, as Lord Scott put it in his judgment on the appeal, 'Gerrymandering—the manipulation of constituency boundaries for party political advantage. In that sense it was corrupt.' Lord Scott's argument continued that, if unchecked, such activity 'engenders cynicism about elections, about politicians and their motives, and damages the reputation of democratic government' (Guardian Unlimited/Society Guardian, 21 December 2001).

Some cases reveal how the framework of privileged position, financial power, access to organizational resources and mobilization of influential others can be combined to protect the guilty and pervert the course of justice. Famously Jonathan Aitkin, from 1992 to 1994 Minister of Defence Procurement in John Major's Conservative government, became entangled in a murky sequence of lies, attempts to avoid censure for involvement in brokering international arms dealings, a failed attempt to sue a national newspaper, and ultimately prosecution for perjury in January 1999 and bankruptcy in May that year. But this fall was not before Aitkin had profited enormously from his business networking with Saudi Arabian clients, directorships of companies, and political positions and connections, all of which were unethically combined for personal profit and advantage. In 2001 the Aitkin affair was overshadowed by the even more dramatic case brought against Jeffrey Archer, the novelist and former Deputy Chair of the Conservative Party, who had been installed in the House of Lords and had, for a while, looked like a popular candidate for the office of Lord Mayor of London. Archer faced trial and was convicted of perjury in a libel case that he had previously brought against the *Daily Star* newspaper. The *Star* had made allegations about Archer having a liaison with a prostitute, a suggestion that met with clear disbelief from the presiding judge in the original court case, who described Archer's wife Mary as 'fragrant' and implied no man would wander if married to such a woman. In fact Archer had arranged a false alibi to provide cover for the fact that he had been with the prostitute and his conviction and sentence to four years imprisonment immediately prompted new questions about his honesty throughout his public career (Rawnsley 2001). Archer's peccadilloes, lies, and eventual criminal perjury are an astonishing tale about a senior figure in public life (Crick 2000). That it might be a tale from one of Archer's novels about the pursuit of profit and power has been widely noted.

In drawing together these examples of political deviance and corruption it is worth emphasizing that while few members of the public may have expectations of probity within the world of professional criminals, the abuse of trust by those in whom society invests considerable faith that they are trustworthy is doubly damaging. Sutherland's (1949: 13) concerns about the impact of the abuse of trust perpetrated by the white-collar criminal should be extended to pinstripe criminals in government and the offices of state: 'The financial loss from white collar crime, great as it is, is less important than the damage to social relations. White-collar crimes [and the crimes and deviance of the political and criminal justice systems] violate trust and therefore create distrust: this lowers morale and produces social disorganization' (our addition). As Levi (1999: 6) suggests, loss of legitimacy in the political and criminal justice systems can occur as a result of a sense of betrayal in that reasonable expectations of system integrity have not been met, resulting in popular perceptions that there is 'one law for the rich and another for the poor'.

Trust and corruption

Whilst the previous discussion concentrated on well-known cases of offending perpetrated by powerful figures in public life it needs to be emphasized that the intention is not to individualize the causes and sources of crime. While there remains a tendency to explain deviant actions by reference to some form of personality or psychological deficits or as 'rotten apples in the barrel' (Croall 2001: 83), such accounts not only preclude any consideration of whether the 'barrel' is rotten but also mask the extent to which recklessness, ambition, egocentricity, and obsession with power are closely associated with business and/or political success (Box 1983). This is not to discount the relevance of individual motivation but rather to argue that choices need to be located in relation to the organizational context in which the offending occurs and the cultural sensibilities that promote or dissuade wrongdoing. For these reasons a number of authors have been drawn towards interrogating the particular features of organizations that affect the distribution of opportunities for illegality (for an overview see Slapper and Tombs 1999).

One particularly salient account is Shapiro's (1990) examination of the 'social organisation of trust' that indicates the ways in which trust is differentially distributed in occupational hierarchies. Her argument is that senior personnel and high-ranking officers are generally conferred with more trust than others lower in the organization and are also presented with considerably more opportunities to abuse that trust. So whilst 'street robbers' steal from their victims through threats or actual violence, 'suite burglars' cultivate social networks and exploit cultural capital to steal through abusing trust rather than brute force. The strength of this analysis lies in its attempt to reconcile individual and collective agency within an account of the structural distribution of trust within organizations (an analysis which should also be extended to the political and criminal justice systems).

This matter of 'trust' also relates to a feature of the organizational dimension of crime already signalled. This is the capacity of organizations, associations, or groups sharing mutual interests to impose secrecy on or manipulate information about their activities. For example, flawed police investigations, faulty prosecutions, and miscarriages of justice have at various times been covered up. Both the police and wider criminal justice system have demonstrated the capacity to manipulate or 'lose' evidence and information. In the context of the

National Health Service, the case of Dr Harold Shipman, convicted of the serial murder of patients in his care, dramatically revealed how trust and expertise can shield members of a professional group from suspicion and investigation over an extended period of time. On the other side of the fence, professional crime groups are aware of targeting by law-enforcement intelligence-gathering including the use of police informants (South 2001b). In response they can strategically leak information into underworld networks with the aim of misinforming and misleading law-enforcement agencies. Governments (legally and illegally) suppress information about certain political embarrassments using national security laws and restrictions on press reporting, and by the use of civil servants who are prepared to lie and act as shields or be 'economical with the truth' (as in the infamous 'Spycatcher' case of 1987–8; Budge et al. 2001: 539). They also mislead by 'leaking' some information having put their desired 'spin' on the message. Businesses may seek to control information about internal crime and victimization in order to protect public image, shareholder confidence, and insurance risk-assessments and may therefore operate a system of private justice that ensures no official record is ever made of a high volume of hidden crime—from high-street shoplifting to boardroom embezzlement. Business bad practices (often disputed as to their legality or illegality) can also be hidden by what secretive companies choose to make public or not and requirements that financial auditors make fair and true reports to protect shareholders, employees, and the market can clearly be circumvented (as noted earlier of the collapse of the US energy giant Enron).

The services of the public sector and charitable organizations are also, unfortunately, deserving of attention here. Since the 1980s a series of scandals has revealed the abuse of trust and the abuse of those in care in homes and institutions run by local Social Services Departments, Health Services, charitable branches of organized religions, and private companies subject to inspection by public authorities. Disturbing accounts of sexual, physical, and emotional abuse of children, older people, and the mentally ill, as well as inhumane punishments and other ill-treatment, have emerged (see Chapter 1). In many such cases, specialist workers, priests, teachers, and others have managed to pursue long careers of malpractice and abuse not least because organizations have covered up, and closed ranks at times when allegations have been made and intervention might have occurred. As numerous investigations and independent inquiries have established, organizational interests contribute to making such crimes possible, meaning vested interests seek to avoid 'rocking the boat', losing status, or costing the organization money.

Conclusion

This chapter has emphasized the importance of recognizing the organizational bases and resources underpinning certain forms of crime, and the centrality of pursuit of profit and/or power. The organizational perspective has been applied to professional, business, political, and state crime and to examples of cross-over phenomena. Finally, it is suggestive that this chapter aimed to move away from the 'idealism' of the neo-Marxist critiques of the 1970s, yet has nonetheless highlighted the contrasts between the crimes of the powerful and the powerless, and the ways in which these are responded to by society and its regulatory institutions.

One perspective touched on above but not explored in depth is concerned with the representation of crime and professional criminals in the media. In the next chapter the changing images of crime, past and present, are reviewed.

Chapter 5

Crime and Popular Culture

Introduction

FEW readers of this book will ever have been inside a prison. Yet no doubt all will be able to imagine the experience. In building a mental picture, the stock of cultural resources drawn upon might range from classic fly-on-the wall documentaries like *Strangeways*, to famous sit-coms such as *Porridge*, through to *Bad Girls*—a recent television drama, or a celebrated film like *Scum* (depending on the reader's age, gender, ethnicity, geography, or viewing preference). The task of this chapter is to consider the representation of crime in popular culture, not least because public understandings of crime are powerfully shaped by the diverse array of criminal narratives that routinely appear on television (from cop shows to documentaries), at the cinema (from *Brighton Rock* to *Reservoir Dogs*), in literature (from Fyodor Dostoyevsky to Elmore Leonard) and in newspapers (from the *Sun* to the *Guardian*).

Consequently, the chapter will cover both representations of crime in the news and as entertainment—though, as will become clear, rigid distinctions between true and fictional accounts of crime are not only hard to sustain in practice, but frequently the differences are imperceptible. This is not to suggest that people are incapable of discriminating between the real and the imaginary, but to insist that both 'truth' and 'fiction' are socially produced and, perhaps more importantly, consumed in an unruly fashion that might refuse the intentions of authors.

The chapter begins with an examination of the ways in which crime news is produced and then turns to a consideration of the representation of crime across a diverse array of mediums. Whilst 'factual' and 'fictional' narratives of crime are discussed in separate sections in this chapter, it cannot be emphasized enough that disparate media audiences commute on a daily basis between books, magazines, newspapers, television, cinema, radio, and so forth in ways that veer from vague distraction to fierce concentration (Carrabine and Longhurst 1999). In particular, as Robert Reiner et al. (2001: 189) suggestively argue, understandings of crime in everyday life are continually informed by representations of crime in popular culture. Consequently, the chapter also discusses the ways in which audiences might relate to criminal narratives that can encompass both fear and fascination.

Producing the news

The dramatization of crime

How the press and broadcast news report crime has been the subject matter of long-standing debates and research. Reiner (1997: 209–10) provides an extensive discussion of these findings, which can be summarized as follows. First, it is clear that news stories about crime are prominent in all parts of the media. For instance, one study compared the coverage of crime across ten national daily newspapers for four weeks from 19 June 1989, where it was found that 'on average, 12.7% of event-orientated news reports were about crime' (Williams and Dickinson 1993: 40). The proportion of space devoted to crime was greater the more 'downmarket' the paper—the smallest proportion of crime news, 5.1 per cent, appeared in the *Guardian*, the largest was 30.4 per cent in the *Sun* (ibid.: 41). Another study found that broadcast news devoted even more attention to crime reports than the press (Cumberbatch et al. 1995: 5–8). There were variations in the proportion of news items which concerned crime between different media operating in different markets. For instance, Independent Radio News carried the most crime news (over 21 per cent of all stories). Radio 1 also featured crime news prominently, but Radios 2 and 4 carried fewer crime event stories (11 per cent), and Radio 5 the least (9 per cent). On television, crime stories were most prominent on Sky News (over 18 per cent) and ITN featured almost as many. BBC1 had fewer crime event pieces (11 per cent). The key finding was that crime news was more frequent than any other category for every medium at each market level (Cumberbatch et al. 1995: 7).

Second, the pattern of crime in the news tends to concentrate overwhelmingly on violent and especially sex crimes (discussed in more detail below). A major claim of these studies is that the media tends to exaggerate the extent to which one might be a victim of crime. For instance, Williams and Dickinson (1993: 40) found that in one month in 1989, 65 per cent of British newspaper stories dealt with personal violent crime, which they compare to the British Crime Survey's (Mayhew et al. 1989) finding that only 6 per cent of crime involves violence. Studies of the provincial press indicate similar forms of exaggeration—Smith (1984: 290) found that offences such as robbery and assault accounted for less than 6 per cent of known crimes in Birmingham, but occupied 52.7 per cent of the space devoted to crime stories in the local press.

Third, there is a clear pattern in the media portrayal of the characteristics of offenders and victims. Most of the earlier studies found that offenders featuring in news reports were typically older and higher status than those routinely processed through the criminal justice system (Roshier 1973; Graber 1980), though from the early 1990s a significant proportion of media space was filled with images of lawless youth 'joyriding', the mounting wickedness of ever younger children, 'yob culture', and persistent young offenders—into which scenario entered Robbie Thompson, Jon Venables, and James Bulger (see Brown 1998: 48–9 for an informative discussion of press reporting in the months leading up to the Bulger murder in February 1993). Of course, also popular are accounts of celebrities experiencing brushes with the law, as in the case of Michael Barrymore in 2001 or political scandals such as the sleaze allegations levelled at Members of Parliament in the 1990s.

Fourth, a consistent finding across studies of news content is the predominance of stories about criminal incidents, rather than discussions of the causes of crime. Thus, crime stories in newspapers tend to be composed of brief accounts of discrete events, with few details on the background context. So what is presented is what Sherizen (1978: 204) describes as an 'information-rich' and 'knowledge-poor' foundation on how to understand crime (cited in Reiner 1997: 201)—a point that is examined in more detail below.

Fifth, the media generally present a very positive image of the success and integrity of the police and the criminal justice system. So whilst there are critical stories exposing wrongdoing by the police and miscarriages of justice, the malpractice tends to be framed in a damage-limitation narrative and is presented as a story of institutional reform. This can be seen clearly in the Stephen Lawrence inquiry where the Metropolitan Police eventually acknowledged the problems of previous practices but sought to safeguard its legitimacy by saying that it is putting its own house in order.

In order to understand why these patterns occur it is vital to turn to a consideration of the ways in which crime news is constructed. The most influential attempt to think through the 'social production of news' is contained in Stuart Hall et al. (1978), *Policing the Crisis*, which emphasized the ways in which politically and economically dominant groups in society define the scope of debate to ensure the reproduction of the dominant ideology and thereby significantly shape the contours of what the public may think (see below; also Chomsky 1988). Perhaps the most obvious way in which news production can be seen to function ideologically lies in the fact that the vast majority of newspapers and television stations subscribe to a broadly conservative political world-view, whatever the leanings of individual journalists might be, and that the post-war period has witnessed the growing concentration of press ownership in the hands of a relatively few right-wing proprietors (Curran and Seaton 1994: 123–6).

Less obviously, but equally importantly, is that news content tends to be filtered through what reporters would define as 'newsworthiness'. In other words, journalists would argue that they can sense what makes a good story. However, these news values are *learnt* and are in many ways a product of the 'newsroom culture' (Scraton et al. 1991: 111). A number of elements have been identified that contribute to the newsworthiness of a story (Chibnall 1977: 22–45). The most central is immediacy. An event has to be new before it becomes 'news'. Dramatization is another—for where an event is visible and spectacular it will be given more emphasis and space in consequence. Personalization refers to the ways in which leading individuals are emphasized at the expense of the context of the events. Titillation is also a prime news value, in which sexually related stories are emphasized or ordinary and mundane events become sexualized. A final element identified is novelty, which really is the search for a new angle on the same old story. Taken together, these elements of newsworthiness help to explain (a) why it is that violent and sex offences predominate in the media and (b) the concentration on higher-status offenders and victims, particularly celebrities. Furthermore, press reports are never simply a reflection of reality, as the two key processes of selection (which aspects of an event are chosen and which omitted) and presentation (the use of a headline, image, and language) compromise the apparent innocence of a story.

A final way in which news production can be seen to function ideologically is through the structural determinants of news-making. What this refers to is the ways in which journalists have 'structured' access to institutional experts. For instance, the police and criminal justice system control much of the information on which crime reporters rely. These institutional sources are what Hall et al. (1978: 57) term the 'primary definers', which provide the initial definition and primary interpretation of the topic in question. This interpretation sets the terms of reference within which all further coverage of debate takes place. A good example of these processes is captured in the following quotation.

The popular image of journalists (elaborated in many movies) as intrepid hunters after hidden truths is hardly realistic. Specialist reporters in particular are closely involved with, and indeed dependent upon their sources. Thus crime reporters identify with the police, defence correspondents with the services, and industrial relations experts with trade unions. But, in addition, journalists, who are better seen as bureaucrats than as buccaneers, begin their work from a stock of plausible, well-defined, and largely unconscious assumptions. Part of their job is to translate untidy reality into neat stories with beginnings, middles, and denouements. (Curran and Seaton 1994: 264–5)

Whilst this view is perhaps overly negative, leaving little space for the acknow-ledgement of the achievements of some journalists in exposing and reporting stories that official and business interests would have preferred to remain unexplored (see Chapter 4), this position is echoed in more recent work. Other commentators have reported on detailed observation of the crime news pro-duction process and qualified the conspiratorial determinism of earlier studies but crucially have not rejected the key insight that political and economic constraints set limits on access for the news media (Ericson et al. 1987, 1989, 1991; Schlesinger and Tumber 1993, 1994). Reiner (1997: 222) characterizes this production of crime news as 'cultural conflict', since it highlights the struggles that take place on newsroom floors between journalists, editors, owners, and sources. Yet while these accounts might portray a more fluid and contingent picture of news production, they do not fundamentally change the role of crime news. It has been argued that in the final instance the 'news media are as much an agency of *policing* as the law-enforcement agencies whose activ-ities and classifications are reported on' (Ericson et al. 1991: 74, emphasis in original). In other words, they 'reproduce order in the process of representing it' (Reiner 1997: 223).

To illustrate the significance of the processes discussed above a consideration of the reporting of sex crime in the press is illuminating. The key contradiction here is that whilst violent sex crimes are widely regarded by the public as particularly abhorrent, reporting tends to focus on a very few disturbed serial rapists, rather than typical rape which tends to be committed by an assailant known to the victim (see Chapter 3). In other words, the construction of the 'sex beast' in popular national newspapers plays an important role in maintaining the threat of 'stranger danger' at the expense of representing 'intimate vio-lence' as a serious social problem. In a wide-ranging examination of the report-ing of sex crime Keith Soothill and Sylvia Walby (1991: 34) emphasized the cen-tral place that the 'sex fiend' occupies in the popular press, which whilst not being a gross misrepresentation of reality is rather 'a selective portrayal of specific facts'.

The contrast between national and local press coverage provides an import-ant first step into understanding the dynamics of sex crime reporting. As these authors (ibid.: 35) argue, national newspapers tend only to retain an interest in a case 'if there is scope for the construction of a sex fiend who continues to wreak havoc on a community', whereas the local press are much less selective and 'on occasions will continue to maintain an interest in a case which seems unconnected with any other'. The most obvious reason for tabloid interest in promoting connections between incidents of sexual assault lies in the fact that a sex beast will sell newspapers.[1] Yet it is also the case that working on atrocious sex crime stories is the closest that most popular national newspaper reporters will ever come to investigative journalism, so that the significance of professional zeal should not be underemphasized. However, while serious investigative journalism challenges official accounts of 'reality', the search for a major sex criminal rarely does so, as 'the press and the police are using the same repertoire of scripts' (ibid.: 35). For instance, if an investigation is going unsuccessfully, the development of a sex fiend theme can provide the police with the resources to sustain a particular line of investigation. Moreover it is argued that 'the sex fiend conforms to their [the police] view of real sex crime. It has the thrill of the chase and is really the only acceptable variant in relation to sex crime from the "cops and robbers" scenario which in the eyes of most police officers is what policing is really about' (ibid.: 35). The police and the press also face a similar problem when the crime remains unsolved and no further atrocities are found. The police cannot maintain an expensive investigation, whilst the press are attuned to the 'boredom factor' of their readers. Consequently the story assumes a much lower profile, as it is not in the interests of the police or the press for an investigation to be seen economically and emotionally to fail.

The coverage of the case of Fred and Rosemary West from February 1994 to 1996 (and continuing) illustrates further themes of relevance. Fred and Rose West systematically raped, sexually tortured, and killed some of their own children and other young women lured to their house in Gloucester. When Fred West hung himself whilst awaiting trial, the news media focused their attention on Rose West and it has been argued that during the period of her trial in autumn 1995,

every denigratory term applicable to a woman was probably applied to Rose by journalists covering the case. She was described variously in the news as: depraved, lesbian, aggressive, violent, menacing, bisexual, likes oral sex, seductive, a prostitute, over-sexed, a child-abuser, nymphomaniac, sordid, monster, she had a four poster bed with the word c**t (sic) carved on the headboard, posed topless, never wore any knickers, liked sex toys, incestuous, who shed tears in silence, no sobs, no sound at all. (Wykes 2001: 177).

This language, whilst careering from the fiendish to the salacious, is always emphasizing the insanity of her conduct, which Maggie Wykes (2001: 178) contrasts with the paucity of information relating to Fred to the extent 'that it was almost as if he was excused from blame'. There are clear parallels here with the media treatment of Ian Brady and Myra Hindley—the latter continuing to receive far more press vilification than the former. The *Daily Mail* (23 November 1995) even proclaimed that 'Rose West and Myra Hindley have formed a macabre friendship in jail . . . the two most evil women in Britain, both openly bisexual—have been seen holding hands in Durham prison' (cited in Wykes 2001: 178). The fact that Fred raped and killed, whilst also running profitable prostitution and pornography businesses, was deemed unworthy of the same level of comment. So much so that the *Sun* (23 November 1995) insisted that Fred was 'only the undertaker' (ibid.: 178).

The particular point to be drawn from this discussion of the press coverage of the case of the Wests is that the emphasis given to Rose's deviant sexuality, at the expense of any extended consideration of Fred's role in the atrocities committed, potentially serves to secure a position for 'other male abuse' as less shocking or threatening 'by perpetuating the myth of home, fathers and family as safe' (ibid.: 178). The more general point is that, in fact, the world is not one where a few deranged individuals are responsible for every rape and sexual assault yet this is the message that the national popular press seems to promote. This world-view is sustained despite decades of feminist research which has consistently demonstrated that women and children are routinely subjected to levels of sexual and violent abuse in their families that most readers of this book would find greatly disturbing.

Moral panics and social theory

So far the discussion has concentrated on a description of crime news content and an account of the structural processes that might produce (and constrain) what can be said in broadcast and print media. The chapter now turns to a more theoretical consideration of the social function of exaggerated crime narratives in the media. From the outset it should be emphasized that arguments over the pernicious effects of media representations of crime have provided a persistent rhetoric of anxiety since the eighteenth and nineteenth centuries (Pearson 1983). The most familiar arguments are advanced by commentators of the Right who condemn the role of the media in encouraging permissiveness, undermining morality, and corroding the national character. According to this view the media sensationalize wrongdoing, glamorize wickedness, and generally erode the hallowed traditions of authority, deference, and respect that characterize the 'British way of life'.

Yet a key theme in liberal and radical criminologies has also been an abiding concern with the power of the mass media, albeit with an altogether different agenda. Since the 1980s, debates surrounding the prevalence of fear of crime (discussed in more detail in Chapter 3) have challenged the more theoretical excesses of this earlier work, which implied that the public are ideologically hoodwinked into misunderstanding crime as a social problem. Whilst there have always been intense episodes of collective anxiety, pious outrage, and organized persecution, with the witch trials of the seventeenth century being the most familiar example and Jewish history providing one of the longer essays in European scapegoating (though African, Indian, and Irish diasporas, amongst others, are no strangers to demonization), it is fair to say that moral panics are a product of the modern condition, not least because of the signifi-cance attached to the role of the mass media in framing social issues. It is equally the case that one of British sociology's more lasting contributions to public discourse is the notion of moral panic. This is now briefly outlined for the purposes of demonstrating not only the theoretical understandings that informed the classic positions but also as a means of questioning the continu-ing relevance of the concept in the light of changing characterizations and ways of experiencing modernity.

As is well known, the key texts are Jock Young's (1971) *The Drugtakers* and Stan Cohen's (1972) *Folk-Devils and Moral Panics*. Whilst they both, in important ways, were building on the work of earlier American labelling studies (see Becker 1964), one of the main differences in this British work was an emphasis on the conflicts between youth subcultures and Establishment forces and con-sequently they adopted a much more collective focus than the American perspectives. The model used to explain how moral panics occur is deviancy amplification,[2] and versions of it are to be found in both books. Cohen (1972: 9) argued that one of the most recurrent types of moral panic in post-war Britain has been associated with various forms of post-war youth culture. Cohen's work showed how the agencies of control, such as the media, the police, and various moral entrepreneurs interacted to create a panic over the Mods and Rockers. He used the notion of deviancy amplification to explain how the petty delinquen-cies of these groups at seaside resorts were blown up into serious threats to law and order.

Jock Young's (1971) book was based on a participant observation study of marijuana users in the Notting Hill area of London in the late 1960s. Young (1971) also used deviancy amplification to describe how the mass media turned marijuana use into a social problem through sensationalist and lurid accounts of the lives of users. In common with other British approaches produced at around this time,[3] Young (1971) regarded drug-taking as a subcultural resolution of problems posed by society. He therefore mounted his critique against the prevalent discourses which viewed drug use as a form of pathology or disease: in his words, 'people do not "catch" drug addiction, they embrace it' (1971: 42, emphasis in original).

The pressing questions that need to be asked are 'why do moral panics occur when they do?' and 'what is their function?' Cohen (1972: 192–3) insisted that moral panics were a product of 'boundary crises' (the term is Erikson's (1966)). They occur when a society has some uncertainty about itself. This ambiguity is resolved through ritualistic confrontations between the deviant group and the community's official agents, whose duty it is to define where the boundaries lie and how much diversity can be tolerated. In effect they clarify the normative contours at times when the boundaries are blurred. In this way moral panics tend to occur when society is undergoing rapid change, when the need to define boundaries is particularly acute.

Young's (1971) argument was that in small-scale societies deviancy amplification was much less likely as everyone has at least some face-to-face contact with deviant members of traditional societies and the information about members is rich and multi-dimensional, whereas modernity produces a significant drop in this sort of information. With severe social segregation there is a lack of direct information about those labelled deviants. This creates a great reliance on the mass media for information. The media's need to give the public what it wants and maintain a circulation in competitive markets means that they constantly play on the normative worries of large sectors of the population, often employing outgroups on which collective fears and anxieties are projected. There is a strong Durkheimian theme here, in that the boundaries of normality and order are reinforced through the condemnation of the deviant. But what Cohen (1972) and Young (1971) both were emphasizing was that this process only occurred in modernity through a considerable distortion of reality.

It is this last point that was to be substantially developed through a theoretically sophisticated, neo-Marxist understanding of ideology by Stuart Hall and his colleagues at the Birmingham Centre for Contemporary Cultural Studies in their (1978) *Policing the Crisis: Mugging, the State, and Law and Order*. The book can be regarded as the landmark text bridging critical criminology and cultural studies, and it is here that the somewhat vague Durkheimian notion of social control is replaced by a more rigorous neo-Marxist concern with state power. Hall et al. (1978) introduced Gramsci's (1971) concept of hegemony to understand the timing of the moral panic that emerged in the early 1970s around mugging. In much of the secondary commentary in criminology on the text, their analysis has been dismissed for claiming that the criminality crisis over mugging was contrived by ruling elites to deflect attention away from the economic crisis facing the British state, whilst ignoring the impact of crime on the working class. For instance, the moral panic identified by Hall et al. was criticized as 'a polemical rather than an analytical concept' (Waddington 1986: 258). Whilst making his case for a 'realistic' approach to crime and control in the 1980s, Jock Young (1987: 338) accused the text of Left 'idealism' and located it in the 'Great Denial' of crime as a force of social distress in decaying inner cities.

The difficulties arise in part from the idea of a moral *panic*, which implies an extraneous, excessive, irrational response to a situation. To be sure Hall et al. insist that the official 'reaction to "mugging" was out of all proportion to any level of actual threat' and that this 'ideological displacement' is their definition of a moral panic (Hall et al. 1978: 29). Nevertheless, what they do painstakingly demonstrate is how the police, media, and judiciary interacted to produce what they termed 'ideological closure' around the issue, in which black youth were cast as folk devils in dominant images of the archetypal mugger, as a scapegoat for all social anxieties produced by the changes to an affluent, but destabilized society. In many respects, the real strength of the book is the way in which it attempts to deconstruct the politics of representation in ways that had not yet been attempted in such an extended fashion. Of course, to many a reader now the discussion of the 'social production of news' will be too conspiratorial, but the focus on the sites of textual construction is one of the lasting legacies of the book.

Regardless of their theoretical orientations these classic studies indicate the *complexity* of explanation. But these accounts were produced nearly 30 years ago, and in many ways describe a very different world from that in which we now live. To address this point, the chapter now turns attention to some defining features of moral panics in late modern Britain that will require considerable theoretical work in the near future if the concept is to have any lasting relevance.

Moral panics and late modernity

There have been a series of criticisms levelled at moral panic theory, which would include McRobbie's (1994) and McRobbie and Thornton's (1995) significant interventions and Young's (1999: 24-6) subsequent questioning of the scapegoating function of moral panics in late modernity. The central themes can be summarized as follows.

The first point concerns their frequency—moral panics have an extremely short shelf life and a rapid rate of turnover, making it extremely difficult to cling to a model that points to their episodic quality, spirals, and flows. Indeed, Sheila Brown (1998: 46-52) goes so far as to say that the 1990s witnessed a 'total panic' around young people from Alcopops through to the film *Trainspotting*, via riots on peripheral council estates to children murdering children. One need not agree with all of her characterizations, but the point remains that we live in very different times from when there was a discrete succession of 'panics'.

The second point is that moral panics are contested. There has been a growth of interest groups and pressure groups who respond to and question media demonization of various social issues and the categorization of people as problems. The influence of such groups allows the media to portray reporting as responsible and providing 'balance'. One example of this is how it is no longer possible to ideologically vilify single mothers without strong voices of dissent. McRobbie (1994: 213) gives the example of the National Council for One Parent Families that played a leading role in diminishing the Conservative Party's demonization of young single mothers and the attempt to further penalize young mothers for having children without being married.

The third point concerns reflexivity. The notion of moral panics now pervades media and political rhetoric. For instance, Sue Cameron on BBC2's *Newsnight* asked 'Is it not the media itself that has helped to create this phenomenon?', the phenomenon being 'new juvenile crime' (cited in McRobbie 1994: 198). It is now a question directly aimed at politicians when, for example, they are perceived as deliberately trying to whip up a moral panic over an issue, as Ann Widdecombe routinely faced over the Conservative Party's use of asylum-seekers as a threat in the run-up to the general election in 2001.

The fourth point is that moral panics have become vital marketing strategies. Thornton (1994: 183) provides a detailed account of the ways in which disapproving 'tabloid coverage legitimates and authenticates youth cultures'. In particular she and McRobbie (1995: 565) have demonstrated how moral panics 'are one of the few marketing strategies open to relatively anonymous instrumental dance music'. Yet it is also the case that the success of a film like *Natural Born Killers* was due largely to the moral panic that accompanied its release in Britain on the back of a number of alleged 'copycat' murders in the United States and Europe—indicating that it is not only subcultural industries that have become versed in the art of selling through 'panic'.

The fifth point is that moral panics can now easily rebound. A good example is Conservative Prime Minister John Major's fraught attempt to take the nation 'Back to Basics' in the mid-1990s, a strategy which famously backfired amid stories of financial sleaze, and a lamentable lack of adherence to 'basic values' by his cabinet colleagues, which were exposed through close media inspection: 'Mistresses abounded, broken families were commonplace, sexual peccadilloes scrutinized, the moral panic rebounded back upon itself' (Young 1999: 25). An illustration of the general point here is that the series of news revelations about political sleaze and corruption were not presented to nor received by the public in terms of a moral panic but rather in terms of a cynical weariness about the apparently routine nature of such 'revelations'.

The sixth and final point relates to diversity in that the 'hard and fast boundaries between "normal" and "deviant" would seem to be less common' (McRobbie and Thornton 1995: 572–3). In many ways this is the most important point that a late modern reconceptualization of theory has to deal with. For whilst the various authors that have been discussed here point to the above changes as being a result of the vast expansion and diversification of the mass media, it is important to recognize that a more wide-ranging account is needed of the social changes that have occurred over the last 30 years that have undermined boundaries, some of which have been detailed in Chapters 3 and 4.

Furthermore, the proliferation of communication technologies has meant that whilst there are new spaces for diverse niche interests there has also been a broader tendency towards the merging of news and entertainment. Yet it is difficult to underestimate the significance of the changes that have occurred in the cultural sphere. These are multi-faceted and include the undermining of the moral certainties that accompanied the pre- and immediate post-war era. As David Garland (2001: 88) puts it, there have been 'radical changes in the norms governing such matters as divorce, sexual conduct, illegitimacy, and drug taking'. In some respects, these changes were wrought by the cultural politics of the 1960s and the formation of new social movements associated with feminism, race, sexuality, and youth culture—though arguably the key legacy of the 1960s is the 'triumph of the individual over society' (Hobsbawm 1994: 334), which would come to be expressed in Margaret Thatcher's infamous insistence that there 'is no such thing as society, only individuals'. Nevertheless, the championing of an egoistic, competitive individualism also sits with a liberal recognition of the right to be different and the development of a potentially more pluralistic politics of 'multiculturalism', albeit one fraught with difficulties (Bhabha 1997). Accompanying these changes has been the emergence of consumption as a primary site of expressing one's identity through lifestyle choices, the elevation of the culture industries as central markers of social change and the declining relevance of church, state, family, and neighbourhood in instituting moral regulation.

In order to grasp the significance of these changes for moral panic theory a number of authors (Jewkes 1999; Reiner et al. 2001; and Thompson 1998) have recently turned to the concept of 'risk society', as formulated by the theorist Ulrich Beck (1992) to understand the anxieties provoked by these transitions from modern to late modern social formations. For instance, it has been argued that the increased frequency of dramatic moral narratives in the mass media in the 1990s (as documented above) is partly a response to the increased pressures of market competition, but is also a key means by which 'the at-risk character of modern society is magnified and is particularly inclined to take the form of moral panics in modern Britain due to factors such as the loss of authority of traditional elites, anxieties about national identity in the face of increasing external influences and internal diversity' (Thompson 1998: 141). It is beyond the scope of this chapter to assess whether Beck's (1992) conceptualization of risk is the most appropriate for understanding the contemporary character of moral panics. Instead this section will conclude with some signposts indicating how future theoretical, and perhaps more importantly, empirical work might best be orientated.

One of the main problems with the classic formulations and the recent attempts to refine the concept of moral panics is captured in Richard Sparks's (2001: 199) telling criticism that they remain committed to a 'style of analysis which treats the detailing of media "contents" or "mythologies" (depending on methodological preference) as a largely self-sufficient activity, and which tends to enter grand and mostly unsustainable generalizations about their hold on public opinion or their ideological predominance'. In other words, how audiences interpret and use the media demands far more attention than has hitherto been received in criminology (notwithstanding the voluminous literature on 'fear of crime')—a point returned to later in this chapter. Nevertheless, the questions raised by this critique can only be answered through detailed empirical research.

The chapter now turns to a consideration of the representation of crime in popular culture. It should be emphasized that this is not intended to be an exhaustive coverage of all forms, nor a comprehensive historical survey. Instead what is offered is a sense of the range of representations whilst indicating some continuities and discontinuities in theme and form. The more general intention is to provide the reader with a glimpse of the diversity of criminal narratives that can regularly be encountered through television viewing, cinema-going, and reading popular literature, which powerfully shape understandings of crime.

Watching the detectives

The origins of detective fiction

Of all the genres of popular fiction the detective story is probably the most studied, partly because its beginnings can be fixed with relative certainty. It is generally agreed that Edgar Allen Poe's 1841 story 'The Murders in the Rue Morgue' provides the distinct innovation of organizing the narrative around the intellectual genius of a detective hero, Auguste Dupin, who reconstructs the scene of a crime and catches the guilty party through the clues and traces left behind. It was this innovation that Conan Doyle was to translate into a commercially successful formula in his Sherlock Holmes stories, the first of which appeared in 1887 (Bennett 1990: 212).

However, it has also been rather grandly claimed that the mystery that marks the beginning of all detective stories has been seen as a basic and universal function of all narratives. For instance, the process of discovery has been compared to the myth of Oedipus, whose discovery of his origins is also a discovery of his crimes (McCracken 1998: 51). So in some respects the detective narrative can be seen as a new form of an old story. In the example of Poe (1980), it is clear that he was also a gifted author of the Gothic horror genre, which can be seen at work in such stories as 'The Pit and the Pendulum', 'The Masque of the Red Death', and 'The Fall of the House of Usher', to name just a few. This was a genre that had emerged in the eighteenth century and was organized around such motifs as suspense, the supernatural, and the pre-modern. Consequently, it has been argued that the innovation that Poe performed was to transform these motifs into his detective fiction in the 1840s. Simultaneously, there was also a 'flourishing trade in broadsheets, ballads, "memoirs" and novels about the exploits of highwaymen like Dick Turpin, Jack Sheppard, and thief-takers like Jonathan Wild' (Reiner 1992: 183) in the eighteenth century, which is explored in illuminating detail by Rawlings (1992).

However, if the focus remains restricted to narrative conventions in the abstract then there will be a failure to understand the historical conditions that produced them (Thompson 1993: 43-4). In other words, an account of the development of detective fiction needs to recognize its social articulations, rather than simply celebrate the individual genius of a particular author. One historical shift that has been understood as particularly important for the emergence of detective fiction is the transformation from arbitrary power to the rule of law. In other words, this genre of fiction emerged at a time when Western countries had recently moved from a judicial process based on torture and confession to one centred on trial by evidence (McCracken 1998: 51). This point can be taken further through an examination of the ways in which detective fiction articulates discourses of individualism, science, and rationality, which were all set in motion in the Enlightenment and in many ways define modernity. Detective stories can also be read as narratives on the urban experience and the development of policing and surveillance. To develop these arguments the work of the literary critic Walter Benjamin is particularly instructive.

For Benjamin, the origins of detective fiction are to be found in the rapid expansion of cities in the nineteenth century and the impersonality this urban sprawl brought to social relations. He suggests that the original concern of the detective story lay with the 'obliteration of the individual's traces in the big city crowd' (Benjamin 1983: 43). On the one hand, the genre lifts the veil of anonymity that the urban mass provides the criminal, through making him knowable by the traces he leaves behind, such as fingerprints, cigar ash, and so on. In other words, the fictional detective subjects the city to a controlling and individualizing gaze in which there is no hiding place for the criminal. But at the same time, the gaze reduces the value of individuality, in that the tell-tale clues left behind are seen not as the product of a unique human being but rather as statistical effects.

The literary context in which Benjamin (1983) discusses Poe's detective stories is through the figure of the *flâneur*, in his broader study of the poet Charles Baudelaire. Historically, the term *flâneur* referred to a group of writers and journalists who in the serial feature sections of Paris newspapers, and in books known as *physiologies*, wrote depictions of city life from a position of spectatorial dominance in the 1830s (Brand 1991: 6). Benjamin's argument is that the *flâneur* was a precursor to the detective as they both suggest that the city can be read. So Poe's achievement was twofold. First, he linked crime with the urban crowd. Second, he provided, in Dupin, a figure who could read and master the dangerous city.[4]

However, what is crucial to Benjamin's argument is that the development of a gaze that could master the city is not just restricted to the world of fiction. In fact it closely corresponded to the new mechanisms of surveillance that rendered the city legible to the gaze of power. This was achieved precisely through the bureaucratic reduction of individuality down to a set of knowable traces. What is remarkable about this is that Benjamin was writing in the 1920s and 1930s, some 50 years before Michel Foucault's (1977) analysis of the principles of panopticism, which literally means the 'all seeing eye'.[5] Foucault has been highly influential in criminology through arguing that the key form of power in modern societies is surveillance. He builds his argument from Bentham's Panopticon, which was designed to be a model prison in which the surveillance of prisoners was to be complete and total. However, Foucault extends this argument to insist that society has become totally transparent to the gaze of power. The Enlightenment forms of discipline and surveillance aim to penetrate deep into the depths of society to transform populations into objects of social administration.

So the argument can be made that the 'private eye' of detective fiction complements this public eye of power, through rendering society totally visible to the gaze of power. In fact, it has been suggested that the classical detective story embodies the totalitarian aspiration of a transparent society rendered visible through the exercise of power and the registration of knowledge (Moretti 1990: 240). Yet, one of the central themes that begins to emerge in the early twentieth century and continues up to contemporary representations of crime on television, at the cinema, and in literature concerns the 'ambivalent but central place of the city in modern sensibility and the place of the individual moral agent in the face of social organizations too extensive to direct or comprehend' (Sparks 1992a: 36). In other words, a far more ambiguous and complex set of relationships obtain between the city, crime, and detection. It is to this shift that the discussion now turns.

The 'Golden Age'

The 'Golden Age' is the term used to refer to the novels of authors like Agatha Christie, Dorothy Sayers, and G. K. Chesterton which were produced in the inter-war period. Here the detective is an eccentric, amateur sleuth, marking an important stage in the development of detective fiction. For this is not only a shift from the dangerous city streets to the English countryside, but also crime, or more accurately the murder mystery, becomes an event that can take place not only among the working class but also amongst the upper reaches of the class structure.

This social milieu means that the 'ordinary' policeman (and it is usually a 'he') has no chance of solving the mystery, since he possesses neither the standing necessary to gain access to, nor the graces to move easily in this social setting. Above all, he is not versed in the arts of performance practised by this social group and is therefore unable to unmask the murderer. The *ordinary* policeman stands by whilst the *extraordinary* detective solves the mystery (or more usually the bungling plod stands in the way of the genius sleuth). Since the ordinary policeman cannot work effectively in this social world the scene is set for someone who can bridge the world of the upper classes and the world of justice. The detective is consequently an ambiguous figure, who is both inside, but with a certain distance from, the social setting of crime (Clarke 2001: 79). Predominantly, this role is occupied by an amateur, or at least someone who is not a member of the police force. Crucially, though, the sleuth remains a *flâneur* who can penetrate the social codes of the elites. For instance, Agatha Christie's Miss Marple is as much a *flâneur* as her urban counterparts. She is able to play the part of the innocent old lady, an anonymous type, yet also possesses the acute observational powers necessary to see what others do not see and thereby solve the mystery.

Whilst there is a shift in tone, from the gloom and menace of Poe and his many imitators, to a more familiar comedy of manners in the Golden Age mysteries and an accompanying change in location to the ubiquitous English country house, there are important continuities with the earlier work. For instance, as Alison Young (1996: 98) argues, the Holmes stories do not deal specifically with a criminal offence, but rather they examine disorder in the respectable bourgeois family, and more often than not, the destructive force of greed upon family relationships. This theme is developed in the inter-war period, while the upper classes present themselves in public as self-confidently imperial, powerful, and respected, where everyone knows their place and acts accordingly, in private they 'keep killing one another—and when one of them is murdered, there is a long queue of likely candidates for the role of chief suspect' (Clarke 2001: 76). In other words, the mystery is an effect of intimate, family relationships going wrong rather than a result of a dangerous world 'out there' and the victim is typically cast unsympathetically and deserving of their fate. The victim is frequently of a 'type'—the harsh, hot-tempered, and stupid father opposed to a marriage, or an unremitting cad whose impending marriage to the decent girl interferes with her preference for an upright young man, or perhaps worst of all the victim has posed as a gentleman but has concealed some dark secret that he has used to exploit the rituals of status (Grella 1988: 96–7).

In stark contrast to the English murder mystery, an entirely different form of detective fiction was being developed in the United States, most famously in the work of Raymond Chandler and his archetypal 'private eye' Philip Marlowe. This genre is usually regarded as 'hard-boiled' detective fiction in that the narrative seeks to offer a sense of social realism in its murky urban settings, its focus on low life and the use of gritty, everyday language (Clarke 2001: 81; see also Hirsch 1981: 26–7 and Messent 1997: 1). This literature also provided the basis for the development of *film noir* in Hollywood in the 1940s and 1950s (Clarens 1997: 192) which offered frequently bleak outlooks on the urban condition as opposed to the musicals, melodramas, and screwball comedies that were being produced in the 1930s. In fact, the term *film noir* was coined by post-war French film critics, once American pictures began to be shown again after the Second World War, when these critics noticed the dramatic contrasts in the content and style of the films that Hollywood produced during and after the War.

In many ways these stories and films returned crime to the mean streets of cities and we can see many motifs that Poe introduced in the 'Murders in the Rue Morgue' as set conventions in hard-boiled fiction and *film noir*. Thus, the figure of the detached, intuitive, and smart investigator and the city as a dark and dangerous setting return to centre stage. Similarly, wealth, power, and status are key elements in these stories and films, but they function in very different ways from the English murder mystery. The imaginary social order of North America here is one where the city provides the context in which money links a variety of social groups, which would include the old rich, businessmen, gangsters, con-men, and corrupt police departments in tangled relationships (Clarke 2001: 82).

The narrative tension in these stories is sustained by the conflict between an amoral, corrupt world and the isolated moral code of the detective. The detective must be socially mobile enough to work in a whole variety of urban settings without becoming contaminated. In fact it has been argued that the Private Investigator is the moral conscience of America—the classic 'everyman' figure, who stands for all the 'little people' who are not part of the centres of power and influence, but whose lives are threatened by their corruption (Clarke 2001: 84–5). Yet, this is perhaps the limits of the genre, as it has been criticized for its conservatism. What this means is that even though it reveals widespread corruption, it is a literary and cinematic form that defends the social system (Messent 1997: 7–8). So that whilst individual crimes might be solved, nothing ever changes in the larger social and political climate.

The police procedural

Since the 1950s the police have been the focus of narrative attention in detective fiction, not least because the 'imaginary social order in which gifted amateurs could carry out investigations under the noses ... of humble policemen could hardly be sustained (except as a pastiche) in the post-war context' (Clarke 2001: 86). James Ellroy, the author of *L.A. Confidential*, has remarked that he 'consciously abandoned the private eye tradition', since the 'last time a private eye investigated a homicide was never' (cited in Messent 1997: 11). This emphasizes the fact that private eyes are quite simply irrelevant to contemporary criminal justice investigations, and that the figure is purely a romantic fantasy. In response, the detective story has moved its social milieu to the occupational world of the police procedural where stories are based in police settings, and detection becomes 'professionalized'. Of course, in some versions the narrative form does not change very much, the same themes are simply moved to the world of the police (Clarke 2001: 86). It still remains a matter of the detective's extraordinary ability to reveal the truth beneath the surface of appearances, albeit now accompanied by the apparatus of organized detection although still displaying personal eccentricities—like Inspector Morse's gruff penchant for fine ale and classical music.

Other versions, like BBC2's series *The Cops*, from the late 1990s, demonstrate much of the mundane, human business of crime-fighting, and in fact the crimes are always secondary to the personal and political struggles between the characters. Whilst this series was highly praised for its critical 'realism', it is important to recognize that it was a reworking of what Reiner (1992: 200) has termed a 'community police narrative' that is as old as television. In the British context, the exemplar was *Dixon of Dock Green*, which came to be displaced by the vigilantism of *The Sweeney*, but staged a highly successful comeback in such series as *Juliet Bravo*, *The Bill*, and *Heartbeat*. In recent years, however, *The Bill* has moved away from its strict portrayal of harmonious relationships within the force and wider society, to enter the terrain of deviant cops, disintegrating domestic lives, and institutional racism that have provided some of the staples of cinematic representations of crime-fighting.

In many respects the archetypal police procedural on screen explores the tensions between the 'good cop' and the occupational world in which he functions. This is very close to the Private Eye form, in which the 'loner' battles against the bureaucracy and incompetence of the police department. The classic example of this is the Dirty Harry series of films. The first, released in 1971, heralded a new innovation of tainted-cop investigation dramas. Harry Callaghan is the police officer dedicated to terminating a serial killer on the loose in San Francisco. To get his man he will rarely play by the book and he defies both his conservative bosses and the political establishment in tracking down the killer. The indignant, crusading policeman embodies both a late 1960s counterculture ideology, through his defiance of authority, and a right-wing distrust of the government.

In fact, one commentator at the time claimed that 'this action genre has always had a certain fascist potential, and now it has finally surfaced' in Dirty Harry (Kael 1972, cited in Sparks 1996: 354). There is no doubt that the film applauds Harry's right-wing vigilantism, and Harry Callaghan, played by Clint Eastwood, is an unbreakable straight arrow who remains completely uncontaminated in his search for the psycho. In later variations on the same narrative pattern, cop and killer become doppelgängers and a far more morally ambiguous story is told, such as in the recent films *Face/Off* (1997) and *Heat* (1995), whereas in the Harry films they remain distinct adversaries in a straightforward struggle between good and evil. And like their hero, the films believe that evil can be contained; whereas in later films like *L.A. Confidential* (1997), malevolence is systemic and no cop operates with Harry's moral purity (Hirsch 1999: 157).

Born to be bad

Much of the crime fiction discussed so far has been concerned with a narrative structure that starts with an opposition between law-abiding citizens and criminals. Yet there is another genre of films that focus on professional criminals, on characters who pursue a criminal way of life before the film or story begins, which would include the classic original gangster films of the 1930s up to the underworld epics of, say, the *Godfather* or *Good Fellas*, or the recent television series *The Sopranos*—which inserted a new dynamic on family relationships into mob tales. Another staple of Hollywood cinema has been the failed heist, which was cleverly reworked in *Reservoir Dogs* and the myriad of imitations that followed in the success of Quentin Tarantino's postmodern reworking of what had become a stale genre. Tarantino also provided a fresh spin to crime films in *Pulp Fiction*, which transformed hit men into likeable, tragicomic heroes.

These American films have been highly successful at the British box office and hence contribute to the British understanding and imagining of crime in contemporary society. However, it is also important to recognize that British crime cinema has a significant history and has made distinctive contributions. Traditionally concentration has been on tough men in seedy low-life worlds of professional crime (such as *Brighton Rock* 1947; *Get Carter* 1971; *The Long Good Friday* 1981; *The Krays* 1990). Whilst many of these films have reached iconic status in the 1990s 'lads' press, Monk (1999) argues that an important shift occurred in British crime film during that decade. Her argument is that the social milieu of crime switched from the underworld to the underclass, or to be more precise a number of key films examined the 'predicament of the jobless underclass male' (Monk 1999: 174). From the feel-good comedy of *The Full Monty* (1997) to the grim heroin drama of *Trainspotting* (1996) such films explored the consequences of the economic decline and social destruction wrought by Thatcherism in places blighted by deindustrialization, where crime is 'normal' and woven into the fabric of everyday life (themes that are examined in more detail in Chapters 3 and 4).

Perhaps the most disturbing British crime film of the 1990s was Danny Boyle's *Shallow Grave* (1994) which served to emphasize the amorality of a 'winner-takes-all' society by detailing the increasing ruthlessness of three thoroughly unpleasant Edinburgh yuppie flatmates, who discover that they can attain instant wealth through concealing the death of a fourth, older flatmate. Whilst Claire Monk (1999: 181) compares the film to Tarantino's trademark 'Nietzschean anti-morality', it is also important to recognize that in both directors' worlds it is professional criminals, and not the police, who dispense 'justice' according to one of the few reliable principles of an underworld code (i.e. you do not double-cross the boss). Whilst there were important changes in the representation of crime in British film during the 1990s, Guy Ritchie's (1998) *Lock, Stock and Two Smoking Barrels* illustrates some significant continuities in that the film recalls the long-running and highly popular television series *Minder*, which frequently played on the humour of small-time villains getting mixed up with ganglords and a largely ineffective Metropolitan Police Force.

Another significant development in crime fiction over the last couple of decades has been the introduction of the serial killer, which highlights the return of the threat of irrationality to the genre. Whilst classical crime fiction derives its narrative tension from the opposing forces of reason and unreason, in much of the detective fiction of the twentieth century, crimes are motivated and their causes can be traced somewhere back to relationships of love, greed, or revenge amongst the principal players in the drama. Yet with the advent of the serial killer, there is the creation of 'innocent victims'. As John Clarke (1996: 83) argues, in this imaginary social order, crime is a totally random event and it appears as if out of nowhere, making violence unpredictable and symbolically much more dangerous than in previous fictional representations of crime. The films and stories lay a great stress on the ways in which the serial killer can pass for normal and will not stand out as a deranged individual. Quite the reverse is the case; he blends invisibly into social life. For instance, the serial killer in *Seven* (1995), played by Kevin Spacey, is referred to only as 'John Doe' (the term used for unnamed corpses).

In the conventional detective story, the murderer is in many respects 'normal' in that they are part of a particular type of social order with predictable motives, such as love, revenge, money, and so on. By contrast, the detective is 'extraordinary', with special qualities that permit a solution where the less brilliant will fail. In the case of the serial killer, this pattern is inverted—it is the murderer who is extraordinary with the ability to appear normal, while the detective is part of a collective enterprise and is increasingly dependent on the abilities of others, such as forensics, psychologists, and so on, to arrive at a solution (Clarke 1996: 84). Yet this theme of inversion is, in many respects, a defining characteristic of Gothic melodrama, in that the 'transgression of all boundaries [is] a conscious narrative agenda' (Simpson 2000: 19) and the oscillation between reassurance and danger sustains the narrative tension in serial killer texts. In other words, the appearance of the serial killer in fiction owes an enormous debt to Gothic horror, which relies heavily on the establishment of normality prior to the terror being unleashed and the ensuing violation of the comforting patterns of daily life.

The theme of transgression has also been developed in what Scott McCracken (1998: 70) defines as postmodern detective fiction. One of the main criticisms of detective fiction, particularly in its 'hard-boiled' guise, is that it only offers a problematic 'white, heterosexual, male' gaze on the world. For instance, it has been argued that 'in detective fiction gender is genre and genre is male' with women only figuring to 'flesh out male desire and shadow male sexual fear' (Messent 1997: 1). Yet during the 1980s and 1990s the genre has broadened its scope to entertain a more pluralist and critical world, where feminist, lesbian, gay, and non-white detectives now operate.[6] Crucially though, these stories are not simply a celebration of how anyone can be a detective but rather they are concerned with the ways in which multiple inequalities are structured around gender, sexuality, and ethnicity. In other words, detectives like V. I. Warshawski, Kate Delafield, and Easy Rawlins transgress the boundaries of conventional detective fiction to reveal the complex, contradictory, and hostile worlds that an Anglocentric, straight, and masculine rationality has created. Whilst these are recent developments in US crime fiction, British television viewers will perhaps be familiar with ITV's *Prime Suspect* series of police procedurals that explored the struggles faced by Detective Inspector Jane Tennyson, played by Helen Mirren, to work in the male occupational culture of the police. Older viewers may recall ITV's *The Gentle Touch*, which centred on Jill Gasgoine's female detective. Further transgressive themes were more recently pursued in BBC1's *Between the Lines*, which featured Siobahn Redmond playing Detective Sergeant Maureen Connell—British television's first lesbian detective. The chapter now turns to a consideration of the remarkable shifts in broadcasting that have occurred over the last decade.

Reality TV

There is an important sense in which the proliferation of 'reality' TV programming (a term which covers 'docu-soaps', lifestyle 'make-overs' and 'factual
entertainment' formats) represents a crisis in the documentary form—the pin-
nacle of public service broadcasting. The reasons for the demise of documentary and the 'daytime-ization' of prime time television are complex but
would include the interplay of the market, the expansion of satellite broadcasting, and the standardization of programming style to maximize audiences
(Palmer 1998: 363). The impact of the market has meant that producers are
required to make more and cheaper programming where a substantial proportion of viewers are turning away from terrestrial broadcasting to watch sport
and film on satellite and cable (Brundson et al. 2001: 31). It is important to locate
this style of programming in the context of these broader transformations, not
simply because the formats share similar modes of address, production values,
and genre hybridity but also because they raise important questions about the
relationships between the media, democracy, and the public sphere.

One of the earliest and best-known reality TV programmes is *Crimewatch UK*,
which was first broadcast in 1984,[7] and continues regularly to attract audiences
of between eight and thirteen million viewers—figures that are close to soap
opera popularity and far greater than the main national news programmes
(Dobash et al. 1998: 38). The success of *Crimewatch* lies in its blurring of the
boundaries between fact, fiction, and entertainment. Fact and public appeal are
merged with dramatization and fiction so that while the programme is
'intended to mobilize audiences to help the police solve crimes, it also enter-
tains, using crime stories with murder, armed robbery with violence, and sexual crime as staple items' (Dobash et al. 1998: 38). However, a key difference
between *Crimewatch* and more recent programmes lies not simply in the latter's
use of CCTV footage as opposed to dramatized reconstruction, but that 'both
the "everyday-ness" of the crimes portrayed . . . and the frequency of their
occurrence in 'everyday life' is highlighted in both the rhetoric and the
aesthetic which are characteristic of programmes such as *Crime Beat, Police
Camera Action* and *Car Wars*' (Brundson et al. 2001: 47). In other words, the argument in Chapter 3 that crime has become a normal 'fact of everyday life' in late
modern Britain, is borne out by the new forms of representation contained in
these post-*Crimewatch* programmes. The passage that follows indicates some of
the ways in which the ordinariness of crime is achieved, in that the

sense of proliferation or volume of 'everyday' crime . . . is reflected in several structures of
repetition set up by these programmes. Not only does their very seriality suggest a relentless stream of crime, but the programmes themselves are organised around the repetitive

replay of similar footage. *Police Camera Action*, for example, is essentially a montage of car chases, punctuated only by Alistair Stewart's direct address to the camera warning us of the dangers of bald tyres and buying stolen vehicles. (Brundson et al. 2001: 47)

In other words, not only is the dull monotony of everyday crime emphasized but 'the address to the viewer as a threatened consumer is key to these programmes' (Brundson et al. 2001: 49), in that the viewer-consumer is continually warned that they must take responsibility for crime prevention.

There is considerable debate over whether these new forms of programming are a more democratic way of representing crime or are part of a broader governmental project activating the citizenship against the figure of the criminal. For instance, Ib Bondebjerg (1996: 29) argues that 'what we are witnessing through hybridization and new reality and access genres is the democratization of an old public service discourse, dominated by experts and a very official kind of talk, and the creation of a new mixed public sphere, where common knowledge and everyday experience play a much larger role'. This position is endorsed by Charlotte Brundson and her colleagues (2001: 50–1) who argue that 'real crime programmes ... could be seen to more thoroughly democratize public service discourse by addressing those crimes which are more likely to affect the viewing public'. In support of this argument they draw a contrast between the 'stolen Porsche of the June 2000 edition of *Crimewatch* [which] is more likely to be replaced by a P-registration Vauxhall Astra in *Police Camera Action*' (ibid.: 50–1). A much more critical reading of reality TV is offered by Gareth Palmer (1998, 2000) who clearly laments the contemporary loss of the documentary project, with its ambition to create an informed citizenry by expanding public understanding through exposing injustice. As he puts it, 'such programming works against the documentary ethos, confirming stereotypes rather than exploring the cracks and fissures in the system and thereby introducing the ambiguity vital to healthy debate' (Palmer 1998: 374). For what it is worth, it is vital that the debate goes beyond issues of representation into the world of social practice and assesses the place of crime in public sensibility and private engagement. The issues surrounding how audiences use the media are discussed below and this section will conclude with some observations on how the significance of these transformations can be theorized.

The discussion of the origins of detective fiction argued that the figure of the detective was closely related to the new forms of discipline and surveillance associated with modernity, through the notion of the panopticon, which implied new forms of power relationships in which the *few see the many* and the penetration of the murky surface of appearances to discover the causes of crime. This metaphor of detection remains a highly significant theme in contemporary fiction. Yet it is important to recognize that accompanying these processes are complementary forms of what Thomas Mathiesen (1997: 219) has described as synopticism, that enables the *many to see the few*. Mathiesen's (1997) arguments are important as they allow a consideration of the development of the mass media in ways that can make sense of the close corollaries between the spectacle of crime in popular culture and the rigorous deployment of surveillance technologies in public and private space. In this regard reality TV would seem to be the latest manifestation of this trend, not simply because the programming relies on grainy CCTV footage and insists that the public must take responsibility for crime control, but rather that the gaze of the viewer is crucial to understanding the place of crime. Mathiesen (1997) goes so far as to describe his thesis as the 'viewer society', to emphasize the significance of synopticism. Yet whilst he has raised some important insights there is little discussion of *viewing*, and it is such matters that are now addressed.

Unruly audiences

Whilst the preceding discussion has attempted to offer a wide-ranging account of crime narratives, there are few guarantees that readers will have consumed or read such narratives in the same way. Much of the criminological literature has concentrated on the role of the media in generating fear. Rather less effort has been extended to a questioning of why it is that so many of us are fascinated with crime as a spectacle, or to addressing the question of how it is that the meaning(s) of a text are produced, circulated, and consumed. Out of the many approaches to understanding the place of the audience in relationship to the text there are two that offer considerable promise in enabling an understanding of the *pleasures* of crime.

Psychoanalysis: pleasure and fear

The discipline that has directly confronted the issues of desire, fantasy, the imaginary, and the real is psychoanalysis. In cultural, film, and literary theory there are well-developed psychoanalytical traditions that examine the processes through which audiences identify with what they see on screen or read in books. Indeed, texts are capable of being read in a multiplicity of ways. Yet as Sparks (1996: 358) argues a particularly pressing question is: Why do we read or view with such pleasure scenes or passages that ought to disturb and shock our emotional sensibilities?

At one level, there are issues here about the processes of identification that occur when we place ourselves in the position of particular characters, either at specific moments or throughout a film. On another level the significance of 'looking' is important. In what is regarded as a landmark essay in feminist film theory Laura Mulvey (1975) analysed the ways in which visual pleasures are organized in narrative cinema through spectatorship. Typically, the gendered pleasures that derive from the spectatorial male gaze are rendered through voyeurism (the sexual attraction of the threatened or threatening woman) and narcissism (identifying with the masculine hero). In Janey Place's (1990) reappraisal of *film noir*, a genre that has received extensive criticism for its deeply misogynist narrative formula, she focuses on the distinctive visual style that often overwhelms the narrative, with consequences that can disrupt the male fantasy of the plot: 'Visually, *film noir* is fluid, sensual, extraordinarily expressive, making the sexually expressive woman, which is its dominant image of woman, extremely powerful. It is not their inevitable demise we remember but rather their strong, dangerous, and above all, exciting sexuality' (Place 1990: 153). Such work points towards a move away from psychoanalysis to a focus on the active female audience and the differing social contexts in which texts are consumed (discussed in more detail below), as we now turn to another area in which psychoanalytical thinking might contribute to understanding pleasure.

Earlier in this chapter it was argued that the appearance of the serial killer in detective fiction owes an enormous debt to Gothic horror—a genre that delights in the spectacle of fear and whose success depends on the inability of a reader or viewer to make sense of the source of terror. In McCracken's (1998) discussion of Gothic horror it is noted that the conventions rely heavily upon the initial establishment of normality before the violation of comforting patterns of daily life can begin and McCracken draws on Sigmund Freud's (1958) essay on 'The Uncanny'—a term covering the unfamiliar, weird, eerie, creepy, and dismal to account for the experiences addressed in reading horror stories. As such the unease provoked by 'the uncanny' is difficult to recreate in academic prose but the general point here is to suggest that whilst Jack Katz's (1988) groundbreaking work on the pleasure, excitement, fun, and risk-taking dimensions of crime has begun to be addressed in criminology, what is also needed is a consideration of the seductions of being scared—for what every unsettling horror story dictates is that the true monsters lie not outside but within the self. It is with the investigation of such matters that the psychoanalytical preoccupation with subjectivity offers considerable promise.

Sociology: text and context

The second approach to understanding the 'pleasures of crime' is resolutely more sociological in character and arises from a dissatisfaction with the ways in which audiences have been characterized in the work of the Frankfurt School—an influential group of scholars highly critical of popular culture in the mid-twentieth century and subsequent theoretical developments, from structuralism and semiology through to postmodernism. It is beyond the scope of this chapter to offer a full discussion of the implications of these various theoretical perspectives and instead the focus must be on an illustration of how criminology might usefully benefit from an engagement with such work.

The work of the French critic Roland Barthes (1993) is significant as it demonstrates how cultural theory has shifted from a structuralist concern with the ideological functions of texts (which is explored in his celebrated readings of popular culture as 'mythologies') to a post-structuralist recognition that socially positioned audiences interpret texts in a multiplicity of ways that can wildly diverge from the author's intentions.[8] This is developed in Stuart Hall's (1977) early work on television and the press. Hall argued that while the formal properties of media texts are organized to 'prefer' one way of being read, which is that most in accord with dominant ideological systems, this does not prevent other possible readings which are 'negotiated' and/or the 'oppositional'. These arguments were subsequently taken up in David Morley's (1980) empirical research on the current affairs programme *Nationwide*, which indicated how the different readings were crucially mediated by social position.

This research has been highly influential in sociological studies of audiences and seems to have informed Reiner et al.'s (2000, 2001) work. This, highly significantly, is one of the first criminological studies to undertake a wide-scale historical (1945–91) content analysis of media representations of crime across film, newspapers, and television in Britain. At the same time it attempts to address the issues of audience interpretation through using focus groups in which selected images and texts were used to stimulate discussion of the meanings attributed to them and 'to encourage general discussion about crime, social change, notions of authority and responsibility' (Reiner et al. 2000: 111). Their findings were summarized as follows:

people varied in which type of crime fiction they enjoyed, but most liked fiction involving an intellectual puzzle. Young women are particularly keen on media which are realistic and offer them information (about the nature, consequences and prevention of crime). Men preferred action plots, with fast pace, special effects and humour. Most people were ambivalent about press crime reporting, wanting to know but not to be voyeuristic. Older people recalled past media largely in terms of notorious events, prominent drama series and television and film stars, and little was recalled of specific narratives. Young people showed little interest in past media and much enthusiasm for contemporary media. (ibid.: 119)

Gender and generation significantly inform audience positioning in relation to media representations of crime. For instance, 'young women are aware of their potential victim status, particularly their vulnerability to male violence, and so they welcomed coverage of such crimes', whereas neither 'younger nor older men in our groups would accept views of themselves as potential victims' (Reiner et al. 2001: 189–90). Moreover the younger 'men were particularly interested in forms of crime media in which the criminal was as much a focus as the law enforcers and in which the moral boundaries between the two were ambiguous or unresolved' (ibid.: 190).

Recent work in cultural studies has taken a much more ethnographic stance and researched diffuse audiences in their social settings to reveal the complex patterns and rhythms of everyday life (see Abercrombie and Longhurst 1998 for an overview). One particularly salient example is Joke Hermes's (2000, with Stello 2000) research on a small, disparate group of Dutch crime fiction readers, which proposes that these readers share an 'interpretive community' that enables the readers to form a sense of who they are. However, it is her more general argument that is crucial here, for she insists that there is a tendency to 'overrate the meaningfulness of any single text once it is part of an everyday setting' (Hermes 2000: 352). Future research on crime and the media could usefully pursue this kind of examination of nuanced understandings of crime narratives in the popular imagination and particular places.

Conclusion

This chapter began with a consideration of the ways in which crime is dramatized in broadcast and press reporting through an examination of the ways in which crime news is produced. In particular, attention was drawn to the ways in which the reporting of sex crime is attracted to constructing the figure of the 'sex beast' to the neglect of representing 'intimate violence' as a serious social problem. The discussion then shifted to a theoretical consideration of the function of moral panics and outlined a series of criticisms levelled against the concept, followed by an analysis of persistent themes found in fictional representations of crime in literature, film, and television. The final section turned to the vexing issue of how audiences interpret texts and explored recent examples of theoretical and methodological approaches that suggest a move from close text-based analysis to situating media consumption in the complex patterns of everyday life.

Chapter 6

Crime and Its Futures

ONCLUSIONS can offer a variety of ways of ending a book. Here two opportunities are taken—to look back and to look forward. First, looking back means
reiterating what this book has and has not attempted to achieve. However,
rather than merely summarizing preceding chapters it may be more interesting
to remind readers of key themes, to draw attention to issues and directions
arising, and then lead on from these to look forward a little. So, the second part
of this concluding chapter will note some recent trends concerning crime in
modern Britain and flag a number of areas where we believe future work will
either be useful, or indeed may come to be essential, for the criminology of
modern Britain.

This book has focused on crime but as noted in Chapter 1 and evident
throughout, it is impossible (as well as undesirable) to completely sever the
subject of crime from control. Nonetheless, to focus on crime is perhaps an
overdue exercise, for so much criminology is, rather surprisingly, more about
control than it is about crime. Here chapters have described and documented
chronologies and characteristics of crime, official and popular responses, and
various examples of the forms and formations of crime, from the everyday to
the sensational. Arguably, the four directions pursued here—examining crime
and its historical roots, its everyday nature, its organizational bases, and its
cultural representations—mean this book offers a different kind of account of
crime in modern Britain to those available elsewhere.

This book has not attempted to provide a review of the criminal justice system
or the law of crime. Nor has it been, in terms of its focus, a review of criminological theory. Many other texts perform these functions very well, although in
turn they may be less comprehensive and informative about forms of crime per
se. In many places in preceding chapters, discussion of pertinent criminal justice, legislative and theoretical contexts and developments has been provided
but it is assumed that this book will be complementary to other studies.

At the outset of Chapter 1 it was suggested that this book would address the following questions: In what ways have patterns and cultural representations of crime changed over time? What kinds of crime have been subject to most political and popular attention? What kinds of crime have been overlooked and why? What are some of the explanations that have been put forward to account for the high crime levels in Britain? Why do we fear the reality of crime so much while consuming representations of it so avidly? By and large these questions have been answered.

History and crime

This book has covered a time-span that is deliberately broad and used definitions of 'modern Britain' that are designedly flexible. In so doing, it has hopefully pointed to the importance of taking a long view of crime. Current debates about crime among politicians, journalists, and academics often overlook historical experiences. They can therefore tend to imply that today's society is more fractured, that today's cities are more dangerous, that today's young people are more violent, that today's entrepreneurs and politicians are more corrupt than those of earlier times. To argue that historical experiences of crime should be taken into account in criminological, sociological, and policy work is not to argue that 'nothing has changed' or conversely, to argue that each 'succeeding' historically identifiable period or epoch is somehow very different to the last. Rather, it is to argue that claims about important social changes should be made in relation to a wider historical context. Clearly, the dramatic increase in recorded crime since the Second World War is a social change that needs to be explained but attempts to develop explanations should beware of assuming certain things about earlier societies or oversimplifying their often highly complex social dynamics. Eighteenth-, nineteenth-, and twentieth-century communities (and their predecessors) were all greatly worried about and fascinated by crime at an elite and a popular level. They all sought to develop new ways to deal with what they often felt to be new kinds of crimes and new breeds of criminal and all periodically feared that they were facing 'unprecedented' threats to their safety, property, and values. So, while there were, of course, very many differences between life in 1800 and life in 2000, the more precise nature of those differences could be exposed through a more active engagement between historians, criminologists, sociologists, and policy-framers.

Historical writing on crime has changed a great deal since the 1970s. As Chapter 2 showed, the early focus on social crime as a product of class conflict has given way to more nuanced investigations of wider varieties of crimes and criminals. Historians are still very much concerned to understand the changing relationship between crime and the economy but are now much more likely to consider the effects of other variables, such as gender, age, ethnicity, and sexuality, alongside the effects of class position. Recent work on historical masculinities and crime, with its emphasis on the ways in which different groups of men have offended and been punished at different times, has clearly demonstrated the value of this more plural approach. Further, administrative histories of the changing criminal justice system have given way to histories which are less concerned with legal mechanisms than with the complex power relationships that support certain forms of policing and punishment over others. Likewise, histories of criminological thought that have been based on the changing role of particular academic institutions and individual theorists are beginning to be supplemented by histories of the spread of other kinds of knowledge about crime, such as that generated by criminal justice workers, different kinds of reform and welfare organizations, journalists and other writers, and offenders themselves.

Many areas remain to be explored within the history of crime in modern Britain. More work on histories of colonial crime, underworld crime, corporate crime, intimate crime, and wartime crime, to name but a few, would all contribute a great deal to our understandings of the variety and complexity of modern criminalities. Such work would not provide simple answers but it would help to illuminate the ways in which present experiences of crime are invariably somehow connected to those of the past.

Everyday crime

This book has deliberately juxtaposed 'crime as exceptional' against 'crime as normal' social phenomena through examining the prevalence of crime and people's varying experiences of crime (as perpetrators, victims, and/or concerned citizens) in the particular settings of their daily life. The 'everyday ness' of crime is evident in the vast range of illegal and deviant activities committed by the general public who neither see themselves nor tend to be viewed as criminals, 'ordinary' people who take for granted certain kinds of law-breaking in the hidden and petty-criminal economies of everyday survival, 'respectable' people who are involved in 'part-time crime' (Ditton 1977) in the normal circumstances of their everyday jobs, and those who simply get a buzz out of leading life 'on the edge'. It is also reflected in the routine (though not always reported/recorded) experience of different forms of abuse, violence, harassment, and property crime committed against, but also by, the young and the old, men and women, the poor and the rich, and different ethnic groups. Our discussion of the social distribution of different forms of crime risks suggests that some groups more than others will most frequently be victims of crime but this does not imply that members of vulnerable categories cannot also be perpetrators of crime. People's worries about crime and incivilities of various kinds inevitably take their toll upon the quality of life (McCabe and Raine 1997). Yet, whether expressed levels of fear of crime actually reflect 'objective' levels of risk, or whether such concerns are best understood in the changing social context of a range of everyday troubles, conflicts, prejudices, and insecurities, is still subject to debate. Furthermore, popular understandings of crime and the moral judgements involved—for instance, who is to blame and what is to be done about it—are embedded not only in day-to-day talk about crime but also in the everyday language of politics and punishment.

Many areas of everyday crime require further systematic investigation, notably hate crimes against immigrants and minorities (see Iganski 1999) and the increased blurring of boundaries between employment and unemployment, work and illegality, and the hidden sectors of the economy and more conventional crime activities (see Ruggiero and South 1997). Such work would contribute to a critical rethinking of the nuanced meanings and experiences of crime especially at a time when the increasing polarization of the world economy and accelerated movement of migrant workers (including the trafficking in human beings within and to Europe) have opened up new 'racialized geographies of disadvantage' (Gilroy 1987) and new processes of criminalization (as in the differentiated provision of more hazardous—and hence more likely to be detected and penalized—criminal opportunities offered to migrants and minorities).

Organizational forms of crime

The term 'organized crime' conventionally describes vertical and horizontal organizational arrangements in which criminals are brought together to participate in formalized or semi-formalized and continuing criminal enterprises. Many commentators have challenged this image of organized crime as all-pervasive, or conforming to Mafia-type models of the kind promoted in studies from the USA (particularly in the 1950s and 1960s, the classic example being Cressey 1969) or as found in numerous media representations. Various writers (Hobbs 1997; Woodiwiss 1988) have provided authoritative critiques of this kind of model and literature. Instead there is considerable evidence and analysis showing that Britain does not have the kind of 'organized crime' that is associated with use of the term in the American literature but rather that Britain has a tradition—and new varieties—of professional criminals acting in organizational and associational forms (McIntosh 1975; Hobbs 1995; Winlow 2001). While the international connections and activities of such groups align with wider processes of globalization and the transformation of market societies (Taylor 1999), the importance of the roots and localized character of these actors and their networks needs to be remembered. As Hobbs (1998) shows by usefully employing the idea of 'glocalization' (Robertson 1995), localized professional crime ventures can connect to global crime but their local as well as their transnational character needs to be emphasized.[1]

Business crime and political crime are areas of study that have been relatively neglected by British criminology but have recently 'come in from the cold'. In criminology, key writers like Levi, Nelken, and Clarke have investigated forms of business crime and, alongside others such as Ruggiero and Punch, elaborated on connections between 'crimes of the suite' and crimes of political office. The cross-over connections revealed within and beyond nation-states are important, but there remains a considerable amount of work to be done here.

One further underdeveloped area, explored in Chapters 2 and 3 and certainly relevant to the forms of crime discussed in Chapter 4, is the 'maleness' or masculinity of crimes of power and profit. This subject has received some pioneering attention but deserves more. Masculinity is central to much business and professional organizational crime. In the legal business world, financial journalism, films such as *Wall Street* and accounts of 'success' offered by corporate leaders (Roper 1994; Punch 2000b: 253–70) the intense masculinity of 'doing business' (Messerschmidt 1993; Levi 1994) is frequently emphasized. For Messerschmidt (1993: 133–4): 'the fact that men control the activities of management . . . is critical to understanding corporate crime. . . . men recruit men who share similar norms, attitudes, values and standards of behaviour. . . . Foremost among those is the ability to compromise personal principles in order to move up the ladder.' Arguably, all of this also applies to the largely masculine, especially in higher echelons, 'insider worlds' of professional and political crime.

Crime and popular culture

'Factual' and 'fictional' narratives of crime powerfully shape public understandings of crime. As should be clear from Chapter 5, the relationships between crime and the media have been the subject of long-standing debates and controversies, particularly with regard to whether the news media generate harm through dramatizing crime and distorting reality. The topic of crime is also a source of entertainment and Chapter 5 explored the range of representations of crime found in literature, film, and television. Whilst certain themes persist across a range of genres (including the place of surveillance in rendering societies visible to the gaze of power), it is important to recognize that there is a real poverty of empirical research on the seductions of crime for media audiences.

Nevertheless, there has been a series of recent statements insisting that a 'cultural criminology' offers a fresh way of interrogating representations of crime and disorder (Ferrell and Sanders 1995; Ferrell and Websdale 1999; Presdee 2000). On the one hand, such new directions for criminology should be welcomed as potentially offering new perspectives and sources of revitalization for the field. On the other hand, while this is not the place to offer a detailed critique of such work, it can be argued that it remains romantically committed to a version of cultural theory that has received extensive criticism over the last 25 years. Even so, what should be emphasized is that the disciplines of criminology and cultural studies have much to learn from each other and if a 'cultural criminology' is to emerge then it must be one that recognizes the respective limitations of both cultural studies and criminology.[2]

A key media technology that has been discussed only briefly so far (Chapter 4) is the Internet, part of an information revolution that has implications for representations of crime as well as offering sites for committing and being a victim of crime (returned to below). Today, 'most major news producers use online digests and many journalists depend on the WWW for research and for publication' (Wykes 2001: 6), which means that the news media are increasingly, if unequally, integrated into a global journalism electronic network. How the further development of global journalism frames and reports crime will be an important area for future research.

These summaries of chapters have looked at some of the main points and areas covered. They have also begun the process of looking forward, noting omissions in this text as well as some of the limitations of the study of crime in Britain more generally. The next section continues along these lines, offering a modest exercise in futurology and a selective listing of future areas for research.

Crime trends in the early twenty-first century

Moving on from the historical and the contemporary, can a synthesis of ideas about the 'future of crime' be offered? Naturally, any such exercise will always be a 'hostage to fortune'. Furthermore, as Reiner (2000) has indicated, if one draws upon the recent lamentable history of increasing crime rates, diversifying forms of criminality, publicly expressed fears and anxieties, and relative-to-complete failure of various government and criminal justice efforts to solve or resolve crime problems, then—almost inevitably—any projection forward will tend to look rather bleak if not downright dismal and dystopian.

One summary scenario (South 1997) might run as follows. Commentators of left, liberal and right persuasions might agree that domestically, the increasing growth of socially excluded, marginal groups in society will lead to more property crime, burglary, shoplifting, theft from the person, and similar crimes (see Chapter 3). Traditionally, where any such political consensus would quickly end would be in trying to reach agreement about deeper 'causes' of such trends, although since the 1990s, the convergence between political parties on the subject of crime and its remedies may mean disagreements are no longer as deeply entrenched as they once were (Carrabine et al. 2000). Drawing upon the evidence and arguments of this book, an extension of the present into the future would suggest that a consumer-oriented society, fuelled by diversity of choice, advertising, and aspiration, price-cut wars in supermarkets, and designer-label exclusivity in the fashion industry, will continue primarily to serve the needs and desires of those who can afford to live in such a society and who can take advantage of its diversity and cornucopia of possibilities. These are the 'included'—the employed, settled, house-holding, financially and onto-logically secure individuals and families, who benefit from the advantageous booms of the economic cycle, are generally able to ride out and survive the downturns, and are not greatly troubled by the crimes and incivilities of every day life (although they may engage in some of them). But for those ill-placed in such a society, the outgroup or 'excluded' (Young 1999; and see earlier discussions in Chapters 2 and 4), all these benefits are elusive and it should be unsurprising that it is members of this group who are, and will probably remain, those most prolifically involved in small-scale property crime.

Concerning the crimes of the middle and managerial classes, some Western trends suggest that business organizations will increasingly be both targets for, and perpetrators of, criminality. Such trends are related to access to organizational resources, to the pressures of domestic and global competition, to the continued erosion of the bases and virtues of trust, and to the inability of late modern market capitalism to regulate corporate activity (see Chapter 4).

The freeing of business and capital from the constraints of the institutional regulations of modernity and the opening of gateways to the globalization of commerce and consumption (Ritzer 1993), the diversification of leisure and pleasure opportunities, and the acceleration of the lived experience of time and space (Adam 1990) have all been features of a shift to a new late modernity or what some call postmodernity (Owen 1997). In this context, the cultural is often celebrated over the socio-economic because consumption practices (legal and illegal) and media representations have achieved such dominance and prominence in everyday life. In thinking about crime and deviance in the future therefore, new spheres of consumption and media will merit increased attention. For example, the rise of the new consumption-oriented 'nocturnal economy' is part of the rejuvenation of various inner-city areas in Britain and throughout the Western world. It reflects the late modern creation of the 24-hour global day of the international financial market, as well as the 24/7 (24 hours per day, 7 days per week) characterization of the alertness and energy now deemed necessary to survive in the legal or illegal marketplaces of deals and hustles.[3] However, while for some the nocturnal economy simply means the all-night opening of convivial leisure spaces, in other respects it opens up new spaces for crime. Alcohol-related violence among customers, drug dealing, and the circulation of 'bootleg booze' (Hall 2000/2001: 10) are common problems, while the incidence of murders linked to competition for the lucrative door-security contracts of pubs and clubs rose in the 1990s (Thompson 2001c).

Drug-related crime is likely to continue to increase in the future, the profits generating significant developments in criminal organization and further diversification into legitimate commerce (Dorn et al. 1992). The present offers few pointers for significant future intervention against, or reshaping of, the drug economy. The main legal controls on drug consumption stem from the 1971 Misuse of Drugs Act. At over 30 years old, this is now a piece of legislation likely to see some revision in the future. The signs are that some liberalization will occur, particularly in relation to rescheduling the 'seriousness' of cannabis use and redefining it as a class C rather than class B drug. But as any review of the history of drugs shows, while rationality and moderation occasionally surface in politics and policy these are easily forgotten as soon as another new form of drug-taking comes along and is demonized. In the twenty-first century new drugs but very familiar responses will undoubtedly present themselves.

Drug trafficking is a complex business and in its local as well as global dimensions seems resistant to enforcement efforts aimed at eradication. At various international levels, the blurring of criminal and legitimate enterprise will increasingly be significant while changes in global politics and finance, trade and migration, will mean more crime and fraud, terrorism, and extortion, directed against governments, the transnational corporate sector, and against trade alliances (for example, the European Union; see Ruggiero et al. 1998: 6; and NAFTA, the North American Free Trade Association, see Jamieson et al. 1998). British criminology seems to have provided relatively few case studies of cross-border crime and transnational criminality but has paid greater attention to the policy and operational responses of the law-enforcement system and case studies of the control of crime across borders.[4] The latter provides the evidence that such activity is ongoing, that it clearly affects Britain, and that it is likely to continue to do so.

As armed conflicts in Eastern Europe, as well as Africa and Asia have demonstrated, crimes of war and violations of human rights will be increasingly important issues, with implications for Britain. Following the terrorist attacks on New York and Washington on 11 September 2001, the Prime Minister suggested that Britain and all developed nations must now take more seriously their international obligations to intervene to prevent crimes of war, genocide, and terrorism. Similarly, domestically and globally, crimes against the environment such as pollution and environmental exploitation, and resulting problems such as damage to public health and victimization of local populations, will increasingly be matters for international crime and control agendas (South 1998). The media and law-enforcement organizations now anticipate that terrorism will be the major new transnational crime of the twenty-first century. Certainly, future accounts of globalization and crime will no longer be adequate unless they address a whole new agenda for criminology, including the new terrorism, the criminology of war (Jamieson 1998), and crimes against humanity, human rights (Cohen 2001), and the environment.

It is equally the case that any future discussion of crime cannot risk underestimating the significance of the Internet. For some commentators cybercrime might simply be old crime in a new bottle but it is important to recognize that there is not one cyberspace but many, which could include 'a library, a telephone, a public park, a local bar, a shopping mall, a broadcast medium, a print medium, a medical clinic, a private living room, and a public educational institution' (Biegel 2001: 28) to name but a few possible cyberspaces. This sense of diversity is also present in the types of activity that might be regarded as criminal, which would include hacking (encompassing simple mischief through to political protest), on-line fraud, creating and distributing child pornography, websites espousing hate, and copyright violations.

For the future study of crime in modern Britain, many further areas deserve and need more investigation. To list just a few: crime and the nation state—for example, on the one hand, the extension of British/Western definitions of crime to the wider world, from the colonial period to the export of 'Western' ideas about human rights, and on the other, the reshaping of British definitions of crime by 'outside' agencies, for example, the EU; crime and politics—the question of what will be the longer-term effects of New Labour policies that set out to be 'tough on crime, tough on the causes of crime'; new work on crime and the body, on masculinities and femininities, on the relationships between humanity and the environment, and on attempts to overcome the social/ positivist divide. This brief list is by no means exhaustive and the suggested topics undoubtedly reflect the extension of discussions in preceding chapters and the concerns and interests of the authors. Any thoughtful survey of the everyday realities of contemporary crime and of the horizons of life in the twenty-first century will easily produce more types and topics of research to add to the list.

Crime has always been with us and Reiner (2000: 87) suggests that:

a continuation of high rates of routine crime, and the variety of security and control measures adopted to contain or reduce them, offers a highly dystopian image of the future. We are already getting accustomed to everyday routines geared around crime prevention, with varying tactics and success depending on social location. In essence there is a vicious circle of interdependence between social divisions and exclusion, crime and control strategy. Growing social divisions fuel rising crime, which in turn generates control strategies that accentuate social exclusion. In a variety of interlocking ways crime and reactions to crime both exacerbate the social divisions that generated them.

This future dystopia may be the direction in which the evidence points but it remains worthwhile to hope otherwise and for British criminology to aspire to make a positive contribution to the achievement of a better, if not crime-free, society. It is still possible that the exercise of the 'criminological imagination' and the development of a more just and humane society can, at the very least, reduce some of the causes, burdens, harms, and hurt of crime in modern Britain.

Notes

Notes to Chapter 1

1 Staples in two senses—as a key component of the media diet on daily offer, and in the Durkheimian sense of binding society together through a shared experience that safely removes external threats beyond the boundaries of morality and security that we collectively seek to maintain.

2 A more detailed discussion of these trends can be found in recent overviews, Emsley 1996a and 1997; Gatrell 1990; Maguire 1997.

3 Similarly, Home Office research indicated that in order to reduce the crime rate by only 1 per cent, the prison population in England and Wales would have to increase by 25 per cent, or more than 12,000 people (*Independent*, 25 Oct. 1993).

4 See e.g. M. Anderson et al. (1995). For the official view of such relations see the web sites of e.g. the Home Office (**www.homeoffice.gov.uk/**), the Metropolitan police (**www.met.police.uk**) and the European Union (**www.europarl.eu.int**). For extensive critical commentary on such developments, see the journal *Statewatch*.

5 The number of criminological studies of criminal justice workers is too vast to list here, but key studies include Emsley (1996b) and Reiner (1978, 1992, 1997) on the police; Babington (1999) on magistrates; Page (1992) and Mair (1997) on probation officers.

Notes to Chapter 2

1 The early work of British feminist criminologists also considered histories of women's experiences of crime and control from the late nineteenth century onwards (Heidensohn 1968, 1996; Smart 1976). In general criminologists tend to use the work of Lombroso and Ferrero (1895) and critics of their particular brand of biological positivism as a starting point for discussions of women and crime, whereas historians of crime tend to take a much broader view.

2 The 1991 Criminal Justice Act replaced the juvenile court with a new 'youth court' and extends the court's jurisdiction to include the 17-year-olds.

3 By contrast, Chapter 4 focuses on those who have access to conventional and unconventional economic and organizational resources and who exploit these in the pursuit of profit and/or power.

Notes to Chapter 3

1 Apart from works under the category of 'True Crime', only a few critical studies of murder and murderers exist—see, e.g. Newburn and Stanko (1994); Radford and Russell (1992); and Collier (1998).

2 All indictable offences and certain summary offences such as assault on a police constable and criminal damage (Home Office 1999).

3 Prior to 1972, the peak age was 14 for both males and females, rising to 15 years for males following the raising of the school leaving age from 15 to 16 in 1972, and then to 18 in 1988. For females the age fluctuated between 14 and 15 rising to 18 in 1997. It has been suggested that such changes may reflect differences in the types of offences and the use of informal methods of disposal, rather than in actual offending behaviour (Home Office 1999).

Notes to Chapter 4

1 The latter case returned to the courts in 2001 in a failed appeal to overturn the convictions of the principal offenders.

2 Hughes and Langan are discussing 'corporate crime' yet find it useful for purposes of definition to refer to 'business organizations'. As discussed further below, this chapter adopts the term business crime to also include corporate and white-collar crime.

3 The case of 'blue collar' crime or fiddles and thefts associated with the hidden economy of everyday life is referred to in Chapter 3. But there is clearly a blurred line between the individual taking advantage of the 'perks of the job' and more organized and syndicated forms of crime (see below).

4 The title of a police detective series of the time.

5 For example Chossudovsky (1996: 27) quotes a *Time* magazine report (29 July 1991: 22): ' "If BCCI is such an embarrassment to the US that forthright investigations are not being pursued it has a lot to do with the blind eye the US turned to heroin trafficking in Pakistan" said a US intelligence officer.' A blind eye was turned because US foreign and security policy sought to maintain strategic influence in this area in response to fears of growing influence from Russia and China. Heroin trafficking was a concern of other departments of US government who in any case might have been less concerned about the destination of this heroin which was more likely to be Europe, US supply still largely coming from the Golden Triangle and latterly Latin America.

6 In Britain the civil liberties groups Liberty, Amnesty International, and INQUEST are involved in campaigns while *Statewatch* is a left-of-centre regular news report that meticulously draws on official and public news stories to record such matters.

Notes to Chapter 5

1 See Holland (1998) for a more general discussion of the 'sexualization' of 'soft news' (features on the family, romance, and domesticity, which had been developed by the Victorian press) from the 1970s, to understand some of the ways in which 'sex sells'.

2 The concept was initially advanced by Wilkins (1964) and in many respects the idea of media exaggeration would have avoided some of the unfortunate connotations that the term moral *panic* came to assume, in that the public response was regarded as irrational.

3 Which were also developed by Phil Cohen (1972) and in the collection edited by

Stuart Hall and Tony Jefferson (1976) and which have proved to be highly influential readings of youth subcultures—see Chapter 2 for further details.

4 This is suggested in his short story 'The Man of the Crowd' that was published in 1840, a couple of years before the Dupin mysteries—though significantly the man of the crowd is someone who cannot be read by the the the dilettante *flâneur* narrating the story and after 24 hours on the Man's trail the narrator comes to the conclusion that he must be 'the genius of deep crime' (Poe 1980: 104). Dupin would come to stand as the figure that could transcend the Crowd.

5 Note also that the real (although subsequently fictionalized) detective agency founded by Alan Pinkerton in the United States in 1830 adopted as its motto 'the Eye that never sleeps' (South 1995: 17).

6 Important criminological discussions of feminist crime writing are contained in Naffine (1996: ch. 5) and Young (1996: ch. 4), whereas Munt's (1994) collection of essays offers a sense of the diversity of gender politics contained in this new form.

7 The idea of television assisting the police in their enquiries is not new, as for some 30 years a programme called *Police 5*, presented by Shaw Taylor, ran in the London area. However, this was a five-minute slot, and ran more like a news bulletin (Schlesinger and Tumber 1993: 19).

8 This argument goes further in Jacques Derrida's (1976) notion of deconstruction that emphasizes the inherent instability of meaning. It is also important to recognize that Barthes also came to dismiss that form of bourgeois literary criticism which claims that the full meaning of a text is to be found in discovering the motivations of the author behind the work—an enterprise he would subsequently condemn through famously announcing 'The Death of the Author' (Barthes 1977). The price to pay for the author's demise is at the light expense of the birth of the reader. Whilst Barthes (1977: 148) is aware that this does not mean a simple championing of 'reader's rights', it does mean that attention has turned from understanding the text as in control of the reader to seeing meaning as the product of socially positioned audiences.

Notes to Chapter 6

1 As Robertson (1995) shows we cannot sensibly think of 'the global' without including 'the local' for the former has systematic properties arising from the attributes of the local units (ibid.: 34; Hobbs 1998: 419), and this is reflected in studies of organized crime in which, as Hobbs (1998: 419) observes, 'current research indicates that even the classic "international" criminal organisations function as interdependent local units'.

2 A good example of the possibilities in this kind of work is offered in Leach and Kearon's (2001) discussion of burglary where they use theoretical work on the body to grasp fully the feelings of abjection that many victims of house theft experience.

3 The term 24/7 seems to have risen from the street scene in the USA to more general use in youth culture and business jargon.

4 See Sheptycki's series of studies of the development of transnational policing
   and relationship to the growth of cross-border and globalizing crime. Much of
   this draws on empirical study of Britain and European neighbours: Sheptycki
   2000b.

References

Abercrombie, N., and Longhurst, B. (1998), *Audiences: A Sociological Theory of Performance and Imagination*, London: Sage.

Ackland, J. W. (1982), *Girls in Care: A Case Study of Residential Treatment*, Aldershot: Gower.

ACMD (1998), 'Drug Misuse and the Environment: A Summary', Supplement to *Druglink*, 13: 4.

Adam B. (1990), *Time and Social Theory*, Cambridge: Polity Press.

Adler, F. (1975), *Sisters in Crime: The Rise of the New Female Criminal*, New York: McGraw-Hill.

Akhtar, S., and South, N. (2000), 'Hidden from Heroin's History: Heroin Use and Dealing within an English Asian Community', in M. Natarajan and M. Hough (eds), *Illegal Drug Markets: From Research to Prevention Policy*, Crime Prevention Studies, vol. 11, Monsey, NY: Criminal Justice Press.

Amnesty International (1984), *Torture in the Eighties*, London: Amnesty International.

—— (2001), *USA and the Death Penalty*, Media Briefings February 2001. (Available online **www.amnesty.org.uk**. Accessed 4 Jan. 2002.)

Anderson, M., den Boer, M., Cullen, P., Gilmore, W., Raab, C., and Walker, N. (1995), *Policing the European Union*, Oxford: Clarendon Press.

Anderson, S., Kinsey, R., Loader, I., and Smith, C. (1994), *Cautionary Tales: Young People, Crime and Policing in Edinburgh*, Aldershot: Avebury.

Archer, J. (1990), *By a Flash and a Scare: Incendiarism, Animal Maiming and Poaching in East Anglia 1815–1870*, Oxford: Clarendon Press.

—— Orr, D., and Roylance, C. L. (2001), *Violence in Liverpool and Manchester, 1850–1914* (presented on ESRC Violence Research Programme website, **www1.rhbnc.ac.uk/sociopolitical-science/VRP).**

Arnot, M., and Usborne, C. (eds) (1999), *Gender and Crime in Modern Europe*, London: UCL Press.

Asahi Shimbun (2001), *Japan Almanac 2001*, Tokyo: Asahi Shimbun Publishing Company.

Aust, R. and Simmons, J. (2002), *Rural Crime*, Home Office Statistical Bulletin 1/02, London: Home Office.

Babington, A. (1999), *A House in Bow Street: Crime and the Magistracy, London 1740–1881*, 2nd edn, Chichester: Barry Rose Law.

Bailey, V. (1987), *Delinquency and Citizenship: Reclaiming the Young Offender, 1914–1948*, Oxford: Clarendon Press.

Barclay, G. (1995), *Digest 3: Information on the Criminal Justice System in England and Wales*, London: Home Office.

Barclay, G., Tavares, C., and Siddique, A. (2001), *International Comparisons of Criminal Justice Statistics 1999*, Home Office Statistics Bulletin, Issue 6/01 May, London: Home Office.

Barthes, R. (1977), *Image—Music—Text*, London: Fontana Press.

—— (1993, orig. pub. 1957), *Mythologies*, London: Vintage.

Bartlett, D. (1999), 'Corruption and Lying in a Parliamentary Democracy: British Politics at the End of the Twentieth Century', *Crime, Law and Social Change*, 30: 205–35.

Bartley, P. (2000), *Prostitution: Prevention and Reform in England, 1860–1914*, London: Routledge.

Bayley, D. (1991), *Forces of Order: Policing Modern Japan*, Berkeley: University of California Press.

Bean, P. (ed.) (1993), *Cocaine and Crack: Supply and Use*, Basingstoke: Macmillan.

Beattie, J. (1975), 'The Criminality of Women in Eighteenth Century England', *Journal of Social History*, 8: 80–116.

—— (1986), *Crime and the Courts in England 1660–1800*, Oxford: Clarendon Press.

Beck, U. (1992), *Risk Society: Towards a New Modernity*, London: Sage.

Becker, H. (1964), *Outsiders*, New York: Free Press.

Behlmer, G. K. (1982), *Child Abuse and Moral Reform in England 1870–1908*, Stanford, Calif: Stanford University Press.

Beirne, P. (1993), *Inventing Criminology: Essays on the Rise of Homo Criminalis*, Albany, NY: State University of New York Press.

—— (ed.) (1994), *The Origins and Growth of Criminology: Essays on Intellectual History, 1760–1945*, Aldershot: Dartmouth.

Benjamin, W. (1983), *Charles Baudelaire: A Lyric Poet in the Era of High Capitalism*, London: Verso.

Bennett, T. (1990), 'Knowledge, Power, Ideology: Detective Fiction', in Bennett (ed.), *Popular Fiction: Technology, Ideology, Production, Reading*, London: Routledge.

Bernard, T. J. (1992), *The Cycle of Juvenile Justice*, Oxford and New York: Oxford University Press.

Berthoud, R. (1997), 'Income and Standards of Living', in Modood *et al.* (1997).

Bhaba, H. (1997), 'Culture's In-Between', in Hall and du Gay (eds), *Questions of Cultural Identity*, London: Sage.

Biegel, S. (2001), *Beyond Our Control? Confronting the Limits of Our Legal System in the Age of Cyber Space*, Cambridge, Mass.: Massachusetts Institute of Technology.

Biggs, S., Phillipson, C., and Kingston, P. (1995), *Elder Abuse in Perspective*, Buckingham: Open University.

Block, A (1991), *The Business of Crime*, Boulder, Colo.: Westview Press.

Blok, A. (1972), 'The Peasant and the Brigand: Social Banditry Reconsidered', *Comparative Studies in Society and History*, 14: 494–503.

Body-Gendrot, S. (2000), *The Social Control of Cities? A Comparative Perspective*, Oxford: Blackwell.

Bondebjerg, I. (1996), 'Public Discourse/Private Fascination: Hybridization in 'True-Life-Story' Genres', *Media, Culture and Society*, 18: 27–34.

Bosworth, M. (1999), *Engendering Resistance: Agency and Power in Women's Prisons*, Brookfield, Vt.: Ashgate.

—— (2001), 'The Past as a Foreign Country: Some Methodological Implications of Doing Historical Criminology', *British Journal of Criminology*, 41/3: 431–42.

Bottomley, K., and Coleman, C. (1981), *Understanding Crime Rates*, Farnborough: Saxon House.

Bottoms, A. E., Claytor, A., and Wiles, P. (1992), 'Housing Markets and Residential Community Crime Careers: A Case Study from Sheffield', in D. Evans et al., *Crime, Policing and Place: Essays in Environmental Criminology*, London: Routledge.

Box, S. (1983), *Power, Crime and Mystification*, London: Routledge.

—— and Hale, C. (1983), 'Liberation and Female Criminality in England and Wales', *British Journal of Criminology*, 23/1: 35–49.

—— —— (1984), 'Liberation/Emancipation, Economic Marginalization or Less Chivalry', *Criminology*, 22: 473–97.

Boys, A., Dobson, J., Marsden, J., and Strang, J. (2001), *Cocaine Trends: A Qualitative Study of Young People and Cocaine Use*, London: National Addiction Centre.

Braithwaite, J. (1989), *Crime, Shame and Re-integration*, Cambridge: Cambridge University Press.

Brand, D. (1991), *The Spectator and the City in Nineteenth Century Literature*, Cambridge: Cambridge University Press.

Briggs, R. (1996), *Witches and Neighbours: The Social and Cultural Context of European Witchcraft*, London: HarperCollins.

British Medical Journal (1999), 'BMA warns of arrival of genetic weapons', *BMJ*, 30 Jan. 1999, p. 318.

Brogden, M., and Nijhar, P. (2000), *Crime, Abuse and the Elderly*, Devon: Willan Publishing.

Brown, B. (1990), 'Reassessing the Critique of Biologism', in Gelsthorpe and Morris (eds) (1990).

Brown, C. (1984), *Black and White in Britain: The Third PSI Survey*, London: Policy Studies Institute.

Brown, J. (1978), 'Social Control and the Modernisation of Social Policy', in P. Thane (ed.), *The Origins of Social Policy*, London: Croom Helm.

Brown, S. (1994), *Whose Challenge? Youth, Crime and Everyday Life in Middlesborough*, published report to Middlesborough City Challenge Partnership, Middlesborough: Middlesborough City Challenge.

—— (1998), *Understanding Youth and Crime: Listening to Youth?* Buckingham: Open University Press.

Brownlee, I. (1998), 'New Labour—New Penology? Punitive Rhetoric and the Limits of Managerialism in Criminal Justice Policy', *Journal of Law and Society*, 25/3: 313–35.

Brundson, C., Johnson, C., Moseley, R., and Wheatley, H. (2001), 'Factual

Entertainment on British Television: The Midlands TV Research Group's "8–9 Project"', in *European Journal of Cultural Studies*, 4/1: 29–62.

Budd, T. (1999), *Violence at Work: Findings from the British Crime Survey*, London: Home Office.

—— and Mattinson, J. (2000), *The Extent and Nature of Stalking: Findings from the 1998 British Crime Survey*, Home Office Research Study No. 210, London: Home Office.

—— and Sims, L. (2001), *Antisocial Behaviour and Disorder: Findings from the 2000 British Crime Survey*, Findings 145, London: Home Office.

Budge, I., Crewe I., McKay, D., and Newton, K. (eds) (2001), *The New British Politics*, Harlow: Longman.

Burt, C. (1925), *The Young Delinquent*, London: University of London Press.

Butler, J. (1993), 'Endangered/Endangering: Schematic Racism and White Paranoia', in R. Gooding-Williams (ed.), *Reading Rodney King/Reading Urban Uprising*, New York: Routledge.

Cain, M. (1990), 'Towards Transgression: New Directions in Feminist Criminology', *International Journal of the Sociology of Law*, 18/1: 1–18.

Calder, A. (1991), *The Myth of the Blitz*, London: Cape.

Campbell, B. (1993), *Goliath: Britain's Dangerous Places*, London: Methuen.

Campbell, D. (1994), *The Underworld*, London: BBC Books.

Carlen, P. (1988), *Women, Crime and Poverty*, Milton Keynes: Open University Press.

—— (1996), *Jigsaw: A Political Criminology of Youth Homelessness*, Buckingham: Open University Press.

—— (1998), *Sledgehammer. Women's Imprisonment at the Millennium*, Basingstoke: Macmillan.

—— and Worrall, A. (eds) (1987), *Gender, Crime, and Justice*, Milton Keynes: Open University Press.

Carrabine, E., and Longhurst, B. (1999), 'Mosaics of Omnivorousness: Suburban Youth and Popular Music', in *New Formations*, 38: 125–40.

——, Lee, M., and South, N. (2000), 'Social Wrongs and Human Rights in Late Modern Britain: Social Exclusion, Crime Control, and Prospects for a Public Criminology', *Social Justice*, 27/2: 193–211.

Carroll-Burke, P. (2000), *Colonial Discipline: The Making of the Irish Convict System*, Dublin: Four Courts Press.

Carter, P. (2001), *Men and the Emergence of Polite Society, Britain 1660–1800*, Harlow: Longman.

Cashmore, E., and McLaughlin, E. (eds) (1991), *Out of Order? Policing Black People*, London: Routledge.

Chappell, M. (1997), *Redcaps: Britain's Provost Troops and Military Police*, London: Osprey.

Chibnall, S. (1977), *Law and Order News*, London: Tavistock.

Chigwada-Bailey, R. (1997), *Black Women's Experience of Criminal Justice: A Discourse of Disadvantage*, Winchester: Waterside Press.

Chomsky, N. (1988), *Manufacturing Consent: The Political Economy of the Mass Media*, New York: Pantheon Books.

Chossudovsky, M. (1996), 'The Business of Crime and the Crimes of Business', *Covert Action Quarterly*, 58 (Fall): 24–30.

Christie, N. (1986), 'The Ideal Victim', in E. Fattah (ed.), *From Crime Policy to Victim Policy*, Basingstoke: Macmillan.

Clancy, A., Hough, M., Aust, R., and Kershaw, C. (2001), *Crime, Policing and Justice: the Experience of Ethnic Minorities. Findings from the 2000 British Crime Survey*. Home Office Research Study 223, London: Home Office.

Clarens, C. (1997), *Crime Movies*, New York: Da Capo Press.

Clark, A. (1987), *Women's Silence, Men's Violence: Sexual Assault in England 1770–1845*, London: Pandora.

Clarke (1990), *Business Crime: Its Nature and Control*, Cambridge: Polity Press.

Clarke, J. (1996), 'Crime and Social Order: Interrogating the Detective Story', in J. Muncie and E. McLaughlin (eds), *The Problem of Crime*, London: Sage.

—— (2001), 'The Pleasures of Crime: Interrogating the Detective Story', in J. Muncie and E. McLaughlin (eds), *The Problem of Crime*, London: Sage. 2nd edn.

——, Cochrane, A., and McLaughlin, E. (eds) (1994), *Managing Social Policy*, London: Sage.

Clarke, M. (1990), *Business Crime: Its Nature and Control*, Cambridge: Polity Press.

Cloward, R. A., and Ohlin, L. (1960), *Delinquency and Opportunity*, New York: The Free Press.

Cockburn, J. S. (1991), 'Patterns of Violence in English Society: Homicide in Kent 1560–1985', *Past and Present*, 131: 70–106.

Cockburn, J. S., and Green, T. A. (eds) (1988), *Twelve Good Men and True: The Criminal Trial Jury in England, 1200–1800*, Princeton: Princeton University Press.

Cohen, P. (1972), 'Sub-Cultural Conflict and Working Class Community', *Working Papers in Cultural Studies*, No. 2.

Cohen, S. (1972), *Folk-Devils and Moral Panics: The Creation of the Mods and Rockers*, London: McGibbon and Kee.

—— (1973), 'The Failures of Criminology', *Listener*, 8 Nov.: 622–5.

—— (1981), 'Footprints on the Sand: A Further Report on Criminology and Sociology of Deviance in Britain', in Fitzgerald et al. (eds) (1981).

—— (1993), 'Human Rights and Crimes of the State: The Culture of Denial', *Australian and New Zealand Journal of Criminology*, 26/2: 97–115.

—— (1996), 'Crime and Politics: Spot the Difference', in *British Journal of Sociology*, 47/1: 1–21.

—— (2001), *States of Denial: Knowing about Atrocities and Suffering*, Cambridge: Polity Press.

Coleman, C., and Moynihan, J. (1996), *Understanding Crime Data: Haunted by the Dark Figure*, Buckingham: Open University Press.

Collier, R. (1998), *Masculinities, Crime and Criminology: Men, Heterosexuality and the Criminal(ised) Other*, London: Sage.

Collison, M. (1996), 'In Search of the High Life: Drugs, Crime, Masculinity and Consumption', *British Journal of Criminology*, 36/3: 428–44.

Connell, R. W. (1987), *Gender and Power*, Cambridge: Polity Press.

—— (1995), *Masculinities*, Cambridge: Polity Press.

Cook, D. (1989), *Rich Law, Poor Law: Differential Responses to Tax and Supplementary Benefit Fraud*, Buckingham: Open University Press.

Coomber, R. (1997a), 'Vim in the Veins—Fantasy or Fact: The Adulteration of Illicit Drugs', *Addiction Research*, 5/3: 195–212.

—— (1997b), 'The Adulteration of Drugs: What Dealers Do, What Dealers Think', *Addictions Research*, 5/4: 297–306.

Cooter, R. (ed.) (1992), *In the Name of the Child: Health and Welfare 1880–1940*, London: Routledge.

Corkery, J. (2000), *Drug Seizure and Offender Statistics, UK, 1998*, Statistical Bulletin, 3/00, London: Home Office.

Cox, P. (2002), 'Race, Delinquency and Difference in Twentieth Century Britain', in P. Cox and H. Shore (eds), *Becoming Delinquent: British and European Youth, 1650–1950*, Aldershot: Ashgate.

—— (forthcoming), *Bad Girls: Gender, Justice and Welfare in Britain, 1900–1950*, London: Palgrave.

—— and Shore, H. (eds) (2002), *Becoming Delinquent: British and European Youth, 1650–1950*, Aldershot: Ashgate.

Craine, S. (1997), 'The "Black Magic Roundabout": Cyclical Transitions, Social Exclusion and Alternative Careers', in R. MacDonald (ed.), *Youth, the 'Underclass' and Social Exclusion*, London: Routledge.

Crawford, A. (1998), *Crime Prevention and Community Safety. Politics, Policies and Practices*, London: Longman.

——, Jones, T., Woodhouse, T., and Young, J. (1990), *Second Islington Crime Survey*, London: Middlesex Polytechnic.

Cressey, D. (1969), *Theft of the Nation: The Structure and Operations of Organized Crime in America*, New York: Harper & Row.

Crick, M. (2000), *Jeffrey Archer: Stranger than Fiction*, London: Fourth Estate.

Croall, H. (1992), *White Collar Crime*, Buckingham: Open University Press.

—— (1998), *Crime and Society in Britain*, London: Longman.

—— (2001), *Understanding White Collar Crime*, Buckingham: Open University Press.

Crowther, C. (1997), 'Policing the Underclass: A Critical Consideration of the Current Agenda', *Scarman Centre for the Study of Public Order, Occasional Paper*, 12, Leicester: University of Leicester.

—— (2000), *Policing Urban Poverty*, Basingstoke: Macmillan.

Cumberbatch, G., Woods, S., and Maguire, A. (1995), *Crime in the News: Television, Radio and Newspapers: A Report for BBC Broadcasting Research*, Birmingham: Aston University, Communications Research Group.

Curran, J., and Seaton, J. (1994), *Power Without Responsibility: The Press and Broadcasting in Britain*, London: Routledge.

Currie, E. (1996), *Is America Winning the War on Crime and Should Britain Follow its Example?* London: NACRO.

Davies, A. (1999), ' "These Viragoes Are No Less Cruel Than the Lads": Young Women, Gangs and Violence in Late Victorian Manchester and Salford', *British Journal of Criminology*, 39: 72–89.

—— (2000), 'Youth Gangs, Gender and Violence, 1870–1900', in S. D'Cruze (ed.), *Everyday Violence in Britain, 1850–1950: Gender and Class*, Harlow: Longman.

Davis, J. (1980), 'The London Garotting Panic of 1862: A Moral Panic and the Creation of a Criminal Class in Mid-Victorian England', in V. A. C. Gatrell, B. Lenman, and G. Parker (eds), *Crime and the Law: The Social History of Crime in Western Europe since 1500*, London: Europa Publications.

—— (1989a), 'From "Rookeries" to Communities: Race, Poverty and Policing in London, 1850–1985', *History Workshop*, 27: 66–85.

—— (1989b), 'Jennings Buildings and the Royal Borough: The Construction of the Underclass in Mid-Victorian England', in D. Feldman and G. Stedman Jones (eds), *Metropolis—London: Histories and Representations since 1800*, London: Routledge.

Davis, M. (1990), *City of Quartz: Excavating the Future in Los Angeles*, London: Vintage.

D'Cruze, S. (1998), *Crimes of Outrage: Sex, Violence and Victorian Working Women*, London: UCL Press.

De Haan, W. (1990), *The Politics of Redress*, London: Unwin Hyman.

Dennis, N. (ed.) (1997), *Zero Tolerance: Policing a Free Society*, London: Institute of Economic Affairs.

Derrida, J. (1976), *Of Grammatology*, Baltimore: Johns Hopkins University Press.

Ditton, J. (1977), *Part-Time Crime: An Ethnography of Fiddling and Pilferage*, London: Macmillan.

——, Bannister, J., Gilchrist, E., and Farrall, S. (1999), 'Afraid or Angry? Recalibrating the "Fear of Crime" ', *International Review of Victimology*, 6/2: 83–99.

Doan, L. (1998), ' "Acts of Female Indecency": Sexology's Intervention in Legislating Lesbianism', in L. Bland and L. Doan (eds), *Sexology in Culture: Labelling Bodies and Desires*, Cambridge: Polity Press.

Dobash, R. E., Schlesinger, P., Dobash, R., and Weaver, C. (1998), ' "Crimewatch UK": Women's Interpretations of Televised Violence', in H. Fishman and G. Cavender (eds), *Entertaining Crime: Television Reality Programs*, New York: Aldine de Gruyter.

Doggett, M. (1992), *Marriage, Wife-Beating and the Law in Victorian England*, London: Weidenfeld & Nicolson.

Doig, A. (1984), *Corruption and Misconduct in Contemporary British Politics*, Harmondsworth: Penguin.

—— (1996), 'From Lynskey to Nolan: The Corruption of British Politics and Public Service', in Levi and Nelken (eds) (1996).

Donziger, S. (ed.) (1996), *The Real War on Crime*, New York: Harper Perennial.

Dorn, N., and South, N. (1990), 'Drug Markets and Law Enforcement', *British Journal of Criminology*, 30/2: 171–88.

—— (eds) (1987), *A Land Fit for Heroin?: Drug Policies, Prevention and Practice*, Basingstoke: Macmillan.

Dorn, N., Murji, K., and South, N. (1992), *Traffickers: Drug Markets and Law Enforcement*, London: Routledge.

Downes, D., and Morgan, R. (1997), ' "Dumping the Hostages to Fortunes'? The politics of Law and Order in Post-War Britain', in M. Maguire, R. Morgan, and R. Reiner (eds), *The Oxford Handbook of Criminology*, Oxford: Clarendon Press.

—— and Rock, P. (1988), *Understanding Deviance: A Guide to the Sociology of Crime and Rule Breaking*, 2nd edn, Oxford: Clarendon Press.

Durkheim, E. (1964, first published 1895), *The Rules of Sociological Method*, New York: The Free Press.

Dyer, C. (2001), 'Law Section: Let's Hear it for the Judge', *Guardian*, 16 Jan., G2, p. 16.

Eales, J. (1998), *Women in Early Modern England, 1500–1700*, London: UCL Press.

Eddy, P., Walden, S., with Sabogal, H. (1989), *The Cocaine Wars*, London: Arrow.

Eldridge, J. (1973), *Sociology and Industrial Life*, London: Nelson University Paperbacks.

Elias, N. (1939/1994), *The Civilizing Process*, Oxford: Blackwell.

Emsley, C. (1996a), *Crime and Society in England, 1750–1900*, 2nd edn, London: Longman.

—— (1996b), *The English Police: A Political and Social History*, 2nd edn, London: Longman.

—— (1997), 'The History of Crime and Crime Control Institutions', in Maguire, Morgan, and Reiner (eds) (1997).

—— and Knafla, L. A. (eds) (1996), *Crime and Histories of Crime: Studies in the Historiography of Crime and Criminal Justice in Modern History*, Westport, Conn., and London: Greenwood Press.

Ericson, R., Baranek, P., and Chan, J. (1987), *Visualising Deviance*, Milton Keynes: Open University Press.

——, Baranek, P., and Chan, J. (1989), *Negotiating Control*, Milton Keynes: Open University Press.

——, Baranek, P., and Chan, J. (1991), *Representing Order*, Milton Keynes: Open University Press.

Erikson, K. (1966), *Wayward Puritans: A Study in the Sociology of Deviance*, New York: John Wiley.

Farer, T. (ed.) (1999), *Transnational Crime in the Americas*, New York: Routledge.

Feeley, M. (1994), 'The Decline of Women in the Criminal Process: A Comparative History', *Criminal Justice History*, 15: 235–74.

—— and Little, D. (1991), 'The Vanishing Female: The Decline of Women in the Criminal Process 1687–1912', *Law and Society Review*, 25: 719–57.

Felson, M. (1998), *Crime and Everyday Life*, 2nd edn, Thousand Oaks, Calif.: Pine Forge Press.

Ferrell, J., and Saunders, C. (eds.) (1995), *Cultural Criminology*, Boston: Northeastern University Press.

—— Websdale, N. (eds) (1999), *Making Trouble: Cultural Constructions of Crime, Deviance and Control*, New York: Aldine de Gruyter.

Field, S. (1999), *Trends in Crime Revisited*, Home Office Research Study No. 195, London: Home Office.

Findlay, M. (2000), *The Globalisation of Crime*, Cambridge: Cambridge University Press.

Fine, P. (2001), 'DU test is no fishy tale', *Times Higher Education Supplement*, 2 Feb. 2001, p. 19.

Finzsch, N., and Jütte, R. (eds) (1997), *Institutions of Confinement: Hospitals and Prisons in Western Europe and North America, 1500–1950*, Cambridge: Cambridge University Press.

Fitzgerald, M., and Hale, C. (1996), *Ethnic Minorities, Victimization and Racial Harassment: Findings from the 1988 and 1992 British Crime Surveys*, London, Home Office.

——, McLennan, G., and Pawson, J. (eds) (1981), *Crime and Society: Readings in History and Theory*, London: Routledge.

Flood-Page, G., Campbell, S., Harrington, V., and Miller, J. (2000), *Youth Crime: Findings from the 1998/99 Youth Lifestyles Survey*, Home Office Research Study No. 209, London, Home Office.

Foster, J. (1990), *Villains: Crime and Community in the Inner City*, London: Routledge.

Foucault, M. (1977), *Discipline and Punish: The Birth of the Prison* (trans. by A. Sheridan), London: Allen Lane.

—— (1979), *The History of Sexuality* (trans. by R. Hurley), London: Allen Lane.

Frances, D. (1988), *Contrepreneurs*, Toronto: Macmillan.

Fraser, F. (1994), *Mad Frank*, London: Little Brown.

Freeman, N (1996/7), 'That Was Business—This is Personal: Professions of Violence in English Cinema from Brighton Rock to the Krays', *Close Up: the Electronic Journal of British Cinema*, 1, Winter. (**www.shu.ac.uk/services/lc/closeup**)

Freud, S. (1958), 'The Uncanny', in *On Creativity and the Unconscious: Papers on the Psychology of Art, Literature, Love, Religion*, New York: Harper Row.

Friedrichs, D. O. (1996), *Trusted Criminals: White Collar Crime in Contemporary Society*, Belmont, Calif.: Wadsworth Publishing Company.

Gabor, T. (1994), *Everybody Does It*, Toronto: University of Toronto Press.

Garland, D. (1985), *Punishment and Welfare: A History of Penal Strategies*, Aldershot: Gower.

—— (1997), 'Of Crimes and Criminals: The Development of Criminology in Britain', in Maguire, Morgan, and Reiner (eds) (1997).

—— (2001), *The Culture of Control: Crime and Social Order in Contemporary Society*, Oxford: Oxford University Press.

Gaskill, M. (2000), *Crime and Mentalities in Early Modern England*, Cambridge: Cambridge University Press.

Gatrell, V. A. C. (1990), 'Crime, Authority and the Policeman State', in F. M. L. Thompson (ed.), *Cambridge Social History of Britain,1750–1950*, vol. iii, Cambridge: Cambridge University Press.

—— (1994), *The Hanging Tree: Execution and the English People 1770–1868*, Oxford: Oxford University Press.

Gelsthorpe, L. (1989), *Sexism and the Female Offender*, Aldershot: Gower.

—— and Morris, A. (eds) (1990), *Feminist Perspectives in Criminology*, Milton Keynes: Open University Press.

Giddens, A. (1991), *Modernity and Self Identity*, Cambridge: Polity.

Gilinsky, Y. (1998), 'The Market and Crime in Russia', in V. Ruggiero, N. South, and I. Taylor (eds), *The New European Criminology*, London: Routledge.

Gillard, M. (1996), 'Flawed Squad: Maxwell Verdict Gives Serious Fraud Office a £25m Hangover', *Observer*, Business Section, 21 Jan. 1996, p. 1.

Gilroy, P. (1987), *'There Ain't No Black in the Union Jack': The Cultural Politics of Race and Nation*, London: Hutchinson.

Girling, E., Loader, I., and Sparks, R. (2000), *Crime and Social Change in Middle England. Questions of Order in an English Town*, London: Routledge.

Goodchild, S., and Morrison, J. (2001), 'Police among 10 Held in Drug Raid', *Independent on Sunday*, 29 Apr. 2001, p. 12.

Goodey, J. (1997), 'Boys don't Cry: Masculinities, Fear of Crime, and Fearlessness', *British Journal of Criminology*, 37/3: 401–18.

Gordon, P. (1983), *White Law: Racism in the Police, Courts and Prisons*, London: Pluto Press.

Graber, D. (1980), *Crime News and the Public*, New York: Praeger.

Graham, J., and Bowling, B. (1995), *Young People and Crime*, Home Office Research Study No. 145, London: Home Office.

Gramsci, A. (1971), *Selections from the Prison Notebooks*, London: Lawrence & Wishart.

Green, P. (ed.) (1996), *Drug Couriers: A New Perspective*, London: Quartet.

Grella, G. (1988), 'The Formal Detective Novel', in Winks (ed.) (1988).

Griffiths, P. (1996), *Youth and Authority: Formative Experiences in England, 1560–1640*, Oxford: Clarendon Press.

—— (2002), 'Juvenile Delinquency in Time', in Cox and Shore (eds) (2002).

Gunther, S.-H. (1999), 'Depleted Uranium and the New Face of War', *Third World Resurgence*, 107: 2–3.

Hahn Rafter, N. (1997), *Creating Born Criminals*, Urbana: University of Illinois Press.

—— (ed.) (1988), *White Trash: The Eugenic Family Studies, 1877–1919*, Boston: Northeastern University Press.

Hale, C. (1992), *Fear of Crime: A Review of the Literature*, Canterbury: University of Kent.

—— (1998), 'Crime and the Business Cycle in Post-War Britain Revisited', *British Journal of Criminology*, 38/4: 681–98.

Hall, S. (1977) 'Culture, the Media and "the Ideological Effect" ', in J. Curran, M. Gurevitch, and J. Woollacott (eds), *Culture, Society and the Media*, London: Methuen.

—— (1980), *Drifting into a Law and Order Society*, London: the Cobden Trust.

—— (2000/2001), 'Violence and the Nocturnal Economy', *Criminal Justice Matters*, 42 (Winter): 10–11.

Hall, S. Critcher, C., Jefferson, T., Clarke, J., and Roberts, B. (1978), *Policing the Crisis: Mugging, the State and Law and Order*, London: Macmillan.

Hall, S., and Jefferson, T. (eds) (1976), *Resistance Through Rituals: Youth Subcultures in Post-War Britain*, London: Hutchinson.

Hammerton, J. (1992), *Cruelty and Companionship: Conflict in Nineteenth Century Married Life*, London: Routledge.

Hanmer, J., and Saunders, S. (1984), *Well Founded Fear*, London: Hutchinson.

Harris, P. (2001), 'Gangs "Doctor" Rotten Meat for the Dinner Table', *Observer*, 7 Oct., p. 10.

Harris, R., and Webb, D. (1987), *Welfare, Power and Juvenile Justice: The Social Control of Delinquent Youth*, London: Tavistock.

Hartless, J., Ditton, J., Nair, G., and Phillips, S. (1995), 'More Sinned against than Sinning: A Study of Young Teenagers' Experience of Crime', *British Journal of Criminology*, 35/1: 114–33.

Hay, D. Linebaugh, P., Rule, J.G., Thompson, E. P. and Winslow, C. (eds) (1975), *Albion's Fatal Tree: Crime and Society in Eighteenth Century England*, London: Allen Lane.

Hebdige, D. (1977), *Subcultural Conflict and Criminal Performance in Fulham*, Occasional Paper, Sub and Popular Culture Series, 25, Birmingham: Centre for Contemporary Cultural Studies, University of Birmingham.

—— (1979), *Subculture: The Meaning of Style*, London: Methuen.

Heidensohn, F. (1968), 'The Deviance of Women: A Critique and an Enquiry', *British Journal of Sociology*, 19/2: 160–75.

—— (1996), *Women and Crime*, 2nd edn, London: Macmillan.

Hencke, D. (2001), '£1m of Duty Frees a Week Stolen from Warehouse', *Guardian*, 19 Nov., p. 10.

Hendrick, H. (1994), *Child Welfare. England 1872–1989*, London: Routledge.

Henry, S., and Milovanovic, D. (1996), *Constitutive Criminology: Beyond Postmodernism*, London: Sage.

Her Majesty's Inspectorate of Constabulary (HMIC) (1999), *Police Integrity: Securing and Maintaining Public Confidence*, London: HMSO.

Hermes, J. (2000), 'Of Irritation, Texts and Men: Feminist Audience Studies and Cultural Citizenship', *International Journal of Cultural Studies*, 3/3: 351–67.

—— with Stello, C. (2000), 'Cultural Citizenship and Crime Fiction: Politics and the Interpretive Community', *European Journal of Cultural Studies*, 3/2: 215–32.

Herrup, C. B. (1987), *The Common Peace: Participation and the Criminal Law in Seventeenth-Century England*, Cambridge: Cambridge University Press.

Higginbotham, A. (1989), 'Sin of the Age: Infanticide and Illegitimacy in Victorian London', *Victorian Studies*, 32/3: 319–37.

Higgins, P. (1996), *Heterosexual Dictatorship: Male Homosexuality in Postwar Britain*, London: Fourth Estate.

Hillmore, P. (1993), 'What Price British Justice Now, M'Lud?', *The Observer*, 28 Nov., p. 23.

Hirsch, F. (1981), *Dark Side of the Screen: Film Noir*, New York: Da Capo Press.

—— (1999), *Detours and Lost Highways: A Map of Neo-Noir*, New York: Limelight Editions.

Hirschfield, A., Brown, P., and Todd, P. (1995), 'GIS and the Analysis of Spatially Referenced Crime Data: Experiences in Merseyside UK', *International Journal of Geographical Information Systems*, 9/2: 191–210.

Hobbs, D. (1988), *Doing the Business: Entrepreneurship, Detectives and the Working Class in the East End of London*, Oxford: Clarendon Press.

Hobbs, D., (1995), *Bad Business*, Oxford: Oxford University Press.

—— (1997), 'Criminal Collaboration: Youth Gangs, Subcultures, Professional Criminals, and Organized Crime', in Maguire, Morgan, and Reiner (eds) (1997).

—— (1998), 'Going down the Glocal: the Local Context of Organised Crime', *The Howard Journal of Criminal Justice*, 37/4: 407–22.

Hobsbawm, E. (1972), *Bandits*, Harmondsworth: Penguin.

—— (1994), *Age of Extremes: The Short Twentieth Century 1914–1991*, London: Abacus.

—— and Rudé, G. (1969), *Captain Swing*, London: Lawrence & Wishart.

Holdaway, S. (1996), *Racialization of British Policing*, Basingstoke: Macmillan.

—— and Rock, P. (eds) (1998), *Thinking about Criminology*, London: UCL Press.

Holland, P. (1998), 'The Politics of the Smile: "Soft News" and the Sexualisation of the Popular Press', in C. Carter, G. Branston, and S. Allan (eds) *News, Gender, and Power*, London: Routledge.

Hollands, R. (1995), *Friday Night, Saturday Night: Youth Cultural Identification in the Post-Industrial City*, Newcastle Upon Tyne: Department of Social Policy, University of Newcastle.

Home Office (1989), *Domestic Violence: An Overview*, London: HMSO.

—— (1997), *Criminal Statistics for England and Wales 1996*, Cm 3764, London: Home Office.

—— (1999), *Digest 4: Information on the Criminal Justice System in England and Wales*, Research, Development and Statistics Directorate, London: Home Office.

—— (2000), *Statistics on Race and the Criminal Justice System*, Research, Development and Statistics Directorate, London: Home Office.

—— (2001), *Statistics on Women and the Criminal Justice System*, London: Home Office.

Hope, T. (1985), *Implementing Crime Prevention Measures*, Home Office Research Study No. 86, London: HMSO.

Hough, M. (1995), *Anxieties about Crime: Findings from the 1994 British Crime Survey*, Home Office Research Study, No. 147, London: Home Office.

Houlbrook, M. (2000), 'The Private World of Public Urinals: London 1918–57', *London Journal*, 25: 52–70.

Houlbrook, M. (2002), ' "Lady Austin's Camp Boys": Queer Social Networks in 1930s London', *Gender and History*, 14: 31–61.

Hudson, B. (1987), *Justice Through Punishment*, Basingstoke: Macmillan.

Hughes, G., and Langan, M. (2001), 'Good or Bad Business?: Exploring Corporate and Organized Crime', in Muncie and McLaughlin (eds) (2001).

Humphries, S. (1981), *Hooligans or Rebels? An Oral History of Working Class Childhood and Youth 1889–1939*, Oxford: Basil Blackwell.

Hutton, W. (1995), *The State We're In*, London: Jonathan Cape.

Hyland, J. (1993), *Yesterday's Answers: Development and Decline of Schools for Young Offenders*, London: Whiting & Birch.

Iganski, P. (1999), 'Legislating against Hate: Outlawing Racism and Anti-Semitism in Britain', *Critical Social Policy*, 19/1: 129–41.

Inland Revenue (2001), *Annual Report of the Board of Inland Revenue*, CM5304, London: The Stationery Office. (Available: **www.inlandrevenue.gov.uk**. Accessed 22 Dec. 2001.)

Innes, J., and Styles, J. (1993), 'The Crime Wave: Recent Writing on Crime and Justice in Eighteenth Century England', in A. Wilson (ed.), *Rethinking Social History: English Society 1570–1920 and its Interpretation*, Manchester: Manchester University Press.

Inspectorate of Constabulary (2000), *On the Record*, London: HMSO.

Irwin, J., Schiraldi, V., and Ziedenberg, J. (2000), 'America's One Million Non-Violent Prisoners', *Social Justice*, 27/2: 135–47.

Jackson, L. (2000), *Child Sexual Abuse in Victorian England*, London: Routledge.

Jamieson, R. (1998), 'Towards a Criminology of War in Europe', in Ruggiero, South, and Taylor (eds) (1998).

——, South, N., and Taylor, I. (1998), 'Economic Liberalization and Cross-Border Crime: the North American Free Trade Area and Canada's border with the USA' (parts 1 and 2), *International Journal of the Sociology of Law*, 26/2: 245–72; 3: 285–319.

Jefferson, T. (1993), 'The Racism of Criminalization: Policing and the Reproduction of the Criminal Other', in L. Gelsthorpe and W. McWilliam (eds), *Minority Ethnic Groups and the Criminal Justice System*, Cambridge: University of Cambridge, Institute of Criminology.

—— (1997), 'Masculinities and Crime', in Maguire, Morgan, and Reiner (eds) (1997).

—— and Walker, M. (1993), 'Attitudes to the Police of Ethnic Minorities in a Provincial City', *British Journal of Criminology*, 33/2: 251–66.

Jeffery-Poulter, S. (1991), *Peers, Queers, and Commons: The Struggle for Gay Law Reform from 1950 to the Present*, London: Routledge.

Jewkes, Y. (1999), *Moral Panics in a Risk Society: A Critical Evaluation*, Crime, Order and Policing Occasional Paper Series No. 15, Scarman Centre, Leicester: University of Leicester.

Johnston, L. (2000), *Policing Britain: Risk, Security and Governance*, London: Longman.

Jones, D. (1982), *Crime, Protest, Community, and Police in Nineteenth-Century Britain*, London/Boston: Routledge & Kegan Paul.

Jones, S. (2000), *Understanding Violent Crime*, Buckingham: Open University Press.

Jones, T., Maclean, B., and Young, J. (1986), *The Islington Crime Survey*, Aldershot: Gower.

Jupp, V., Davies, P., and Francis, P. (1999), 'The Features of Invisible Crimes', in Davies et al. (eds), *Invisible Crimes: Their Victims and Their Regulation*, London: Macmillan.

Kalunta-Crumpton, A. (1999), *Race and Drug Trials: The Social Construction of Guilt and Innocence*, Aldershot: Ashgate.

Katz, J. (1988), *Seductions of Crime: Moral and Sensual Attractions in Doing Evil*, New York: Basic Books.

Kearon, A., and Leach, R. (2000), ' "Invasion of the 'Bodysnatchers": Burglary Re-considered', *Theoretical Criminology*, 4/4: 451–72.

Keith, M. (1993), *Race, Riots and Policing: Law and Disorder in a Multi-Racist Society*, London: UCL Press.

Kelly, L. (1988), *Surviving Sexual Violence*, Cambridge: Polity Press.

Kermode, J., and Walker, G. (1994), *Women, Crime and the Courts in Early Modern England*, London: UCL Press.

Kershaw, C., Budd, T., Kinshott, G., Mattinson, J., Mayhew, P. and Myhill, A. (2000), *The 2000 British Crime Survey*, London: Home Office.

Kersten, J. (1993), 'Street Youths, *Bosozoku* and *Yakuza*: Subculture Formation and Social Reactions in Japan', *Crime and Delinquency*, 39/3: 277–95.

King, P. (1996), 'Female Offenders, Work and Life-Cycle Change in Late Eighteenth Century London', *Continuity and Change*, 11/1: 61–90.

—— (1998), 'The Rise of Juvenile Delinquency in England 1780–1840: Changing Patterns of Perception and Prosecution', *Past and Present*, 160: 116–66.

—— (1999), 'Locating Histories of Crime: A Bibliographical Study', *British Journal of Criminology*, 39/1: 161–74.

—— (2000), *Crime, Justice and Discretion in England, 1740–1820*, Oxford: Oxford University Press.

Kinsey, R. (1984), *Merseyside Crime Survey*, Edinburgh: Centre for Criminology, University of Edinburgh.

—— and Anderson, S. (1992), *Crime and the Quality of Life: Public Perceptions and Experiences of Crime in Scotland: Findings from the 1988 British Crime Survey*, Scottish Office Central Research Unit, Edinburgh: HMSO.

Kohn, M. (1992), *Dope Girls: The Birth of the British Drug Underground*, London: Lawrence & Wishart.

Langbein, J. (1983), '*Albion's* Fatal Flaws', *Past and Present*, 98: 96–120.

Lea, J. (1999), 'Social Crime Revisited', *Theoretical Criminology*, 3: 307–26.

Lea, J. (2000), 'The Macpherson Report and the Question of Institutional Racism', *Howard Journal of Criminal Justice*, 39/2: 219–37.

—— and Young, J. (1982), 'The Riots in Britain in 1981: Urban Violence and Political Marginalisation', in D. Cowell, T. Jones, and J. Young (eds), *Policing the Riots*, London: Junction Boho.

—— —— (1984), *What Is To Be Done about Law and Order?* London: Pluto.

Lean, G. (2001), 'Exhaust "Causes Asthma in Children"', *Independent on Sunday*, 14 Jan. 2001, p. 5.

Lee, M. (1998), *Youth, Crime and Police Work*, Basingstoke: Macmillan.

Leonards, C. (2002), 'Border Crossings: Care and the "Criminal Child" in Nineteenth Century European Penal Congresses', in Cox and Shore (eds) (2002).

Leppard, D., Burke, J., and Kelsey, T. (1997), 'Corrupt Police Bug Public in Yard Scandal', *Sunday Times*, 24 Aug. 1997, pp. 1 and 18.

Leps, M.-C. (1992), *Apprehending the Criminal. The Production of Deviance in Nineteenth Century Discourse*, Durham, NC: Duke University Press.

Letkemann, P. (1973), *Crime as Work*, Englewood Cliffs, NJ: Prentice-Hall.

Levi, M. (1981), *The Phantom Capitalists*, London: Gower Press.

—— (1987), *Regulating Fraud*, London: Tavistock.

—— (1991), 'Pecunia Non Olet: Cleansing the Money Launderers from the Temple', *Crime, Law and Social Change*, 16: 217–302.

—— (1994), 'Masculinities and White Collar Crime', in Newburn and Stanko (eds) (1994).

—— (1997), 'Violent Crime', in Maguire, Morgan, and Reiner (eds) (1997).

—— (1998), 'Perspectives on "Organised Crime": an overview', *The Howard Journal of Criminal Justice*, 37/4: 335–45.

—— (199), 'The impact of fraud', *Criminal Justice Matters*, 36: 5–7.

—— and Nelken, D. (eds) (1996), *The Corruption of Politics and the Politics of Corruption*, Oxford: Basil Blackwell.

Levitas, R. (1998), *The Inclusive Society? Social Exclusion and New Labour*, Basingstoke: Macmillan.

Lewis, R. (1989), 'European Markets in Cocaine', *Contemporary Crises*, 13: 35–52.

—— (1994), 'Flexible Hierarchies and Dynamic Disorder: The Trading and Distribution of Illicit Heroin in Britain and Europe', in J. Strang and M. Gossop (eds), *Heroin Addiction and Drug Policy*, Oxford: Oxford University Press.

Liddle, A.M. (1996), 'State, Masculinities and Law: Some Comments on Gender and English State Formation', *British Journal of Criminology*, 36/3: 361–80.

Linebaugh, P. (1976), 'Karl Marx, the Theft of Wood and Working Class Composition', *Crime and Social Justice*, 6: 5–16.

—— (1991), *The London Hanged: Crime and Civil Society in the Eighteenth Century*, London: Allen Lane/Penguin.

Lister, R. (1998), 'From Equality to Social Inclusion: New Labour and the Welfare State', *Critical Social Policy*, 18/2: 493–517.

—— (ed) (1996), *Charles Murray and the Underclass: The Developing Debate*, London: IEA Health and Welfare Unit in association with the *Sunday Times*.

Loader, I. (1996), *Youth, Policing and Democracy*, London: Macmillan.

—— (1997), 'Private Security and the Demand for Protection in Contemporary Britain', *Policing and Society*, 7: 143–62.

Lombroso, C. (1895), *L'Homme criminel*, 2nd edn, Paris: Ancienne Librairie.

—— and Ferrero, W. (1895), *The Female Offender*, London: T. Fisher & Unwin.

Lyon, D. (1994), *The Electronic Eye: The Rise of Surveillance Society*, Minneapolis: University of Minnesota Press.

McAllister, W. (2000), *Drug Diplomacy in the Twentieth Century*, London: Routledge.

McCabe, A., and Raine, J. (1997), *Framing the Debate: The Impact of Crime on Public Health*, Birmingham: The Public Health Alliance.

McCracken, S. (1998), *Pulp: Reading Popular Fiction*, Manchester: Manchester University Press.

McIntosh, M. (1975), *The Organisation of Crime*, London: Macmillan.

Mack, J. (1964), 'Full-time Miscreants, Delinquent Neighbourhoods and Criminal Networks', *British Journal of Sociology*, 15: 38–53.

McLaren, A. (1997), *The Trials of Masculinity: Policing Sexual Boundaries 1870–1930*, Chicago: University of Chicago Press.

McLaughlin, E., and Muncie, J. (1993), 'Juvenile Delinquency', in R. Dallos and E. McLaughlin (eds), *Social Problems and the Family*, London: Sage/Open University Press.

—— —— (1994), 'Managing the Criminal Justice System', in J. Clarke, A. Cochrane and E. McLaughlin (eds) *Managing Social Policy*, London: Sage.

—— and Murji, K. (1998), 'Resistance Through Representation: "Storylines", Advertising and Police Federation Campaigns', *Policing and Society*, 8: 367–99.

McMullan, J. (1984), *The Canting Crew: London's Criminal Underworld, 1550–1700*, New Jersey: Rutgers University Press.

Macpherson, W. (1999), *The Stephen Lawrence Inquiry: Report of an Inquiry by Sir William Macpherson of Cluny*, CM4262, London: The Stationery Office.

McRobbie, A. (1988), *Zoot Suits and Second Hand Dresses*, London: Macmillan.

—— (1994), *Postmodernism and Popular Culture*, London: Routledge.

—— and Thornton, S. (1995), 'Rethinking "Moral Panic" for Multi-mediated Social Worlds', *British Journal of Sociology*, 46/4: 559–74.

Maffesoli, M. (1989), 'The Sociology of Everyday Life (Epistemological Elements)', *Current Sociology*, 37/1: 1–17.

Maguire, M. (1997), 'Crime Statistics, Patterns and Trends: Changing Perceptions and their Implications', in Maguire, Morgan, and Reiner (eds) (1997).

—— (2000), 'Researching "Street Criminals" ', in R. King and E. Wincup (eds), *Doing Research on Crime and Justice*, Oxford: Oxford University Press.

Maguire, M., Morgan, R., and Reiner, R. (eds) (1997), *The Oxford Handbook of Criminology*, 2nd edn, Oxford: Clarendon Press.

Mahood, L. (1990), *The Magdalenes: Prostitution in the Nineteenth Century*, London: Routledge.

—— (1995), *Policing Gender: Class and Family Britain, 1800–1945*, London: UCL Press.

Mair, G. (1997), 'Community Penalties and the Probation Service', in Maguire et al. (eds) (1997).

Mann, D., and Sutton, M. (1998), 'Netcrime—More Change in the Organization of Thieving', *British Journal of Criminology*, 38/2: 201–29.

Mars, G. (1982), *Cheats at Work: An Anthropology of Workplace Crime*, London: George Allen & Unwin.

Massey, D. (1994), *Space, Place and Gender*, Cambridge: Polity Press.

Mathiesen, T. (1997), 'The Viewer Society: Michel Foucault's "Panopticon" Revisited', *Theoretical Criminology*, 1/2: 215–34.

Matthews, R., and Young, J. (eds) (1992), *Issues in Realist Criminology*, London: Sage.

Mauer, M. (1997), *Intended and Unintended Consequences: State Racial Disparities in Imprisonment*, Washington, DC: The Sentencing Project.

Maung, N. A. (1995), *Young People, Victimization and the Police*, Home Office Research Study No. 140, London: Home Office.

Maxfield, M. (1984), *Fear of Crime in England and Wales*, London: Home Office.

Mayhew, P., and Hough, M. (1988), 'The British Crime Survey: Origins and Impact', in M. Maguire and J. Pointing (eds), *Victims of Crime: A New Deal?* Milton Keynes: Open University Press.

——, Elliot, D., and Dowds, L. (1989), *The 1988 British Crime Survey*, Home Office Research Study No. 111, London: HMSO.

Mednick, S., Moffit, T., and Stack, S. (eds) (1987), *The Causes of Crime: New Biological Approaches*, Cambridge: Cambridge University Press.

Merton, R. (1938), 'Social Structure and Anomie', *American Sociological Review*, 3: 672–82.

—— (1957), *Social Theory and Social Structure*, New York: The Free Press.

Messent, P. (1997), 'Introduction: From Private Eye to Police Procedural—the Logic of Contemporary Crime Fiction', in Messent, (ed.), *Criminal Proceedings: The Contemporary American Crime Novel*, London: Pluto Press.

Messerschmidt, J. W. (1993), *Masculinities and Crime: Critique and Reconceptualization of Theory*, Lanham, Md.: Rowman & Littlefield.

—— (1997), *Crime as Structured Action: Gender, Race, Class, and Crime in the Making*, Thousand Oaks, Calif.: Sage.

Michalowski, R., and Kramer, R. (1987), 'The Space between Laws: The Problem of Corporate Crime in a Transnational Context', *Social Problems*, 34/1: 34–53.

Mirrlees-Black, C. (1999), *Domestic Violence: Findings from a New British Crime Survey Self-Completion Questionnaire*, Home Office Research Study No. 191, London: Home Office.

——, Budd, T., Partridge, S., and Mayhew, P. (1998), *The 1998 British Crime Survey*, Home Office Statistical Bulletin 21/98, London: Home Office.

——, Mayhew, P., and Percy, A. (1996), *The 1996 British Crime Survey: England and Wales*, Home Office Statistical Bulletin Issue 19/96, London: Home Office.

Mollen Commission (1994), *Report of the Commission to Investigate Allegations of Police Corruption and the Anti-Corruption Procedures of the Police Department*, New York: Mollen Commission.

Monk, C. (1999), 'From Underworld to Underclass: Crime and British Cinema in the 1990s', in S. Chibnall and R. Murphy (eds), *British Crime Cinema*, London: Routledge.

Mooney, J. (1993), *The North London Domestic Violence Survey*, London: Middlesex University.

Moran, L. J. (1996), *The Homosexual(ity) of Law*, London: Routledge.

Moretti, F. (1990), 'Clues', in T. Bennett (ed.), *Popular Fiction: Technology, Ideology, Production, Reading*, London: Routledge.

Morley, D. (1980), *The Nationwide Audience: Structure and Decoding*, London: British Film Institute.

Morris, A., and Giller, H. (1987), *Understanding Juvenile Justice*, London: Croom Helm.

Morris, L. (1994), *The Dangerous Classes: The Underclass and Citizenship*, London: Routledge.

Morton, J. (1995), *The Underworld in Britain and Ireland*, London: Little Brown.

Morton, J., (2000), 'Krays would never have a hope today', *Daily Express* micro edn, online, 3 Oct. 2000.

Mulvey, L. (1975), 'Visual Pleasure and Narrative Cinema', in *Screen*, 16/3, repr. in T. Bennett et al. (eds) (1981), *Popular Television and Film*, London: British Film Institute.

Muncie, J. (1999), *Youth and Crime: A Critical Introduction*, London: Sage.

—— (2000), 'Decriminalizing Criminology', in G. Lewis et al. (eds), *Rethinking Social Policy*, London: Sage.

—— (2001), 'The Construction and Deconstruction of Crime', in Muncie and McLaughlin (eds) (2001).

—— and McLaughlin, E. (2001) (eds), *The Problem of Crime*, 2nd edn, London: Sage.

Munt, S. (1994) *Murder by the Book? Feminism and the Crime Novel*, London: Routledge.

Murji, K. (1999), 'White Lines: Culture, "Race" and Drugs', in N. South (ed), *Drugs: Cultures, Controls and Everyday Life*, London: Sage.

Murray, C. (1990), *The Emerging British Underclass*, London: IEA Health and Welfare Unit.

Naffine, N. (1996), *Feminism and Criminology*, Philadelphia: Temple University Press.

Nelken, D. (1997), 'White-Collar Crime', in Maguire, Morgan, and Reiner (eds) (1997).

Newburn, T. (1999), *Understanding and Preventing Police Corruption: Lessons from the Literature*, Police Research Series No. 110, London: Home Office.

—— and Stanko, E., 'When Men are Victims: The Failure of Victimology', in Newburn and Stanko (eds) (1994), *Just Boys Doing Business?* London: Routledge.

Nolan, Lord (The Nolan Committee) (1995), *Standards in Public Life*, vol. 1, Cmnd. 28501, London: HMSO.

O'Malley, P. (1999), 'Volatile and Contradictory Punishment', *Theoretical Criminology*, 3/2: 175–96.

Owen, D. (ed.) (1997), *Sociology after Postmodernism*, London and Thousand Oaks, Calif.: Sage.

Page, M. (1992), *Crimefighters of London: A History of the Origins and Development of the London Probation Service 1876–1965*, London: Inner London Probation Service, Benevolent and Educational Trust.

Painter, K. (1991), *Wife Rape, Marriage and the Law*, Manchester: Manchester University.

Palmer, G. (1998), 'The New Spectacle of Crime', in *Information, Communication and Society*, 1/4: 361–81.

—— (2000), 'Governing Through Crime: Surveillance, The Community and Local Crime Programming', in *Policing and Society*, 10: 321–42.

Pantazis, C. (1999), 'The Criminalization of Female Poverty', in Watson and Doyal (eds) (1999).

Park, C. (2001), 'The Three Faces of Retail Theft', *New Zealand Security*, Feb./Mar. 2001 (Available online **www.ecoliving.co.nz/nzsecurity/mag**. Accessed 20 Dec. 2001.)

Parker, H., Aldridge, J. and Measham, F. (1998), *Illegal Leisure: The Normalization of Adolescent Recreational Drug Use*, London: Routledge.

—— and Measham, F. (1994), 'Pick 'n' Mix: Changing Patterns of Illicit Drug Use amongst 1990s Adolescents', *Drugs: Education, Prevention and Policy*, 1/1: 5–13.

Parker, T. (1981), *Rough Justice*, London: Fontana.

Passas, N. (1996), 'The Genesis of the BCCI Scandal', *Journal of Law and Society*, 23: 57–72.

Pearce, F. (1976), *Crimes of the Powerful*, London: Pluto.

—— and Tombs, S. (1998), *Toxic Capitalism: Corporate Crime and the Chemical Industry*, Aldershot: Ashgate.

Pearson, G. (1983), *Hooligan: A History of Respectable Fears*, London: Macmillan.

—— (1987), 'Social Deprivation, Unemployment and Patterns of Heroin Use', in N. Dorn and N. South (eds), *A Land Fit for Heroin? Drug Policies, Prevention and Practice*, Basingstoke: Macmillan.

—— (1994), 'Youth, Crime and Society', in M. Maguire, R. Morgan and R. Reiner (eds), *The Oxford Handbook of Criminology*, Oxford: Oxford University Press.

—— and Patel, K. (1998), 'Drugs, Deprivation and Ethnicity: Outreach among Asian Drug Users in a Northern English City', *Journal of Drug Issues*, 28/1: 199–224.

Pearson, J. (1972), *The Profession of Violence*, London: Grafton.

Pease, K. (1998), *Repeat Victimization: Taking Stock*, Crime Detection and Prevention Paper No. 90, London: Home Office.

Peck, D., and Plant, M. (1986), 'Unemployment and Illegal Drug Use: Concordant Evidence from a Prospective Study and National Trends', *British Medical Journal*, 293: 929–32.

Percy, A. (1998), *Ethnicity and Victimization: Findings from the 1996 British Crime Survey*, Home Office Statistical Bulletin 6/98, London: Home Office.

Philips, D. (1983), ' "A Just Measure of Crime, Authority, Hunters and Blue Locusts": The "Revisionist" Social History of Crime and the Law in Britain, 1780–1850', in S. Cohen and A. Scull (eds), *Social Control and the State: Historical and Comparative Essays*, Oxford: Martin Robertson.

Phythian, M. (1999), 'The Illicit Arms Trade', *Criminal Justice Matters*, 36 (Summer): 8–9.

Pick, D. (1989), *Faces of Degeneration: A European Disorder, c.1848–c.1918*, Cambridge: Cambridge University Press.

Pitts, J. (1988), *The Politics of Juvenile Crime*, London: Sage.

Place, J. (1990), 'Women in *film noir*', in T. Bennett (ed.) (1990).

Poe, E. (1980), *Selected Tales*, Oxford: Oxford University Press.

Povey, D., and Prime, J. (1999), *Recorded Crime Statistics England and Wales, April 1998 to March 1999*, Home Office Statistical Bulletin 18/99, London: Home Office.

—— and colleagues (2001), *Recorded Crime in England and Wales—12 months to March 2001*, London: Home Office.

Presdee, M. (2000), *Cultural Criminology and the Carnival of Crime*, London: Routledge.

Punch, M. (1985), *Conduct Unbecoming*, London: Tavistock.

—— (1996), *Dirty Business: Exploring Corporate Misconduct: Analysis and Cases*, London: Sage.

Punch, M., (2000a), 'Police Corruption and its Prevention', *European Journal on Criminal Policy and Research*, 8: 301-24.

—— (2000b), 'Suite Violence: Why Managers Murder and Corporations Kill', *Crime, Law and Social Change*, 33: 243-80.

Radford, J., and Russell, D. (eds) (1992), *Femicide: the Politics of Woman Killing*, Buckingham: Open University Press.

Radzinowicz, L., and Hood, R. (1986), *A History of the English Criminal Law and its Administration from 1750*, vol. v, *The Emergence of Penal Policy in Victorian and Edwardian England*, London: Stevens & Sons.

Rawlings, P. (1992), *Drunks, Whores and Idle Apprentices: Criminal Biographies of the Eighteenth Century*, London: Routledge.

—— (1999), *Crime and Power: A History of Criminal Justice, 1688-1998*, London: Longman.

Rawlinson, P. (1998), 'Russian Organised Crime: Moving Beyond Ideology', in V. Ruggiero, N. South, and I. Taylor (eds), *The New European Criminology*, London: Routledge.

Rawnsley, A. (2001), 'Comment: The Archer Affair—Shepherd's Pie and Champagne, Anyone?', *Observer*, 22 July, p. 25.

Read, P. (1984), *The Train Robbers: Their Story*, London: W. H. Allen.

Redhead, S. (with D. Wynne and J. O'Connor) (ed.) (1997), *The Clubcultures Reader*, Oxford: Blackwell.

Reiman, J. (2001), *The Rich Get Richer and the Poor get Prison*, Boston: Allyn and Bacon.

Reiner, R. (1978), *The Blue-Coated Worker*, Cambridge: Cambridge University Press.

—— (1985, 1992), *The Politics of the Police*, 1st and 2nd edns, Hemel Hempstead: Wheatsheaf.

—— (1997), 'Media Made Criminality: The Representation of Crime in the Mass Media', in Maguire, Morgan, and Reiner (eds) (1997).

—— (2000), 'Crime and Control in Britain', *Sociology*, 34/1: 71-94.

—— and Cross, M. (1991), *Beyond Law and Order: Criminal Justice Policy and Politics into the 1990s*, Basingstoke: Macmillan.

——, Livingstone, S., and Allen, J. (2000), 'No More Happy Endings? The Media and Popular Concern about Crime since the Second World War', in T. Hope and R. Sparks (eds) *Crime, Risk and Insecurity*, London: Routledge.

—— (2001), 'Casino Culture: Media and Crime in a Winner-Loser Society', in Stenson and Sullivan (eds) (2001).

Reuter, P. (1984), *Disorganised Crime*, Cambridge, Mass.: MIT Press.

—— and Rubinstein, J. (1978), 'Fact, Fancy and Organised Crime', *The Public Interest*, 53: 45-68.

Richardson, C. (1991), *My Manor*, London: Sidgwick & Jackson.

Riddell, P. (1989), *The Thatcher Effect*, Oxford: Blackwell.

Ridley, F., and Doig, A. (1995), *Sleaze: Politicians, Private Interests and Public Reaction*, Oxford: Oxford University Press.

Ritzer, G. (1993), *The McDonaldization of Society: An Investigation into the Changing Character of Contemporary Social Life*, Newbury Park, Calif.: Pine Forge Press.

Robb, G. (1992), *White Collar Crime in Modern England: Financial Fraud and Business Morality 1845-1929*, Cambridge: Cambridge University Press.

Roberts, B. (2002), 'On *Not* Becoming Delinquent: Raising Adolescent Boys in the Dutch Republic, 1600-1750', in Cox and Shore (eds) (2002).

Robertson R. (1995), 'Glocalisation: Time–Space and Homogeneity–Heterogeneity', in M. Featherstone, S. Lash, and R. Robertson (eds), *Global Modernities*, London: Sage.

Robins, D., and Cohen, P. (1978), *Knuckle Sandwich: Growing Up in the Working-Class City*, Harmondsworth: Penguin.

Rock, P. (ed.) (1988), *History of British Criminology*, Oxford: Clarendon Press.

—— (ed.) (1994), *A History of Criminology*, Aldershot: Dartmouth.

Roper, M. (1994), *Masculinity and the British Organization Man Since 1945*, Oxford: Oxford University Press.

Roshier, B. (1973), 'The Selection of Crime in the News by the Press', in S. Cohen and J. Young (eds), *The Manufacture of News*, London: Constable.

Ruggiero, V. (1996), *Organised and Corporate Crime in Europe: Offers that Can't be Refused*, Aldershot: Dartmouth.

—— (1997), 'Trafficking in Human Beings: Slaves in Contemporary Europe', *International Journal of Sociology of Law*, 25/3: 231–44.

—— (2000), 'Transnational Crime: Official and Alternative Fears', *International Journal of the Sociology of Law*, 28: 187–99.

—— and South, N. (1995), *Eurodrugs: Drug Use, Markets and Trafficking in Europe*, London: UCL Press.

—— (1997), 'The Late-Modern city as a Bazaar: Drug Markets, Illegal Enterprise and "the barricades"', *British Journal of Sociology*, 48/1: 55–71.

—— and Taylor, I. (eds) (1998), *The New European Criminology: Crime and Social Order in Europe*, London: Routledge.

Rumbelow, H. (2001), 'Drugs at the Root of Big Increase in Women Jailed', *The Times*, 26 Nov. 2001, p. 4.

Rutter, M., and Giller, H. (1983), *Juvenile Delinquency: Trends and Perspectives*, Harmondsworth: Penguin.

Ryan, M., and Sim, J (1995), 'The Penal System in England and Wales: Round up the Usual Suspects', in M. Ryan, V. Ruggiero, and J. Sim (eds), *Western European Penal Systems: A Critical Anatomy*, London: Sage.

—— and Ward, T. (1992), 'From Positivism to Postmodernism: Some Theoretical and Strategic Reflections on the Evolution of the Penal Lobby in Britain', *International Journal of the Sociology of Law*, 20/4: 321–35.

Samuel, R. (ed.) (1981), *East End Underworld: Chapters in the Life of Arthur Harding*, London: Routledge & Kegan Paul.

Scarman, Lord (1981), *The Brixton Disorders*, London: HMSO.

Schlesinger, P., and Tumber, H. (1993), 'Fighting the War Against Crime: Television, Police and Audience', *British Journal of Criminology*, 33/1: 19–32.

Schlesinger, P., and Tumber, H. (1994), *Reporting Crime: The Media Politics of Criminal Justice*, Oxford: Clarendon Press.

Scraton, P. (ed.) (1987), *Law, Order and the Authoritarian State*, Milton Keynes: Open University Press.

—— and Chadwick, K. (1991), 'The Theoretical and Political Priorities of Critical Criminology', in Stenson and Cowell (eds), *The Politics of Crime Control*, London: Sage.

——, Sim, J., and Skidmore, P. (1991), *Prisons Under Protest*, Milton Keynes: Open University.

Shapiro, H. (1999), 'Dances with Drugs: Pop Music, Drugs and Youth Culture', in N. South (ed), *Drugs: Cultures, Controls and Everyday Life*, London: Sage.

Shapiro, S. (1990), 'Collaring the Crime, not the Criminal: Reconsidering the Concept of White-Collar Crime', in *American Sociological Review*, 55: 346–65.

Sharp, C., Baker, P., Goulden, C., Ramsay, M. and Sondhi, A. (2001), *Drug Misuse Declared in 2000: Key Results from the British Crime Survey*, Findings 149, London: Home Office.

Sharpe, J. A. (1996), *Instruments of Darkness: Witchcraft in England 1550–1750*, London: Hamish Hamilton.

—— (1999), *Crime in Early Modern England, 1550–1750*, 2nd edn, London: Longman.

—— and Dickinson, R. (2001), *Violence in Early Modern England* (presented on ESRC Violence Research Programme website, **www1.rhbnc.ac.uk/sociopolitical-science/VRP**).

Sharpe, P. (ed.) (1998), *Women's Work: The English Experience 1650–1914*, London: Arnold.

Sheptycki, J. (2000a), 'The "Drug War": Learning from the Paradigm Example of Transnational Policing', in Sheptycki (ed.) (2000b).

—— (ed.) (2000b), *Issues in Transnational Policing*, London: Routledge.

Sherizen, S. (1978), 'Social Creation of Crime News: All the News Fitted to Print', in Winick (ed.), *Devience and Mass Media*, Beverly Hills, Calif.: Sage.

Sherman, L.W. (1995), 'Hot Spots of Crime and Criminal Careers of Places', in Eck and Weisburd (eds), *Crime and Place*, New York: Criminal Justice Press.

Shichor, D., and Sechrest, D. K. (1996), *Three Strikes and You're Out: Vengeance as Public Policy*, Thousand Oaks, Calif.: Sage.

Shields, R. (1991), *Places on the Margin: Alternative Geographies of Modernity*, London: Routledge.

Shore, H. (1999a), *Artful Dodgers: Youth and Crime in Early Nineteenth-Century London*, Woodbridge: Boydell.

—— (1999b), 'The Trouble with Boys: Gender and the "Invention" of the Juvenile Offender in Early Nineteenth-Century Britain', in Arnot and Usborne (eds) (1999).

—— (1999c), 'Cross Coves, Buzzers and General Sorts of Prigs: Juvenile Crime and the Criminal "Underworld" in the Early Nineteenth Century', *British Journal of Criminology*, 39/1: 10–24.

—— (forthcoming), *Underworlds: Professional and Organised Crime in London since 1700*, London: Hambledon Books.

Shover, N. (1996), *Great Pretenders: Pursuits and Games of Persistent Thieves*, Boulder, Colo.: Westview Press.

Sibbitt, R. (1997), *The Perpetrators of Racial Harassment and Racial Violence*, Home Office Research Study No. 176, London: Home Office.

Simon, D., and Eitzen, S. (1993), *Elite Deviance*, Boston: Allyn & Bacon.

Simpson, P. (2000), *Psycho Paths: Tracking the Serial Killer Through Contemporary American Film and Fiction*, Illinois: Southern Illinois University Press.

Sindall, R. (1987), 'The London Garotting Panics of 1856 and 1862', *Social History*, 12/3: 351–60.

Slapper, G., and Tombs, S. (1999), *Corporate Crime*, Harlow: Longman.

Smart, C. (1976), *Women, Crime and Criminology: A Feminist Critique*, London: Routledge & Kegan Paul.

—— (1979), 'The New Female Criminal: Reality or Myth?', *British Journal of Criminology*, 19: 50–9.

—— (1990), 'Feminist Approaches to Criminology or Postmodern Woman Meets Atavistic Man', in L. Gelsthorpe and A. Morris (eds) *Feminist Perspective in Criminology*, Milton Keynes: Open University Press.

Smerdon, J., and South, N. (1997), 'Deviant Drivers and "moral hazards": Risk, No-insurance Offending and Some Suggestions for Policy and Practice', *International Journal of Risk, Security and Crime Prevention*, 2/4: 279–90.

Smith, D. J. (1997) 'Ethnic Origins, Crime and Criminal Justice', in M. Maguire, R. Morgan, and R. Reiner (eds), *The Oxford Handbook of Criminology*, 2nd edn, Oxford: Clarendon Press.

Smith, S. (1980), *The Other Nation: The Poor in English Novels of the 1840s and 1850s*, Oxford: Clarendon Press and New York: Oxford University Press.

Smith, S. (1984), 'Crime in the News', in *British Journal of Criminology*, 24/3: 289–95.

Soothill, K., and Walby, S. (1991), *Sex Crime in the News*, London: Routledge.

South, N. (1987), 'Law, Profit and "Private Persons": Private and Public Policing in English History', in C. Shearing and P. Stenning (eds), *Private Policing* (Sage Criminal Justice Systems Annual 23), Beverly Hills and London: Sage.

—— (1992), 'Moving Murky Money: Drug Trafficking, Law Enforcement and the Pursuit of Criminal Profits', in J. Farrington and S. Walklate (eds), *Offenders and Victims: Theory and Policing*, London: British Society of Criminology and the Institute for the Study and Treatment of Delinquency.

—— (1994), 'Privatizing Policing in the European Market: Some Issues for Theory, Policy and Research', *European Sociological Review*, 10/3: 219–33.

—— (1995), 'So What's New? Some Trends in Security and Surveillance', in *Criminal Justice Matters*, 20: 17.

—— (1997), 'Late-Modern Criminology: "Late" as in "Dead" or "Modern" as in "New"?' in Owen (ed.) (1997).

—— (1998), 'Corporate and State Crimes against the Environment' in Ruggiero, South, and Taylor (eds) (1998).

—— (ed) (1999), *Youth, Crime, Deviance and Delinquency*, Vol. 1, Aldershot: Dartmouth.

South, N., (2000), 'Health and Crime: Connecting Public Health and Public Criminology?', Unpublished paper presented to LSE Mannheim Centre seminar, 24 June.

—— (2001a), 'The Police and Policing', in Budge et al. (eds) (2001).

—— (2001b), 'Illicit Markets', in C. Bryant et al. (eds), *The International Encyclopaedia of Criminology and Deviant Behavior*, Washington: Taylor and Frances. (2001).

—— (2001c), 'Police, Security and Information: The Use of Informants and Agents in a Liberal Democracy', in M. Amir and S. Einstein (eds), *Policing, Security and Democracy*, vol. ii, Huntsville, Tex.: Office of International Criminal Justice Press.

Sparks, R. (1992a) *Television and the Drama of Crime: Moral Tales and the Place of Crime in Public Life*, Milton Keynes: Open University Press.

—— (1992b), 'Reason and Unreason in "Left Realism": Some Problems in the Constitution of the Fear of Crime', in Matthews and Young (eds) (1992).

—— (1996), 'Masculinity and Heroism in the Hollywood "Blockbuster": The Culture Industry and Contemporary Images of Crime and Law Enforcement', in *British Journal of Criminology*, 36/3: 348–60.

—— (2001), ' "Bringin' it all back home": Populism, Media Coverage and the Dynamics of Locality and Globality in the Politics of Crime Control', in Stenson and Sullivan (eds) (2001).

Springhall, J. (1986), *Coming of Age: Adolescence in Britain 1860–1960*, Dublin: Gill and Macmillan.

—— (1998), *Youth, Popular Culture and Moral Panics: Penny Gaffs to Gangsta-Rap, 1830–1996*, Basingstoke: Macmillan.

Stanko, E. (1990), *Everyday Violence*, London: Pandora.

—— (2000), 'Rethinking Violence, Rethinking Social Policy', in G. Lewis et al. (eds), *Rethinking Social Policy*, London: Sage.

—— Marian, L., Crisp, D., Manning, R., Smith, J., and Cowan, S. (1998), *Taking Stock*, Uxbridge, Middx.: Brunel University.

Stanley, C. (1992), 'Cultural Contradictions in the Legitimation of Market Practice: Paradox in the Regulation of the City', in L. Budd and S. Whimster (eds), *Global Financing Urban Living: A Study in Metropolitan Change*, London: Routledge.

Statewatch (1994), 'Organised Crime: None Here', *Statewatch*, 4/4: 15.

Stelfox, P. (1998), 'Policing Lower Levels of Organised Crime in England and Wales', *The Howard Journal of Criminal Justice*, 37-4: 393–406.

Stenson, K., and Sullivan, R. (eds) (2001), *Crime, Risk and Justice: The Politics of Crime Control in Liberal Democracies*, Devon: Willan.

Sumner, C. (ed.) (1982), *Crime, Justice and Underdevelopment*, London: Heinemann.

—— (ed.) (1990), *Censure, Politics and Criminal Justice*, Milton Keynes: Open University Press.

Sutherland, E. (1937), *The Professional Thief*, Chicago: University of Chicago Press.

—— (1949), *White-Collar Crime*, New York: Holt, Rinehart and Winston.

Taylor, A. (1993), *Women Drug Users: An Ethnography of a Female Injecting Community*, Oxford: Clarendon Press.

Taylor, H. (1998), 'The Politics of the Rising Crime Statistics of England and Wales 1914–1960', *Crime, History and Societies*, 2/1: 5–28.

Taylor, I. (1992), 'The International Drug Trade and Money Laundering: Border Controls and Other Issues', *European Sociological Review*, 8: 181–93.

—— (1995), 'Private Homes and Public Others: An Analysis of Talk about Crime in Suburban South Manchester in the Mid-1990s', *British Journal of Criminology*, 35/2: 263–85.

—— (1997a), 'The Political Economy of Crime', in Maguire, Morgan, and Reiner (eds) (1997).

—— (1997b), 'Crime, Anxiety and Locality: Responding to the "Condition of England" at the End of the Century', *Theoretical Criminology*, 1/1: 53–75.

—— (1999), *Crime in Context*, Boulder, Colo.: Westview Press.

—— Evans, K., and Fraser, P. (1996), *A Tale of Two Cities: Global Change, Local Feeling and Everyday Life in the North of England—A Study in Manchester and Sheffield*, London: Routledge.

—— and Jamieson, R. (1997), ' "Proper Little Mesters": Nostalgia and Protest in De-industrialised Sheffield', in S. Westwood and J. Williams (eds), *Imagining Cities: Scripts, Signs, Memory*, London: Routledge.

——, Walton, P., and Young, J. (1973), *The New Criminology: For a Social Theory of Deviance*, London: Routledge & Kegan Paul.

Thomas, D., and Loader, B. D. (eds) (2000), *Cybercrime: Law Enforcement, Security and Surveillance in the Information Age*, London: Routledge.

Thompson, E. P. (1963), *The Making of the English Working Class*, London: Victor Gollancz.

—— (1975), *Whigs and Hunters: The Origin of the Black Act*, London: Allen Lane.

Thompson, J. (1993), *Fiction, Crime and Empire: Clues to Modernity and Postmodernity*, Urbana, Ill.: University of Illinois Press.

Thompson, K. (1998), *Moral Panics*, London: Routledge.

Thompson, T. (2001a), 'UK Banker's Link to Arms Plot', *Observer*, 9th Dec.

—— (2001b), 'Homegrown Gangs Shoot to Power on our Violent Streets', *Observer*, 26th Aug., pp. 10–11.

—— (2001c), 'Fear grips Liverpool as Gang Feud Claims its Sixth Victim', *Observer*, 14th Oct., p. 13.

Thomson, M. (1998), *The Problem of Mental Deficiency: Eugenics, Democracy, and Social Policy in Britain c 1870–1959*, Oxford: Clarendon Press.

Thornton, S. (1994), 'Moral Panic, the Media and British Rave Culture', in A. Rose and T. Rose (eds), *Microphone Friends: Youth Music and Youth Culture*, London: Routledge.

Tikoff, V. (2002), 'Before the Reformatory: A Correctional Orphanage in Ancien Regime Seville', in Cox and Shore (eds) (2002).

Tilley, N., Pease, K., Hough, M., and Brown, R. (1999), *Burglary Prevention: Early Lessons from the Crime Reduction Programme*, Policing and Reducing Crime Unit, Crime Reduction Research Series paper 1, London: Home Office.

Tonry, M. (1995), *Malign Neglect. Race, Class and Punishment in America*, Oxford: Oxford University Press.

Tremblay, M. (1986), 'Designing Crime: The Short Life Expectancy and the Workings of a Recent Wave of Credit Card Bank Frauds', *British Journal of Criminology*, 26: 234–53.

Trickett, A., Osborn, D., Seymour, J., and Pease, K. (1992), 'What is Different about High Crime Areas?', *British Journal of Criminology*, 32: 81–9.

Turner, B. (1996), *The Body and Society: Explorations in Social Theory*, 2nd edn, London: Sage.

Valier, C. (1998), 'True Crime Stories. Scientific Methods of Criminal Investigation, Criminology and Historiography', *British Journal of Criminology*, 38/1: 88–105.

van Duyne, P. (1998), 'Money-Laundering: Pavlov's Dog and Beyond', *The Howard Journal of Criminal Justice*, 37/4: 359–76.

—— and Ruggiero, V. (eds) (2000), *Cross Border Crime in a Changing Europe*, Prague: University of Prague Press.

Van Ree, E. (1997), 'Fear of Drugs', *International Journal of Drug Policy*, 8/2: 93–100.

van Swaaningen, R. (1997), *Critical Criminology. Visions from Europe*, London: Sage.

Vickery, A. (1993), 'Golden Age to Separate Spheres? A Review of the Categories and Chronology of English Women's History', *Historical Journal*, 36/2: 383–414.

Waddington, P. (1986), 'Mugging as a Moral Panic: A Question of Proportion', in *British Journal of Sociology*, 37/2: 245–59.

Walker, C., and Starmer, K. (eds) (1993), *Justice in Error*, London: Blackstone.

Walkowitz, J. (1992), *City of Dreadful Delight: Narratives of Sexual Danger in Late Victorian London*, London: Virago.

Wall, D. (1997), 'Policing the Virtual Community: The Internet, Cybercrimes and the Policing of Cyberspace', in P. Francis, P. Davies, and V. Jupp (eds), *Policing Futures*, London: Macmillan.

—— (ed.) (2001), *Crime and the Internet*, London: Routledge.

Watson, L. (1996), *Victims of Violent Crime Recorded by the Police, England and Wales, 1990–1994*, Home Office Statistical Findings, Issue 1/96, London: Home Office.

Watson, S., and Doyal, L. (eds) (1999), *Engendering Social Policy*, Buckingham: Open University Press.

Webb, S. (1907), *Paupers and Old Age Pensions*, London: Fabian Society.

Webster, C. (1997), 'The Construction of British "Asian" Criminality', *International Journal of the Sociology of Law*, 25: 65–86.

Weeks, J. (1977), *Coming Out: Homosexual Politics in Britain, from the Nineteenth Century to the Present*, London/New York: Quartet Books.

—— (1989), *Sex, Politics and Society: The Regulation of Sexuality since 1800*, 2nd edn, London: Longman.

Weiss, R. P. (ed.) (1999), *Social History of Crime, Policing and Punishment*, Aldershot: Ashgate.

White, J. (1986), *The Worst Street in North London: Campbell Bunk, Islington, Between the Wars*, London, Boston: Routledge & Kegan Paul.

Wiener, M. J. (1990), *Reconstructing the Criminal: Culture, Law and Policy in England, 1830–1914*, Cambridge: Cambridge University Press.

—— (1998), 'The Victorian Criminalization of Men', in P. Spierenburg (ed.), *Men and Violence: Gender, Honor, and Rituals in Modern Europe and America*, Columbus: Ohio State University Press.

Wiesner, M. E. (2000), *Women and Gender in Early Modern Europe*, Cambridge: Cambridge University Press.

Wilkins, L. (1964), *Social Deviance: Social Policy, Action and Research*, London: Tavistock.

Williams, G. (1957), *Recruitment to Skilled Trades*, London: Routledge & Kegan Paul.

Williams, P., and Dickinson, J. (1993), 'Fear of Crime: Read All About It? The Relationship Between Newspaper Crime Reporting and Fear of Crime', in *British Journal of Criminology*, 33/1: 33–56.

Winks, R. (ed.) (1988), *Detective Fiction: A Collection of Critical Essays*, Woodstock, Vermount: Countryman Press.

Winlow, S. (2001), *Badfellas: Crime, Tradition and New Masculinities*, Oxford: Berg.

Woodiwiss, M, (1988), *Crime, Crusades and Corruption*, London: Pinter.

Worrall, A. (1990), *Offending Women: Female Lawbreakers and the Criminal Justice System*, London, New York: Routledge.

Wykes, A. (2001), *News, Crime and Culture*, London: Pluto Press.

Young, A. (1996), *Imagining Crime: Textual Outlaws and Criminal Conversations*, London: Sage.

Young, J. (1971), *The Drugtakers*, London: Paladin.

—— (1986), 'The Failure of Criminology: The Need for a Radical Realism', in J. Young and R. Matthews (eds), *Confronting Crime*, London: Sage.

—— (1987), 'The Tasks Facing a Realist Criminology', in *Contemporary Crises*, 11: 337–56.

—— (1992), 'The Rising Demand for Law and Order and our Maginot Lines of Defence against Crime', in N. Abercrombie and A. Warde (eds), *Social Change in Comtemporary Britain*, Cambridge: Polity Press.

—— (1999), *The Exclusive Society: Social Exclusion, Crime and Difference in Late Modernity*, London: Sage.

Zedner, L. (1991), *Women, Crime and Custody in Victorian England*, Oxford: Clarendon Press.

Name Index

Subject Index